Child Sexual Abuse

THERAPY IN PRACTICE SERIES

Edited by Jo Campling

This series of books is aimed at 'therapists' concerned with rehabilitation in a very broad sense. The intended audience particularly includes occupational therapists, physiotherapists and speech therapists, but many titles will also be of interest to nurses, psychologists, medical staff, social workers, teachers or voluntary workers. Some volumes are interdisciplinary, others are aimed at one particular profession. All titles will be comprehensive but concise, and practical but with due reference to relevant theory and evidence. They are not research monographs but focus on professional practice, and will be of value to both students and qualified personnel.

FORTHCOMING TITLES

Child Sexual Abuse
A guide for health professionals

Celia Doyle
Nene College,
Northampton, UK

CHAPMAN & HALL

London · Glasgow · Weinheim · New York · Tokyo · Melbourne · Madras

Published by Chapman & Hall, 2–6 Boundary Row, London SE1 8HN, UK

Chapman & Hall, 2–6 Boundary Row, London SE1 8HN, UK

Blackie Academic & Professional, Wester Cleddens Road, Bishopbriggs, Glasgow G64 2NZ, UK

Chapman & Hall GmbH, Pappelallee 3, 69469 Weinheim, Germany

Chapman & Hall Inc., One Penn Plaza, 41st Floor, New York NY 10119, USA

Chapman & Hall Japan, Thomson Publishing Japan, Hirakawacho Nemoto Building, 6F, 1-7-11 Hirakawa-cho, Chiyoda-ku, Tokyo 102, Japan

Chapman & Hall Australia, Thomas Nelson Australia, 102 Dodds Street, South Melbourne, Victoria 3205, Australia

Chapman & Hall India, R. Seshadri, 32 Second Main Road, CIT East, Madras 600 035, India

Distributed in the USA and Canada by Singular Publishing Group Inc., 4284 41st Street, San Diego, California 92105

First edition 1994

© 1994 Celia Doyle

Typeset in 10/12pt Palatino by Mews Photosetting, Beckenham, Kent
Printed in Great Britain by Page Bros (Norwich) Ltd

ISBN 0 412 46960 X   1 56593 136 X (USA)

A catalogue record for this book is available from the British Library

Library of Congress Catalog Card Number: 94-70273

♾ Printed on permanent acid-free text paper, manufactured in accordance with ANSI/NISO Z39.48–1992 and ANSI/NISO Z39.48–1984 (Permanence of Paper).

Contents

Acknowledgements

My first debt of gratitude is owed to those former colleagues and mentors who initially awakened and then sustained my interest in child protection work, especially Professor John Cooper, Dr Margaret Oates, Dr Peter Barbor and David N. Jones. This is followed by my thanks to my more recent associates, who have provided me with articles, information and challenging ideas; among these are Madeleine Collinge, Liz Brayne, Dr Mike Kiddle and Eddie Brocklesby. I would also like to thank staff at the Gracewell Institute, notably Jenny Still, Jo Fairfield and Hilary Eldridge; and I am grateful to the many students who have so generously exchanged their ideas with me and passed on references, especially Sally Chapman who provided me with the Kirkwood report.

I doubt if this book would have materialized if it had not been for a chance discussion between Rosemary Galleymore and Jo Campling. Jo's encouragement has been a very important factor during the past few years, for which I am very grateful.

A special acknowledgement goes to the many people, young and not-so-young, who have been the victims of child sexual abuse and have shared their experiences and permitted me to use their accounts in my teaching and writing.

My family have, as ever, been a valuable source of support. My brothers, Mike Doyle and Dr Peter Doyle, have helped me in my struggles with my computer, while Peter and my sister-in-law, Belinda, provided essential assistance in reading through all the more technical sections. My mother, Joan Doyle, also provided sterling support by reading and editing the earlier drafts.

Finally a big thank-you to those very special people who have had to put up with a wife and mother deep in thought or staring at a computer screen, surrounded by books and papers. To my husband, John, and my four children many thanks for your patience.

Introduction

The inspiration for much of my writing comes from my direct work with abused children and their families. However, I was prompted to write this book by my experiences as a lecturer in child protection training for a variety of professional workers. I realized from the anxious questions asked and feelings expressed that, despite the fact that many professionals are unlikely to encounter a high incidence of child sexual abuse cases in the course of their careers, the subject is one that provokes considerable concern, confusion and distress.

While front-line investigative personnel – such as child care social workers, specialist police officers, police surgeons and paediatricians – have a number of anxieties about working with child sexual abuse cases, they can usually avail themselves of specific training, detailed books and articles and the support of experienced colleagues to help sustain them through any difficulties.

It is non-investigating workers on the periphery of child protection work, many of whom are health professionals, who are left feeling worried and vulnerable. They may encounter only one or two cases of child sexual abuse during their careers, and because the numbers they have to work with are small, their employers, perhaps understandably, are reluctant to give them any special training in child protection work. The books available are often found to be either too theoretical or, conversely, too basic to provide appropriate guidance; and because immediate colleagues also rarely deal with cases of child sexual abuse, there is little support or guidance to be gleaned from them.

The non-investigating professionals with whom I have worked have often raised queries about what might be described as 'grey' areas. Questions asked include: Is this serious enough to constitute abuse? Will I do more harm than good by intervening? How can I know that the child is telling the truth? It happened several years ago, so is it worth passing on information to the authorities now? Such situations pose difficult dilemmas for these workers. Referring them to their local child protection procedures is not enough because the issues raised cannot always be answered by procedures. This book attempts to address these and similar questions, as well as giving guidance on how best to respond when, as a health worker, you find yourself faced with an instance of child sexual abuse.

It has become evident that professional workers will often make the most appropriate decisions when they have a thorough appreciation of all the issues. For this reason the first four chapters are designed to increase knowledge and understanding of child sexual abuse. The first two chapters encompass basic data such as definitions, rates of abuse, the forms it takes and the settings in which it can occur. The third chapter looks at the motivation and behaviour of the perpetrators. This is a focal chapter because many of the confusions and apparent contradictions relating to sexual offences become intelligible once the attitude and conduct of the abusers are appreciated. The fourth chapter looks at the perspectives of the victims, not only the abused children themselves but also family members and other associates who are exploited by the sex offender; professional workers can themselves become secondary victims. Because in predominantly white societies there are often extra pressures on black and Asian people and those from ethnic minorities, their perspective is included whenever appropriate. Similarly, the additional issues facing children with disabilities are addressed.

While helping to increase understanding, Chapters 5 and 6 also contain suggestions on how to respond before, during and after an investigation of child sexual abuse. Included here is a section on how professionals can help themselves and others to cope as witnesses in court. This is followed by an examination of what can be done to protect abused children from being re-abused and to safeguard all children and prevent sexual abuse generally.

Many professionals, especially those whose main interaction is directly with parents and other adults, may find that while they never come across a case in which a young child is being abused, they have to deal with a number of disclosures from adults who were abused during their own childhood. In all too many cases time has not been a healer and the relevant health workers find they are having to deal with very real, raw and immediate distress despite the fact that the events causing such anguish occurred 10, 20 or 60 years ago. The final chapter deals with the problems faced by adult survivors and suggests some ways in which these can be alleviated.

For those health professionals who would like to pursue the issues further the book concludes with a guide to additional reading (Appendix D). This includes sections on black perspectives and those of people with disabilities; these are both areas that have largely been overlooked until recently, and victims of child sexual abuse from these groups are beginning to speak out and, not before time, demand to be heard.

The cases used as examples throughout the book are either taken from available literature, when references are given, or are drawn from my own experience of many years working in the field of child protection. To preserve confidentiality, identifying details have been altered and, wherever possible, permission to use the account has been obtained from the clients and patients involved.

*To Peter, Belinda, Alexandra
and Charlotte
Belinda will always be a special person*

1

Terms and definitions

A local authority spokeswoman, commenting in 1989 on the difficulties of helping Asian boys who had been sexually abused by a white, HIV-positive male in London, noted that there was no word for 'sexual abuse' in the Bengali language. Similarly, in the English language there is no single word for the exploitation of children encompassed by the phrase 'child sexual abuse', and this term has only been coined in the last quarter of the twentieth century. There are a number of words relating to specific forms of abuse, such as incest, derived from Latin, and paederasty and paedophilia, derived from Greek, whose usage reaches back into the misty haze of antiquity. Such words indicate that sexual exploitation of children has been recognized in society for many centuries, but these terms were not ones in common parlance and were only applied to what was regarded as a small, deviant minority.

Child pornography, prostitution and sexual abuse were perceived to exist in Victorian times, but this knowledge was suppressed so that by the mid-twentieth century these abuses were seen largely as a thing of the past in all but a few countries (Olafson, Corwin and Summit, 1993). It was known that some very young women worked as prostitutes and young men as 'rent boys', but this was not classed as abusive. These were young people being paid for a service. Not a desirable occupation, but not one which caused too much outrage or evoked a widespread protective response.

Incest was seen to be the province of a few deviant families living in remote rural areas, in overcrowded inner cities, or in glorious isolation in aristocratic mansions. As late as the 1950s its prevalence was estimated by Weinberg (1955) to be approximately one per million of the population despite some of the cases highlighted in the early twentieth century by Sigmund Freud (Freud, 1979; Jacobs, 1992), a number of earlier prevalence studies (Hamilton, 1929; Terman, 1938; Landis *et al.*, 1940) and the historical evidence in the case records of welfare agencies of the nineteenth century. These record incest occurring, predominantly between fathers and daughters, in 'ordinary' families (Gordon and O'Keefe, 1984; Gordon, 1986; Olafson, Corwin and Summit, 1993).

Society was also aware that there were a few strangers, bogymen, who would entice innocent children to deserted locations or into their cars in order to molest them and, in a few tragic cases, sexually exploit and kill them. The police would give talks to schoolchildren about the dangers of accepting sweets or lifts from strangers.

In the 1960s two changes in attitude took place. The advent of the sexual revolution of the 'Swinging Sixties' meant that people began to talk more freely about sexual matters. Sex education in school and the use of more explicit terms in the entertainment and news media meant that a greater number of children now had a level of understanding and an available vocabulary to use in communicating with adults about sexual matters.

At the same time Henry Kempe, a leading paediatrician of the day, coined the phrase 'the battered baby syndrome' (Kempe *et al.*, 1962). The arguments put forward by Kempe and his colleagues, coupled with tragedies such as the death of Maria Colwell in 1973 (DHSS, 1974; Howells, 1974), led to the growing recognition that children could be, and were being, physically abused by their parents and carers. Once professionals were prepared to believe the unbelievable, it became more likely that they could accept that children were being sexually exploited by people in positions of trust. Adult survivors and child victims of sexual abuse now felt able to speak out, and this time they were believed and viewed with more sympathy than hitherto. The 1970s saw the gradual realization that child sexual abuse was a legitimate concern for the medical profession and for all child protection agencies.

At first the focus was on child sexual abuse within the family, particularly the father–daughter relationship. However, as more children and survivors began to disclose abuse, other male relatives and a handful of female relatives, as well as substitute carers and non-family acquaintances were also implicated. The term 'incest' could no longer encompass all the sexually exploitive activities coming to light. In 1978 Kempe wrote, prophetically:

> I have chosen to speak on the subject of sexual abuse of children and adolescents as another hidden pediatric problem and a neglected area. More and more clinical problems related to sexual abuse come to our attention every year. In our training and in our practice, we pediatricians are insufficiently aware of the frequency of sexual abuse; it is, I believe, just as common as physical abuse and the failure-to-thrive syndrome.
>
> Just as the 'battered baby syndrome' rang a responsive chord among pediatricians 20 years ago, it is my hope that with this brief discussion I might stimulate a broader awareness among pediatricians of the problems of sexual abuse.

Kempe then gave several examples of child molestation in which the perpetrator was not a family member: a 53-year-old physician accused of touching the genitalia of pre-adolescent male patients; a lawyer who sexually fondled young girls in his neighbourhood; a baby sitter who raped two girls aged 6 and 14 years. Kempe also gave instances of intra-family abuse, such as a judge who had incestuous relationships with his two daughters.

As will be seen in Chapter 3, distinctions between abuse within and outside the family, or between people who abuse close family relatives and those who molest non-family members, are largely artificial.

Children can be physically mistreated in a great variety of ways by many different people, and they can equally be sexually exploited in a diversity of circumstances. This has meant that just as professionals have had to adopt the general term 'physical abuse' to encompass all the specific forms such as non-accidental injury and the battered child syndrome, so they have adopted the phrase 'child sexual abuse' to cover sexual exploitation in its many manifestations.

The phrase itself seems to be straightforward and clear, yet its apparent simplicity hides a multitude of complicated concepts and ethical dilemmas that are still the subject of heated debate. An examination of each of the individual words that make up the phrase will reveal some of the difficulties experienced by professional workers expected to respond to the problem in an effective manner and make the 'right' decisions. So often trying to determine what will be truly helpful and correct is fraught with difficulty.

DEFINITIONS

Child

According to the Oxford English Dictionary (OED) the word 'child' derives from an old Teutonic word for 'root' and means foetus, infant, boy or girl. The definition continues 'the offspring, male or female, of human parents'. The OED adds 'one who is as a child in character, manners, attainments and especially in experience and judgement'.

Although there is a debate in the area of physical abuse over whether a child can be physically maltreated while still unborn, in relation to sexual abuse, with the possible exception of aspects of ritual abuse, this is not a concern. But from birth onwards an infant can be sexually exploited. Until recently evidence that babies and toddlers were being molested was met with incredulity. It has now been accepted that although pre-verbal children cannot ask directly for help, sometimes the facts speak for themselves.

EXAMPLE: A mother and her new-born daughter remained in hospital for ten days and were then discharged home. Six days later the baby was rushed into hospital with severe brain damage. Her natural father had lost his temper and had dashed her head against the floor. On examination, she was found to have damage to the anus caused by the insertion of a large, smooth object. Her father had already served several prison sentences for the sexual abuse of young children. The victim in this instance was a 16-day-old baby. How much earlier the abuse might have started had the baby been born at home is a matter for speculation.

Towards the other end of the age spectrum, the appropriateness of the use of the word 'child' becomes less clear.

Many cultures identify childhood as the stage of development from birth to puberty, which occurs around the age of 12. However, adulthood in some countries and in some eras in history does or did not start until the age of 25. Until the late 1960s, the 21st birthday was the age of majority in the UK, and in many countries the age of 18 is now seen as the start of adulthood. People aged between 12 and 18 are therefore neither properly children nor properly adult. They are generally referred to as adolescents, teenagers or young people.

How far younger adolescents should be allowed to indulge in sexual activities and to what extent they should be protected from exploitation is open to debate. In many countries the age of consent is as low as 12. Other societies, despite a higher age of consent, may be reluctant to intervene in the sexual activities of a couple of 14-year-olds. Where youthful marriages are permitted, the difficulties inherent in early sexual unions may still be acknowledged. Aristotle, an ancient Greek philosopher and the son of a doctor, opposed early wedlock: 'In all states where it is the custom for men and women to marry young the inhabitants are imperfectly developed and small of stature.' (Barker, 1946). Aristotle may not have been medically accurate, but he distinguished between what is physically possible and what is morally or practically desirable.

In early adolescence bodily changes demonstrate that young people are physically ready for sexual relationships. Moreover, they tend to become naturally more absorbed in sexual matters than are younger children. Pre-adolescent youngsters may show a curiosity in bodily matters that adults define as sexual, but they usually have a host of other developmental tasks that demand their attention.

Health professionals, especially those such as secondary school nurses who deal with adolescent problems, are faced with a dilemma when trying to decide whether a particular teenager is being abused or is being introduced to natural sexual exploration. While some young people have thoroughly enjoyed early erotic encounters, others have recorded that, when involved in intimate activities by someone more powerful, they have felt in every way as vulnerable and exploited as a small child.

The last part of the OED definition is an important one. If an adolescent is reduced to the vulnerable state of a young child, is made to feel relatively powerless and helpless and is unable to give 'informed consent', then he or she is being abused. The same is true of people with learning difficulties who may have reached the age of majority but are, due to developmental limitations, similar to children in ability, experience and judgement.

In conclusion, the word 'child' in association with 'sexual abuse' can cover any person from birth to adulthood – usually the age of 18. It may not be a suitable phrase to apply in relation to adults who have learning difficulties or mental handicap because this would diminish their adult status. Nevertheless, many of the dynamics of child sexual abuse also apply to vulnerable adults. Health professionals working with them may find the theories and guidance on intervention relating to child sexual abuse useful in their work.

Sexual

This word is defined by the OED as 'of or pertaining to organs of sex' and 'relative to the physical intercourse between the sexes or the gratification of sexual appetites'.

The act of touching a child's genitals may have no sexual connotations. Doctors and nurses, in particular, have to do so in the course of administering medical treatment. Babies and toddlers have to be helped to clean their private parts, as might older children with certain disabilities. In defining if an action is abusive it has to be determined whether the person responsible for the act was performing it for his or her own sexual gratification. Questions to ask include: Did the person have the excitement of sexual arousal while touching the child? Does he or she obtain pleasure from rehearsing the scene before and/or after the event? Does the activity have to be kept secret? If the answer to all these questions is 'no' then abuse is unlikely to be present.

Sexual activity need not be restricted to physical contact. It can include exposing the genitalia, talking in a sexual way or involvement in pornography. A proportion of the population gains considerable sexual gratification by using telephone chat lines such as 'Horny Couples', 'Kitten Call' or 'Lust After Me'. When these non-touching sexual activities involve children or vulnerable young people they are abusive.

In her book on the sexual exploitation of children, Judith Ennew (1986) describes several photographs of children. These include: (i) a 'small-breasted, possibly pre-teen girl lying across a bed unclothed. Adult presence indicated only by an erect penis'; (ii) a 'naked little girl crouching with her genitals spread wide towards the camera'; (iii) 'naked pre-pubertal girls standing, holding signs saying "fuck" and "me"'. These pictures have clear sexual connotations although no actual physical contact is evident.

Abuse

As a noun 'abuse' is defined by the OED as 'improper use, perversion, a corrupt practice, deceit, violation, defilement'. The verb 'to abuse' is given as 'to take bad advantage of, to violate'.

Abuse does not exist where there is mutual consent and the activities are mutually satisfying. Children of roughly the same age engaging in sexual games in which there is no coercion, shame or suffering are not abusing one another. By definition, in child abuse there has to be at least one person, perhaps more, taking 'bad advantage' of a child.

Some perpetrators will maintain that their victims consented to the activities, maybe even initiating some sexual contact. However, such consent has to be 'informed'. Children and young people will rarely be aware of the longer-term physical and emotional effects of activities over which they have no ultimate control. They may be attracted by a short-term advantage, such as a present or display of affection. One child, frightened of the dark, welcomed her brother's night-time visits:

> At night I had to go to bed, switch off the light and go straight to sleep ... I would lie there terrified because I could hear the floorboards creak outside my door and I was sure that a man with a gun was coming to shoot me ...
>
> My fears were relieved a little when I was about 6 because Frank started to come to my room in the evening to cuddle me ... I loved Frank's reassuring embraces and felt so grateful to him.
>
> *(Doyle, 1990)*

Frank, her brother, gradually increased the amount of sexual contact until he was penetrating her vaginally, anally and orally. This left her with a lifetime's legacy of shame and guilt.

Many youngsters are forced to accept sexual relations in order to cope with life. Graham Gaskin was a child who, after the death of his mother, was taken into care and placed in one abusive situation after another. He would run away from the institutions purporting to care for him and find whatever accommodation he could. Desperate for somewhere to live, he was invited by friends to stay with them. The flat was owned by a man called Jeremy. Graham recalled:

> I just lay there and let him do what he wanted, short of penetration. It's not hard to see why homosexuals call their lads rent boys, John, Phil and I paid for living in the flat by taking turns sleeping with Jeremy.
>
> (*MacVeigh*, 1982)

Sexual activities are therefore abusive if one person with greater power, whether due to age, physique, status, understanding or knowledge, takes advantage of another person's vulnerability, fears, weaknesses, lack of understanding, helplessness or need. This can include playing on a person's character weaknesses: a 'greedy' child who accepts sex in return for bars of chocolate is as much a victim as one who is forced at knife-point.

Abuse is also present if mutual consent is absent. This consent must be 'informed' and it must be freely given. Children cannot know the dangers and risks, whether emotional or physical, of engaging in sexual relationships where they are the vulnerable partner. In these circumstances they cannot give informed consent.

Child sexual abuse

Taking into account the discussion above, child sex abuse could be defined as: an activity, relating to the sex organs, engaged in for sexual gratification which takes advantage of, violates or deceives children or young people.

There have been a number of other definitions of the phrase which are worth examining. An early one that has been widely used is that of Schechter and Roberge (1976);

The involvement of dependent, developmentally immature children and adolescents in sexual activities they do not truly comprehend, to which they are unable to give informed consent, or that violate the social taboos of family roles.

This definition introduced the concept of informed consent. Another particularly useful word is 'dependent'. It is the dependent nature of children and young people that makes child sexual abuse a particular problem. Often the abuse is perpetrated by the very people on whom the victims rely, such as parents. Furthermore, children may be trapped in abusive situations because they believe that disclosure will endanger, distress or alienate their carers. A sister may be unable to tell her parents about her brother's abusive activities because she fears they will reject her. Similarly, a boy may not be able to tell his parents that his football coach is molesting him in case they stop the coaching sessions he needs to get into his chosen team. Child molesters use and abuse this inherent dependency of children and young people, which is itself often part of the attraction of sex with children.

A longer definition was given by the Standing Committee on the Sexual Abuse of Children (SCOSAC) in 1984:

Any child below the age of consent may be deemed to have been sexually abused when a sexually mature person has, by design or by neglect of their usual societal or specific responsibilities in relation to the child, engaged or permitted the engagement of that child in any activity of a sexual nature which is intended to lead to the sexual gratification of the sexually mature person. This definition pertains whether or not this activity involves explicit coercion by any means, whether or not it involves genital or physical contact, whether or not it is initiated by the child and whether or not there is a discernible harmful outcome in the short term.

One of the problems of this definition is that it refers to the perpetrator as 'sexually mature'. A 10-year-old boy may not be so defined, and yet if he forces himself sexually on his 5-year-old sister he is clearly abusing her and she is equally clearly the victim. Another contentious aspect is its inclusion of the neglect of responsibilities. This might seem to suggest that carers who fail to protect their charges are as culpable as those who actively perpetrate abuse. 'Collusive' mothers, acting consciously or unconsciously, have been blamed for the molestation of their children by their partners. This is open to challenge and Chapters 3 and 4 examine this issue in some depth.

On a positive point, the SCOSAC definition includes as abusive activities that may not involve coercion and may be initiated by a child with no obvious resultant harm. One important feature of abuse is that damage to the child is not the only issue. An activity becomes abusive if it exploits a child for the sexual gratification of the person with greater maturity and hence more power.

A further definition was given by Baker and Duncan when they conducted a survey to establish the general scale of child sexual abuse in the UK in 1985:

> A child (anyone under 16 years) is sexually abused when another person, who is sexually mature, involves the child in any activity which the other person expects to lead to their sexual arousal. This might involve intercourse, touching, exposure of the sexual organs, showing porno-graphic material or talking about sexual things in an erotic way.

This includes the concept of sexual gratification and makes it clear that non-touching forms of sexual activity can be abusive. Some offenders, in an attempt to defend themselves, have maintained that youngsters are able to describe sexual experiences because they have seen sexually explicit video material. This is not a particularly adequate defence, the reason being that adults are abusing young children by providing them with access to pornographic material. Youngsters cannot give informed consent about whether they want to watch such material.

Michelle Elliot (1986) provides a similar definition:

> Any sexual exploitation of a child under the age of 16 for the sexual pleasure or gratification of an adult or significantly older person. This ranges from obscene telephone calls, indecent exposure and voyeurism such as spying on a child undressing, to fondling, taking pornographic pictures, intercourse or attempted intercourse, rape, incest or child

prostitution. It may be a single incident or events which occur over a number of years.

The only reservation in relation to Elliot's definition is that abuse could be perpetrated by a person of the same age or slightly younger than the victim.

EXAMPLE: A 14-year-old gang leader, who had himself been sexualized when younger, forced a 15-year-old boy to have sex with him. The younger boy, who had a powerful personality with considerable leadership skills, would terrorize any boys in the neighbourhood who were not his gang members. The 15-year-old was new to the area, friendless and from an uncaring family. He had a desperate need for acceptance and protection and so could not refuse the sexual initiation into the gang that the leader inflicted on him.

Similarly Anna Salter (1988) argues 'common sense will indicate that a particular situation is abusive, for example manipulated consent of a retarded child by a nonretarded child of a similar age'.

A different definition was used by a research team looking at sexual abuse in Northern Ireland:

A child, anyone under 17 years, is sexually abused when one or more persons involves the child in any activity for the purpose of their own sexual arousal.
    This might involve intercourse, touching, exposure of the sexual organs, showing pornographic material or talking about sexual things in an erotic way, etc.

(*The Research Team*, 1990, p. 15)

Although similar to the one given by Elliot, this definition chooses under 17 rather than under 16 years to denote a child.

What emerges from a review of these definitions is that the phrase 'child sexual abuse' covers the sexual mistreatment of both children and young people. It is not confined within the family and household; a perpetrator can be anyone who exploits another's vulnerability to gain sexual gratification. Finally, it can include activities which do not involve direct touching.

SPECIFIC TERMS

Terms, particularly relating to sensitive topics, are used in specific ways and are carefully chosen to convey particular concepts. There is always a difficulty with the choice of words. What is acceptable in one decade can soon be endowed with negative connotations, be associated with discrimination and be unacceptable in the next, e.g. imbecile. What may be a useful technical word can become so misused in popular parlance that it causes confusion and conflict, e.g. hysterical, neurotic.

Terms can sometimes be invented to cover relatively newly-discovered phenomena, but more often words already in existence have to be adapted. Because child sexual abuse has become a topic of discussion and debate only relatively recently, many words have had to be chosen and adapted.

The different adaptations and uses of terms can be very confusing for health profesionals trying to extend their knowledge of the topic by reading books, articles and research. It therefore seems appropriate to examine some of the terms in current usage and look at how and why they are used.

Victim

This is the word used to denote the person who has been abused by the activities of others. It is defined in the OED as 'a person who is put to death or subjected to torture by another; one who suffers severely in body or property through cruel or oppressive treatment; one who suffers some injury, hardship or loss, is badly treated or taken advantage of'.

This is therefore an appropriate term, especially as one of the key elements of child sexual abuse is that of 'being taken advantage of'. The word 'victim', however, should be used sparingly and with care. It already has some negative connotations. The use of the phrase 'innocent victims' led to the logical assumption that there are some victims who are not 'innocent'. Nowhere has this been more prevalent than in the area of sexual crimes and child abuse. In relation to physical abuse even infants are viewed as 'contributing' to the abuse (Friedrich and Boriskin, 1976; Muller, McCluskey-Fawcett and Irving, 1993). While it may be correct to see some children as rendered more vulnerable to particular forms of abuse, it is unhelpful to use terms such as 'contribute to' and 'provoke'. A victim in relation to child sexual abuse is in no way responsible for, or in any way contributing to, the exploitive activities of the perpetrators.

Victims can be seen as weak, and weakness tends to be despised in many societies. This is why it is a term that can sometimes cause offence. In men value is placed on strength rather than frailty, which could be why many boys and men have found it difficult to acknowledge they have been abused; the word 'victim' is not one they wish to have applied to themselves. However, in the context of child sexual abuse it is perpetrators who are weak – not strong enough to control their own behaviour, they have to control someone else instead.

Co-victim

The person who is directly abused is not the only victim. Other siblings in the family or children in the vicinity may suffer because of the activities of the perpetrator. One woman joined a therapy group for adult survivors. She engaged in all the activities, expressing much the same thoughts and feelings as the other members. She had not been directly sexually abused as a child but at night-time she witnessed her sisters being molested by their father. She recalled:

> My father would creep into our room, ostensibly to tuck us in but he seemed to be trying to see who was in the deepest sleep. Sometimes he would stay by our bedside for 2 minutes, sometimes 15. At that stage he didn't touch me but there was always the fear, the dread, wondering if it was going to be my turn. If one of the other two woke he would say, 'Shh, you're only dreaming, go back to sleep'. Living in fear was the worst thing.
>
> *(Doyle, 1990, p. 20)*

Non-abusing parents, siblings and friends of sexually abused children can all be picked out or targeted and then groomed by abusers to prevent them from protecting and seeking help for the child. This can leave them with feelings of guilt, shame, powerlessness and anger similar to those experienced by the direct victims. The trust and vulnerabilities of members of the child's circle of family and friends are exploited and abused by perpetrators in the same way that they will exploit and abuse the trust and vulnerability of the child. It is therefore appropriate to use the term co-victim for those who, though not the recipients of direct mistreatment, are nevertheless indirectly involved and manipulated by the perpetrator in order to gratify his or her needs.

Survivor

'Survivor' is the term applied to adults who were the victims of child sexual abuse. To survive is 'to continue to live after the death of another, or after the end or cessation of something or condition or the occurrence of some event' (OED).

The phrase 'adults sexually abused as children' is a long and unwieldy one. Abbreviations such as ASACs or AMACs (adults molested as children) only have meaning for people with a special interest in child abuse and sound rather impersonal. The word 'survivor' accurately describes people who, despite having been subjected to negative occurrences and events in their childhood, live on. Not all children who are sexually abused do: some are killed by the offender; a number commit suicide; others die from medical conditions relating to the abuse. Some adults continue to be sexually mistreated, trapped in an abusive situation; they remain victims rather than survivors.

On the whole the word has the same positive connotations as it has when applied to those who survive disasters such as natural calamities, plane crashes, terrorist attacks and concentration camps. It is a celebration of the fact that although perpetrators rob their victims of a carefree childhood they cannot take away their right to a satisfactory adulthood.

It is accepted that some adults abused as children do not want the term to be applied to them. They resent being 'labelled'. There is still discrimination against people who were sexually abused, as though in some way the abuse was 'provoked' or 'deserved' and the moral deficiency lay in the child and not in the perpetrator.

Throughout this book the word 'survivor' will be used to indicate those adults sexually exploited as children who are no longer victims and who have asserted their right to a satisfactory adult life. It is used to denote a positive state of being, even if the adult is still coping with some of the emotional aftermath of having been abused.

Abuser

This is one of the terms used to denote the person mistreating the victim. An abuser is one who acts specifically in relation to the following meanings of abuse, 'to take bad advantage of; to misuse anyone's confidence; to violate' (OED). The term is largely used interchangeably with 'perpetrator' and 'offender'.

Perpetrator

The word 'perpetrator' is used in relation to the person or people who are directly abusing a child or children. Although it can be applied to the person responsible for any form of mistreatment, it tends to relate to those committing child sexual abuse. It is not used to refer to other adults who may have played a role but were not directly involved, such as a non-abusing parent who was aware of the abuse but felt unable to intervene.

A perpetrator is defined as one who 'performs, executes or commits a crime or evil deed or anything treated as shocking, an atrocity' (OED). Given this definition, 'perpetrator' is an apt word to use in relation to child sexual abuse.

Offender

An offender is one who offends or commits an offence. To offend is 'to stumble morally; to commit a sin, crime or fault; to sin against, to wrong; to violate' (OED). An offence is defined as 'a stumbling block, an attack or assault, hurt, harm, injury, damage, a breach of law' (OED).

Most sexually abusive acts against children are unlawful. Therefore the abuser has committed an offence. For this reason 'offender' has become an alternative to the overworked word 'abuser'. There are a few instances of abusive behaviour, such as speaking in sexual innuendoes to a child, where the illegality of the act is not clear, but on the whole 'offender' is a satisfactory alternative to 'abuser' and 'perpetrator'. Additionally, it has the merit of emphasizing the unlawfulness of the activities.

Paedophile and paedophilia

These words derive from the Greek 'paedo' for child and 'philo' for loving or dear. 'Paedophile' seems to have been first used in the nineteenth century by a German psychiatrist, Richard von Kraft-Ebing, to describe a person, male or female, who is sexually attracted to children of either or both sexes (de Young, 1982). In American publications it is usually spelt 'pedophile'.

Different researchers and writers use the term in different ways. Mary de Young (1982) distinguished between people who abuse family members, whom she labelled 'incestuous', and those who molest outside the family, whom she calls 'paedophiles' or 'child molesters'. She also restricted the use of the term to an adult who engages in sexual contact with children under the age of 12. She maintains: 'sexual behaviour with youngsters between the ages of 13 and 16 is more properly referred to as hebephilia ("love of youth") and has different origins and dynamics than pedophilia'. This last statement is open to question and is more fully discussed in Chapter 3.

Occasionally the word 'paedohebephilia' is used to refer to adults who engage in sexual activities with youngsters of all ages from infancy to 16. However, the term 'paedophile' is often used instead.

The stereotypical image of the paedophile is a man who preys on children regularly and as part of his lifestyle. This is the way it is defined by Kathleen Coulborne Faller (1990):

> The term 'pedophile' is narrowly defined in this book and not used for sex offenders in general. These are persons whose primary sexual orientation is to children and who, during the course of their sexual careers, are likely to have scores and even hundreds of victims. Many had a sexual experience in their childhood that has led to their fixation on children. Often it is a sexual encounter that the pedophile

does not define as abusive but as pleasurable. I have never encountered a female perpetrator who fits this definition of pedophile.

Other researchers and clinicians have refined the use of the term. Nicholas Groth identifies different categories of abusers. He would call Faller's type a 'fixated child offender' who 'is a person who has, from adolescence, been sexually attracted primarily or exclusively to significantly younger people, and this attraction has persisted throughout his life, regardless of what other sexual experiences he has had' (1978). A 'regressed child offender' is one who 'originally preferred peers or adult partners for sexual gratification. However, when these adult relationships became conflictual in some important respect, the adult became replaced by the child as the focus of this person's sexual interests and desires' (Groth, 1978). This led to the general adoption of the terms 'fixated paedophile' and 'regressed paedophile'. Although quite a useful distinction in some circumstances, researchers and clinicians (Bolton, Jr, Morris and MacEachron, 1989; Conte 1990) have pointed to its limitations because a number of perpetrators do not fit neatly into one or other category. Nor can a fixated offender be said to pose more of a risk or be less amenable to treatment than a regressed one, and vice versa. Groth himself acknowledges that this is a 'very complex, multidetermined behavior' (1978).

Clinical experience has shown practitioners that many perpetrators will molest both their own children and non-family members. The differentiation between related and non-related offenders is too blurred to make a useful distinction between incest perpetrators and non-family paedophiles. Furthermore, it is now recognized that while many offenders have a preferred age group they may still abuse children across the age ranges. de Younge's assertion that there are different origins and dynamics in relation to people who molest adolescents is found to be wanting.

'Paedophile' is a term that may be used to refer to adults who sexually abuse children of any age whether related or unrelated. Finally, one succinct yet useful definition of paedophilia is 'sexual deviation which drives an adult to seek sexual gratification by involving children' (Riley, 1991).

Paederast and paederasty

'Paederast' is again derived from two Greek words one for 'boy' and the other for 'lover'. It refers specifically to sexual relations between an adult male and a boy. In ancient Greece the love of boys or young men by older men was accepted and relatively common. Plato, addressing his brother, wrote: 'You ought not to have forgotten that any boy in the bloom of youth will arouse some sting of passion in a man of your amorous temperament and seem worthy of his attentions . . . you will carry pretence and extravagance to any length, sooner than reject a single one that is in the flower of his youth' (Cornford, 1941).

The word 'paederasty' is now rarely used although the relationship still exists. Although offenders may target children of the preferred gender, many will abuse any available youngster. There are indications that some male offenders attracted to boys are not interested in sexual relations with adult male partners (Groth and Oliveri, 1989). Just as some heterosexual males can become child sexual abusers, there are inevitably some homosexual men involved in the sexual abuse of children. However, there is no evidence that the majority of homosexual men are sexually oriented towards young boys. Groth (1978) specifically states: 'There were no homosexual, adult-orientated, offenders in our sample who turned to children'.

There is no single word in common parlance to describe sexual relations between an adult female and a girl, although such relations exist. Again, there is no evidence that the majority of lesbian women are sexually attracted to young girls. It is worth stating and restating that child sexual abuse should be not used as an excuse for 'homophobia'.

Child molester

This term is often used interchangeably with paedophile (de Young, 1982; Groth, 1978). In the USA, in particular, the word 'molest', as a verb or noun, is used to cover all forms of child sexual abuse. In the UK, however, the word tends to imply behaviour that is annoying rather than abusive.

Some authors such as Groth (1978) make a distinction between child molesters and child rapists. Those in the first group commit 'sex-pressure offences', are seen as non-violent and use enticement and deception. Those in the second group use threats, intimidation and physical violence. Although useful on occasions, clinical experience has found a blurring of this distinction as it appears that many abusers will use different methods in different situations.

EXAMPLE: One man treated one of his stepdaughters as a princess, buying her very expensive presents. Towards his second stepdaughter he was violent, punitive and sadistic. To his own daughter he was the loving father who enticed her through his proclamations of tender love, care and protection. He sexually abused all three over a prolonged period.

Paraphiliac

This term is often used in American works on child sexual abuse. It tends to embrace a wide spectrum of people who commit sexual offences. It includes offences with other adults and animals, not just with children. Fay Honey Knopp (1985) defines them as chronic and compulsive sexual offenders adding:

Paraphiliacs find unusual or bizarre imagery or acts necessary for sexual excitement, and their behaviour tends to be involuntarily repetitive. The paraphilias include pedophilia, exhibitionism, voyeurism, sexual masochism, sexual sadism, fetishism, transvestism, zoophilia, frotteurism and telephone scatologia.

In their research on non-incarcerated paraphiliacs Abel *et al.* (1987) argued that their clinical experience led them to conclude that unusual or bizarre imagery or acts were not necessary for sexual excitement. They included in their study people who had fantasies or participated in behaviours that were repetitive and involved preference for (a) the use of a non-human object; (b) real or simulated suffering or humiliation; (c) the use of non-consenting partners.

Child sex abusers, whatever word is used to describe them, commit a broad range of exploitive acts in a wide variety of settings. These variations will be discussed in the next chapter.

2

Forms and settings

Unimaginable though it may be to those who are unfamiliar with sexual offending behaviour, children are subjected to almost every form of sexual activity known and abuse can take place in a wide variety of settings.

FORMS OF ABUSE

Sexual abuse can include both touching and non-touching. Some people maintain that non-contact activities are annoying but not abusive. If they do not violate a child's body then they are less serious than those that do. Some consider that touch which falls short of penetration is not as important as intercourse. The law tends to support this view. In the UK at present the maximum penalty for acts of gross indecency on a child under 14 years is two years in prison, but there is a maximum of life imprisonment for sexual intercourse with a girl under 13 years. Professionals who work with child victims and survivors would argue that all cases, including non-contact ones, in which the vulnerable are sexually exploited are abusive and any attempt to rank forms of abuse in a hierarchy of importance is invidious. It is the circumstances in which the abuse occurs that makes it more or less significant.

Non-contact abuse

Voyeurism

This is a way of obtaining sexual satisfaction by watching children who are naked or undressing, or by looking at their genitals. Sometimes it does not involve a relationship with the child, who may be unaware of what is happening. 'I'm quite happy to . . . go round and see girls playing, and then to catch a glimpse of the lower portion of their knickers while they're playing . . . if their skirts are raised, that would also give me – hmm – a sexual relief' (Li, 1990, p. 277). Although in some cases this leads to more intrusive abuse. It can also have a devastating effect on the victims if they become aware of the offender's behaviour. Two sisters aged 10 and 13 years were mortified to find that their father had drilled a number of holes between his bedroom and theirs in order to watch them dressing and undressing.

Sometimes a relationship develops and the children are persuaded to undress in front of the offender. One perpetrator explained: 'The oldest of the girls suggested we play doctors and nurses to the youngest girl, and it was the oldest girl who then exposed the youngest girl to me' (Li, West and Woodhouse, 1990).

Voyeurism also encompasses the observation of sexual acts involving children. Some perpetrators have watched while children are forced or persuaded to have sexual relations with adults, other children or animals.

Exhibitionism

This term is used to describe the exposure of the genitals as a deliberate act to gain satisfaction. The colloquial term 'flasher' tends to be applied to a male stranger who exposes his penis in a relatively public place.

> I was about 9 years old . . . My brother and his pal had let me tag along with them . . . We were sitting having our crisps and lemonade when this man came along wheeling a bike . . . Then he turned round and faced us, opened his trousers and pulled out his penis. It seemed enormous. He came towards me, telling me to hold it. We all turned and ran . . . I think we all felt we had done something wrong. It's something I've never forgotten.
>
> *(Bain and Sanders, 1990)*

Exhibitionism can be accompanied by masturbation.

EXAMPLE: Laura was a very distressed young woman. She felt that a lot of her problems related to the behaviour of her stepfather. When she was about 9 years old he started to wait until she was alone with him in the car and, while driving, he would take out his penis and masturbate in front of her. He seemed to derive enjoyment from her embarrassment and distress. She felt trapped, threatened and humiliated by this activity.

Closely related to exhibitionism is a form of reverse voyeurism where the child is made to watch the sexual activities of adults or pornographic material. Sometimes this is a deliberate action on the part of adults; force or coercion might be used. In other cases the adults are behaving with gross insensitivity because they are titillated by the activities and have insufficient empathy and concern for the children to protect them from exposure to experiences that cause them confusion, fear and distress. To fail to protect in this egocentric and uncaring manner is as abusive as if compulsion is deliberately used.

Pornography

Children can be exploited for the use of pornography without having to be touched. Examples from Ennew's research have already been described in Chapter 1. Children may be required to dress in erotic clothes or pose in sexual positions.

Verbal abuse and coprolalia or scatologia

Non-touch abuse also includes verbal abuse. Talking to a child in a sexual manner can be intimidating. Abusers can humiliate and terrorize children by making sexual threats. Coprolalia and scatologia refers to the utterance of sexual obscenities, usually as a deliberate abusive act (although victims of Tourette syndrome may use obscene speech involuntarily). In cases where the abuse is deliberate the telephone is frequently used.

EXAMPLE: A 10-year-old girl who answered the phone was told her throat would be cut if she put down the phone or told anyone what was said. The caller, an adult male, then made all sorts of indecent suggestions. The girl was terrified.

She felt the perpetrator was somehow close by and knew what she was doing. Subsequently, she had nightmares and felt unsafe and insecure. It was many years before she could use the telephone with confidence once more.

Contact abuse

Fondling

This tends to refer to the touching of the genitals, including the vaginal area, the penis and the breasts of older girls. It can include the tops of the thighs and bottom. In all cases the reason for the touching is the sexual gratification of the perpetrator. 'Fondling' is defined in the OED as 'affectionate handling'. This gives the impression of gentle, caring gestures, which can be far from accurate. Although sometimes giving pleasure to the child, it can be intrusive, humiliating and frightening:

> I must have been 11 or 12 years old because my breasts had just begun to develop. One day, when I was hanging about [a neighbouring farm] as usual, the farmer made some teasing remark about this and grabbed me and rubbed them with his hands. His teenage son and one of the farm labourers were there and they all laughed. All I remember after that was me running and running, with my face burning. I felt so ashamed and embarrassed and dirty . . . It did have a lasting effect on me because something was spoiled then.
>
> (*Bain and Sanders, 1990*)

Masturbation

This is often more specific than fondling and usually involves the penis or vaginal area, although it can involve the anus. For example, Martin had been anally penetrated by his father. 'He did not begin genital masturbation until he left home for college . . . However, from early adolescence Martin engaged in frequent and vigorous anal masturbation, accompanied by fantasies of digital penetration by "another person".' (Berry, 1975).

Strictly speaking, masturbation refers to sexual stimulation of a person's own genitals and is normally a solitary occupation. However, the term 'mutual masturbation' has been used to describe the achievement of sexual arousal, excitement and satisfaction by one person manually rubbing the genitals of another. Children can be forced or enticed to rub a perpetrator's genitals. Mhairi remembers her grandfather: 'He would take his trousers down and make me rub his penis. I couldn't understand what was going on, but I remember being really frightened about this' (Bain and Sanders, 1990). It can also occur the other way round. Ben was sexually abused by his uncle: 'He put his hand on my genitals and began to rub and fondle them. I felt something happening I couldn't understand ... This was my first experience of masturbation ... Later that night I experienced utter revulsion towards myself' (Ben, 1991).

Frottage

Closely allied to masturbation, frottage is the name given to the obtaining of sexual gratification by rubbing against the sexually desired person.

Simulated intercourse

Perpetrators may also achieve a masturbatory experience by rubbing against a child who is perhaps sitting on their knee. A development of this is simulated intercourse. This involves the close contact of the genitals of the perpetrator with the victim with a rhythmical thrusting. If male, the offender may rub his penis between the child's legs. Simulated intercourse can be either vaginal or anal.

Penetration

In many cases penetration is either attempted or achieved, and again it can be vaginal or anal. It is often a very painful experience for the victim. Maya Angelou, raped at the age of 8, recalled a 'breaking and entering when even the senses were torn apart ... I had started to burn between my legs more than the time I'd wasted Sloan's Liniment on myself ... the insides of my thighs throbbed' (Angelou, 1984).

Ben was anally raped by his uncle when he was 14 years old. 'The pain didn't actually come immediately. It grew gradually, then rapidly, and it became a stabbing of hot searing pain' (Ben, 1991). Both girls and boys can be subjected to anal penetration.

It is not uncommon to find anal intercourse being used as a form of punishment. When Donald was about 8 years old his father became angry with him. 'He took me up to the bedroom. I thought I was in for the usual leathering but this time when he took my pants down he abused me with his prick instead. When he finished, he said that's what I would get if I didn't do what I was told' (Bain and Sanders, 1990).

Digital penetration refers to the insertion of fingers. 'Fingering' is sometimes used to indicate any sexual touching with the fingers, but is very often applied to penetration of the anus or vagina by the fingers. Between the ages of 3 and 8 Martin 'frequently showered with his father, who, while washing the patient, would regularly insert his finger into the child's anus. The patient experienced the anal fingering as intrusive and controlling, sometimes as frightening, but also as sensually pleasurable' (Berry, 1975).

Children can be forced to penetrate their abusers. Eleanor was abused by her mother. 'She took my hands and guided them towards her genitals . . . She told me that inside the hole was a warm cosy nest where I had first been . . . Slowly with my tiny child's hands I tried to do as she wanted. Her breathing grew heavy and faster and eventually she threw back her head and let out a large scream. A climax of course but I could not understand what was happening' (Elliot, 1993).

The term 'intercourse', either vaginal or anal, is usually reserved for penetration by the penis. However, children can have all manner of objects inserted into the vagina or anus. These have included bottles, knives, pencils, rose stems, enemas when there was no medical necessity and sticks. Lynne Marie's mother 'picked up a large stick and shoved it inside my vagina' (Elliot, 1993). Kathy Evert recalls her mother's abuse: 'She would insert the end of the hose in me and my insides would flood with cold water. It hurt . . . ''Hold it in'', she demanded, sometimes holding my buttocks together' (Evert and Bijkesk, 1987).

Flagellation

Beating and whipping children, or being beaten by them, can give some adults sexual satisfaction. Beating on the bare buttocks or removing clothing or forcing children to do so is a form of sexual abuse because the perpetrator gains sexual satisfaction. Many perpetrators would deny this, maintaining they were disciplining the child. Equally, many children, although confused, embarrassed, humiliated, uncomfortable and made to feel guilty, do not fully realize the sexual component, and have great difficulty in articulating it even if they do.

On the other hand, some perpetrators and their victims are fully aware and prepared to acknowledge the sexual component. George gained immense sexual arousal and satisfaction from beating girls and being beaten by them. 'The most significant sexual experience I had in childhood, was the one previously described, with the woman chasing her daughters around the lawn and whipping them . . . from that moment I have always wanted to spank girls, and have been fascinated by their underwear' (Li, West and Woodhouse, 1990).

Some children learn to enjoy the activity. Alan was evacuated during the war to his Aunt Maggie who had a friend, Amy. 'Amy was in the habit of spanking her daughter over her knee and shortly after I was moved there she started spanking me. Once when over her knee she put her hand on my penis and said ''It's getting hard, come and look at this''. My aunt Maggie came and they rubbed my penis until it was sore . . . I was always spanked every day. I hesitate to use the word abused because I soon began to like it' (Elliot, 1993).

Flagellation may be associated with other sado-masochistic activities in which pain is inflicted on the child or vice versa in ways other than beating.

Oral sex

Kissing, while sounding relatively innocuous, can be sexualized and frequently children are frightened by the ferocity and passion of what is very different from the non-sexual gentle embrace more usually given to children. Susan, aged 9, was grabbed by a man who helped her parents. 'He was trying to hold me down and he was kissing me hard. I struggled and somehow got away and ran upstairs to my room. I was shaking like a leaf' (Bain and Sanders, 1990).

Kissing while inserting the tongue into another's mouth is commonly referred to as tongue or 'French' kissing.

Breasts can be kissed, sucked, bitten and licked when the victim is a pubescent girl or the perpetrator is female and asks or forces the victim to kiss, suck, bite or lick her breasts.

There are various forms of oral–genital sex. Fellatio occurs when a perpetrator forces the child to lick, kiss, bite or suck his penis or when the victim's penis is put in the offender's mouth, bitten or sucked. Sometimes children are forced by adults to engage in fellatio with other youngsters.

When a girl's vagina is sucked, licked, bitten or kissed, or the tongue is placed as far as possible into the vagina the activity is called 'cunnilingus'. A child may be persuaded or coerced by a woman to place the tongue in her vaginal area, while perpetrators of either sex may make children engage in this activity with each other.

Analingus refers to licking or kissing the anus. As with the other oral–genital activities it may be performed on a child, or the victim may have to perform it on the perpetrator. Children may be encouraged or forced to relate in this way to other children.

Bondage, bestiality and fetishism

There are other activities that can accompany any of the contact ones described. Perpetrators can indulge in bondage, tying up or being tied up by children. Masking tape is sometimes used as binding or a gag. Offenders occasionally engage in bestiality – sexual activities with animals. Dressing up in sexually alluring or strange clothes might be demanded. This can be a type of fetishism, which is defined as an unusual sexual fixation on particular parts of the body or garments. One man was sexually aroused by small boys in shorts and school uniform. He was discovered to have a house full of boys' preparatory school uniforms, which he would ask his victims to dress in before molesting them.

Smearing food, semen or faeces on children is not unknown. Some perpetrators gain sexual satisfaction from urinating over children or vice versa, and drinking or making the child drink urine. This form of gratification is called urophilia, undinism or, most commonly, urolagnia.

Necrophilia is sexual gratification obtained from relations with corpses. Although, as far as is known, rare in relation to paedophilia, there are evident dangers if necrophilia is combined with a sexual orientation towards children. It could be the motivation behind a few of the cases where a child is killed by the abuser.

Common to all the forms of abuse above is the possibility of filming or photographing the activities, either for private viewing or to sell as child pornography.

SETTINGS FOR CHILD SEXUAL ABUSE

There are a considerable number of different settings in which child sexual abuse can take place. Sometimes it occurs in the victim's home or that of a family member, sometimes within their local community, sometimes in institutions. Common settings will be considered in this section.

One of the main distinctions in much of the research is between abuse within the family and that which happens outside family circles. The distinction is often blurred as children can be involved by relatives in both family and non-family sexual activities. Furthermore, it is increasingly acknowledged that a significant number of perpetrators exploit related and non-related children.

Family settings

'Incest' can be used generally to indicate any sexual abuse within the family. In the USA and the UK, there are Incest Survivors Groups. These are not confined to people who have been abused in the strict legal sense of the term. On the other hand, incest has sometimes been used to refer narrowly just to father–daughter relationships, and some of the early work on sexual abuse tended to emphasize this form of abuse to the exclusion of others. However, increasingly it has been recognized that father–daughter incest is the tip of the iceberg, and now the term 'child sexual abuse' is preferable, with the use of 'incest' being reserved for specific illegal acts. Nevertheless, in much of the literature, especially American writing, 'incest' still denotes any form of sexual abuse with related children.

Under English and Welsh law incest as an offence is confined to blood relationships and excludes step-parents, foster-parents and adoptive-parents. It covers a man who indulges in sexual intercourse with a woman he knows to be his granddaughter, daughter, sister (including half-sister) or mother. It also covers a woman who consents to sexual intercourse with her grandfather, father, brother (including half-brother) or son. The relative mentioned need not be a minor, therefore the laws do not always relate to child abuse.

These incest laws exclude sexual intercourse or other sexual activities between same gender relatives. A boy being subjected to anal penetration or other sexual abuse by a male relative comes under the law relating to buggery or indecency with children. Two kinds of buggery are distinguished: (a) sodomy, which is sexual intercourse involving the anus between males or between a male and a female; (b) bestiality, which is a similar activity with animals, or as the OED delicately defines it an 'unnatural connection with a beast'.

On the whole writers, researchers and professionals working with child sexual abuse do not confine themselves to strict legal definitions and therefore there are several references to father–son incest (Dixon, Arnold and Calestro, 1978; Halpern, 1987; Pierce, 1987), and the phrase can mean any form of sexual abuse, not just anal penetration. Sometimes the phrase 'homosexual incest' is used, although it is an unfortunate term. A proportion of the fathers will abuse both sons and daughters – 'a father sexually abused all six children in his family, including four sons' (Pierce, 1987) – or only abuse sons because only sons are available. The phrase might also imply that the victim was homosexual, but it is unrealistic to fix a label of sexual orientation on a child or young person in early adolescence. It can also feed into the fears that homosexual fathers will automatically abuse their sons. However, there is no reason why a man who is sexually oriented to other adult men would be interested in sexual activities with children.

To add to the confusion, some publications (Freund and Kuban, 1993) refer to homosexual men who are oriented towards mature males as 'androphilic'. However, in medical works this can refer to parasites that thrive on humans as opposed to other species. Similarly, 'gynophilic', sometimes used to refer to men who are sexually aroused by mature females, can also mean satyriasis, hypersexuality occuring in males.

Abuse within the family includes a wide range of perpetrators. Research shows that the majority of family offenders are fathers. In one survey fathers comprised 20% of the total, but because only 43% were family members, fathers represented nearly half the 'related' perpetrators (Mrazek, Lynch and Bentovim, 1981). In a Great Ormond Street Hospital study (Bentovim *et al.*, 1988) 46% were parents, but as only 2% of the total were women the parents referred to were predominantly fathers. In the Northern Ireland study (The Research Team, 1990) 13.5% of victims were abused by their fathers, which was nearly half the total of cases where the abuser was a relative.

Stepfathers, including mothers' cohabitees, seemed to be the second largest group which, because there are proportionally fewer stepfathers than natural fathers, means they are over-represented. The figure tends to be about 25% of all family perpetrators (The Research Team, 1990; Bentovim *et al.*, 1988; Mrazek, Lynch and Bentovim, 1981). The Research Team's Northern Ireland (1990) study shows a fairly high proportion of uncles being involved, with brothers also implicated in significant numbers. Other relatives include mothers, sisters, grandfathers and grandmothers as well as cousins and aunts. 'My aunt used to come and baby-sit when my mum and dad were out . . . She started touching me and putting her finger inside me. I remember getting really scared at this' (Bain and Sanders, 1990).

The laws of incest in England and Wales do not recognize the offence of a grandmother having sexual intercourse with her grandchild. Grandmothers can, however, be perpetrators. It is known that women can offend and there is no reason why they would automatically stop abusing children on reaching their half-century.

EXAMPLE: One child, abused by her older brother, was asked what her brother did to her. Her reply was that it was the same as he did with 'grandma'. The grandmother had not only engaged in mutual masturbation with her 13-year-old grandson, but had on numerous occasions purposefully watched him anally abuse his 6-year-old sister.

Sometimes children are abused by relatives who are not living in the family home. They may visit uncles, aunts and grandparents. On some occasions children have been groomed so effectively by the abuser that they visit willingly. At other times children show distress before and after seeing the relatives. Elaine and her family used to visit an aunt in the holidays. She was enticed into a shed by her elder cousin and thereafter regularly abused by him. 'My cousin was threatening to tell my mother about what I was doing in the shed, unless I went in there with him ... so I started pretending to be sick when we were due to visit my aunt' (Bain and Sanders, 1990).

Some youngsters are abused in cases of divorce or separation while on access visits to one parent. 'From the time they split up, I went for summer holidays to my dad's ... By the time I was 14 he was having intercourse with me. Sometimes he used to call me by my mum's name when this was happening ... I think he was trying to get back at mum through me' (Bain and Sanders, 1990). If there is a custody battle raging or a lot of ill feeling there is the suspicion that the child has been primed to make allegations against one parent. However, the evidence points to the fact that false allegations in this context are relatively rare (Faller, 1990).

Conversely, children can be abused in the family context by a non-relative. Mention has already been made of step-parents or parent's cohabitees. Sometimes it is difficult to distinguish between a lodger and a cohabitee. However, there are clearly cases of lodgers who are not cohabitees abusing children. Sylvia Fraser (1989) recalls being abused by Mr Brown who, with his wife and small son, rented two rooms in her father's house. The issues relating to foster-families and house parents are discussed in Chapter 3.

Baby-sitters are also a possible source of sexual abuse, yet a fuss made by a child about being left with a baby-sitter may be dismissed as sheer awkwardness on the part of the child.

In some cases, children are abused by several members of of the family in several households:

EXAMPLE: In one extended family the grandfather was initially sent to prison for incest with two of his daughters. He was later charged with indecent assault against his grandchildren who visited him. However, his own children exploited their offspring and the youngsters molested each other. Meanwhile, one child in the family was being sexually mistreated by her uncle, stepfather, father, grandfather and older brother as well as being abused by a lodger. Sexual activity with any available partner was part of the family tradition; women and girls, men and boys were all victims and perpetrators. Adults from sexually abusive backgrounds with records of interfering with their own relatives have married into the family.

A considerable number of specialist professionals and many facilities have been allocated to this case, but abuse is so deeply ingrained in the extended family tradition that the professionals find it difficult not to be overwhelmed by the apparently intractable situation.

Neighbourhood and community settings

One great fear, overshadowing probably the majority of parents, is of their child being abused by a stranger. Most research studies have shown that many abused children know their assailant. Stranger abuse accounted for 14% in a BBC survey (La Fontaine, 1990) and 4.7% in the Northern Ireland study (The Research Team, 1990). However, in the Baker and Duncan study (1985) 51% of the victims had been abused by 'strangers'. In Finkelhor's sample (1984), stranger abuse ranged from 33% to 45%; he speculated that there may be an under-representation of abuse from relatives because of the reluctance of children to tell their parents of abuse within the family. In a study examining 501 case records, Carnie, Waterhouse and Dobash (1993) found that strangers constituted only 10% of the sample. Some research projects either under-record or do not record the number of strangers involved because the statistics are gathered from agencies dealing specifically or predominantly with family problems.

Strangers who abuse are often described as 'loners'. They may abuse a child in a semi-public place, such as in the remote corner of a park. Occasionally, they take the children to their houses.

> A 13-year-old boy was brought to the Pediatric Clinic by his distraught mother after he had returned home from a mysterious two-week absence. It was discovered that the boy had been kept in the home of an old man. Though fed and clothed he was repeatedly sodomized and forced to masturbate and commit fellatio on his abductor.
>
> (*Kaufman* et al.*, 1976*)

Sometimes couples work together and it is not unknown for a woman working with a man to entice a child into a car or other vulnerable situation. Occasionally children are abused by groups. 'A 13-year-old girl was brought to the emergency room by her mother after an alleged gang rape. The patient was vaginally and rectally assaulted and forced to commit fellatio on nine young adult males' (Kaufman *et al.*, 1976).

Children can be abused by strangers in their own home. In the 1980s and 1990s in the UK there was a spate of individuals and couples gaining access to children in their own homes by convincing the parents they were health professionals or social workers. In most cases the activities were confined to looking at or touching the children's genitals. Children can also be assaulted and raped in their homes by violent strangers who break in. Again, the perpetrators may work alone or in couples or gangs.

> The three [men] ... continued to roam the area, Art, the leader of the group, being determined to "get into a house". After much searching, they came upon another residence ... The members of the family, all of whom were white, father, mother and a son and daughter, both in adolescence, were awaked and tied up ... The mother and daughter were raped by each of their captors.
>
> (*Hamilton, 1979*)

In a large proportion of cases the perpetrator is an acquaintance of the child, but not a relative or family member. Sometimes perpetrators are older children in the community whose own games become sexually coercive and abusive to younger or weaker

children. On occasion the offender is a neighbour who lives
alone, a lonely grandfather-figure perhaps. But some
perpetrators have families and children visiting because they
know the abuser's own children.

EXAMPLE: Hector played sexual games with his son. When
the boy made friends his father would persuade him to bring
them home to tea. If Hector was sexually aroused by a
particular friend and the child was prepared to join in the
games, his son was allowed to retain his friendship. The
child's playmates were determined entirely by the father's
sexual proclivities.

Other perpetrators gain a position of trust in the community
and have a legitimate reason for befriending children. They
may have a status that inspires confidence. Offenders have
ranged from a sports club coach to a Sunday school teacher.
In a study of six sex rings, Burgess, Groth and McCausland
(1981) listed three Boy Scout leaders. The list of possible
abusers in this context is considerable.

Day schools and care settings have come under greater
scrutiny in recent years (Kelly, Brant and Waterman, 1993).
In the USA there has been increasing concern about day care.
Faller (1990) writes: 'In less than five years, day care has been
transformed from an acceptable solution for mothers who must
find someone to look after their children while they work to
a potential hazard for children because of the risk of maltreatment, especially sexual mistreatment while in day care'. Faller
undertook a study of 48 cases from 20 centres. Finkelhor,
Williams and Burns (1988) were involved in a more extensive
study. Over a three-year period they expected to find about
60 to 75 cases. In fact, they uncovered 270 cases involving an
estimated 1300 children. Despite the large numbers, the researchers point out that, statistically, children are still more likely
to be abused in their own homes.

In the two studies the centres in which abuse occurred varied
in size from the small family-based unit similar to a child-
minder, to the large, organized and well-established centre.
Perpetrators included the directors of the centres, other care
staff, non-care staff and relatives of employees. Some cases
involved a single child abused by a lone perpetrator, at the
other extreme all the staff sexually abused children in group

activities. The abuse took a variety of forms including fellatio, cunnilingus, digital and object penetration and anal or vaginal intercourse. In several cases there was ritual abuse, which will be discussed further in the following sections. There has been no British survey, but health professionals everywhere must be alert to the possibility of the sexual abuse of very young children in day care settings and schools.

Ritual and organized abuse

Both ritual and organized abuse can involve family members, community members or the two combined. There is some confusion over the various terms. 'Ritual abuse' is sometimes used to indicate any type of set routine that gives the perpetrator a sense of sexual excitement or fulfilment. However, the phrase now has a specific meaning: 'the involvement of children in physical, psychological or sexual abuse associated with repeated activities ("ritual") which purport to relate the abuse to contexts of a religious, magical or supernatural kind' (McFadyen, Hanks and James, 1993).

The term 'organized abuse' is sometimes applied to certain types of neighbourhood ritual abuse. Here, however, it will be used to describe those 'sex rings' and other forms of abuse that involve recruitment and networking devoid of the supernatural or religious element. The phrase 'sex initiation rings' is also used in publications (Burgess, Groth and McCausland, 1981). The term 'organized ritual abuse' can be used to indicate ritualistic activities taking place in networks, in contrast to solitary or disparate perpetrators of ritual abuse. It is worth emphasizing that not all adults engaging in cult or satanic activities are child sex abusers.

Sometimes ritual abuse is confined to an individual or nuclear family. The cases that have come to light recently have tended to involve the extended family and/or a neighbourhood network. Some members of a cult or network are born into it, others are recruited by relatives, neighbours or significant people in the area. Often members are respected and leading members of a community. In a study of five neighbourhood cults, Snow and Sorensen (1990) found they were in areas of white, middle- or upper-class professionals and blue-collar workers. Four districts were urban and one rural, but all five bordered on open tracts of land such as canyons, gullies, fields or cemeteries.

Finkelhor, Williams and Burns (1988) found a significant number of ritual activities in the day care settings that they studied. Most cases involved groups of perpetrators. Finkelhor and his associates proposed a threefold typology.

1. True cult-based ritualistic abuse – the sexual abuse is not the perpetrator's primary goal but is part of an elaborate belief system and an attempt to create spiritual or social systems through practices that are sexually, emotionally and physically abusive. Satanic organizations, which advocate the negation and corruption of goodness and innocence, could fall into this category.
2. Pseudoritualistic abuse – here the primary goal is child sexual abuse but the ritual, threats of supernatural powers and bizarre activities are all used to coerce, intimidate and discredit the victims.
3. Psychopathological ritualism – the perpetrators hold delusional and obsessional ideas with supernatural, mystical or religious contents. This is more likely to occur with individual perpetrators than with groups.

A fourth type could be added – 'hedonistic ritualistic abuse' – where the perpetrators obtain a special pleasure and excitement from supernatural activities rather like children having Hallowe'en parties. This is combined with the pleasure and excitement they derive from sexual activities with children. To the adults it may be a party or a bigger, better form of the games they played as children; to the victims it is not a game but a terrifying ordeal.

It is also possible, in group or neighbourhood activities, that individual members represent different types. For example, people with delusional and obsessive ideas, or paedophiles who cynically recognize the advantages of using rituals to ensure their victim's silence, may be readily persuaded to join a category 1 organization.

Child victims and adult survivors of ritualistic abuse describe common features that are clearly abusive. Characteristics include: ceremonies that require sexual activities between children and adults, or with other children; the involvement of animals, sexually or as objects to be mutilated or killed; the real or simulated sacrifice of humans, especially babies, and the ingestion of blood, urine, semen, faeces, drugs or magic potions. Sometimes there will be dressing up in special robes and masks and the use of candles, chanting and occult symbols. The victims may be confined in cupboards or coffins. They may be beaten, berated and deliberately humiliated. Children are terrorized into compliance and silence by magical and supernatural threats.

Victims and specialist workers alike have had problems convincing a sceptical public, incredulous journalists, dubious professionals and a doubtful judiciary that ritual abuse exists. 'The more horrible and bizarre a child's allegations, the less likely that he will be believed' (Kelly, 1988). If children have been repeatedly terrorized or drugged their accounts will be confused and contradictory. Adults, particularly those in category 2, may simulate bizarre events such as the murder of a baby. When children then describe what they saw, no bones are found or the infant is shown to be alive and well. This discredits the rest of their testimony.

Gonzalez *et al.* (1993) found that ritual abuse experiences were the last that children would disclose during therapy. They pose the question: 'Are ritualistic aspects of abuse harder for kids to talk about or harder for mental health workers to hear about? It is possible that this particularly gruesome area raises such discomfort for therapists that they give inadvertent subtle cues to children suggesting that they are not ready to hear about it.'

Adult survivors of ritualistic abuse who are willing to talk about their experiences are likely to be disturbed and distressed, and are therefore readily labelled 'neurotic' or 'personality disordered'. They are dismissed as incompetent witnesses who are imagining, exaggerating and living in a world of fantasy. A group of parents, 'Adult Children Accusing Parents', is claiming that their adult offspring are suffering from the 'False Memory Syndrome'. They maintain that therapists are putting words in the mouths of their clients and the memories of their children are inaccurate (Rickford, 1993). When the memories of adults who suffered relatively 'undramatic' events can be called into question so powerfully, it makes it that much easier to dismiss the recollections of adults recalling bizarre incidents.

There is less scepticism about organized sex rings devoid of satanic ritual or supernatural aspects. There have been a number of successful joint police/child-protection-agency operations to uncover these rings. The 'joint investigation by police and social workers cracked open a major network of child sexual abuse, and culminated in the recent jailing of 14 men for sexual offences against teenage boys' (Redding, 1989). Rings are defined as consisting of 'an adult perpetrator (or perpetrators) and several child victims who are aware of each other's participation' (Wild and Wynne, 1986).

Some rings are relatively small scale, with just one adult and several children. Other rings develop into complex networks involving several adults and many children, and may be organized in order to provide child pornography or child prostitutes. Sometimes children recruit other children, with maybe one child acting as ringleader. 'Mary was the ringleader and she put pressure on her friends to go over to his house' (Burgess, Groth and McCausland, 1981). Occasionally, if the adult perpetrator is removed from the scene, then the most dominant and yet most dependent children in the ring will seek a replacement perpetrator.

Children are persuaded to join and remain members through threats, bribery and peer pressure (Wild and Wynne, 1986). Rings may consist of boys, girls or both. The most likely ages are 6–12 years in sex rings, however, as noted by Finkelhor, Williams and Burns (1988), pre-school children in day care settings can be abused on an organized basis.

In the case of ritual abuse the ritual itself acts as an indoctrination into a belief system and an inculcation into group practices (McFadyen, Hanks and James, 1933). However, in both ritual and non-ritual organized abuse children, particularly those who have had a long-standing membership, may be given roles that require them to abuse other children. This gives them an identity within the group, a loyalty towards it and a responsibility for its maintenance.

Institutional abuse

Wild and Wynne (1986) noted that several rings operated in children's homes or hostels. Other institutions catering for children include schools, especially boarding schools, hospitals, juvenile penal establishments and day or residential facilities for children with mental or physical disabilities.

Children in these establishments are particularly vulnerable because of the nature of institutions. In recent years the risks inherent in residential care have been highlighted by a number of scandals. In 1985, the officer in charge of a Lewisham (south London) children's home was convicted of offences involving indecent photography of young children. His superiors had been aware of unacceptable behaviour for six years but had done nothing (Lawson, 1985). At the same time, a report by Hughes, Patterson and Whalley (1986) examined homosexual acts and prostitution in nine boys' homes or hostels in Northern Ireland. Again, there were allegations of an official 'cover-up'.

The trial of Frank Beck and associates in Leicester (England) in 1991 placed the matter firmly in the professional, political and public domain. As head of a number of children's homes and a respected figure in the local Social Services Department, he abused a considerable number of children in care throughout a lengthy career. On 29th November, 1991 he 'was found guilty on 17 counts involving sexual and physical assault. Those convictions included four for offences of buggery and one for an offence of rape' (Kirkwood, 1993).

Perpetrators like Beck and colleagues are attracted to work or volunteer to help in children's residential facilities because they are consciously or unconsciously aware that they will have fairly easy access to children who, on the whole, are emotionally isolated. In evidence to the subsequent Kirkwood Inquiry one young person said: 'I am sure it's difficult to understand why I kept going back to see him [Beck] after I had been sexually assaulted, but I was naïve, very lonely and it was the only place I felt secure and had friends' (Kirkwood, 1993).

Institutions themselves engender compliance in the inmates. Residents have very little control over their lives, little autonomy and few choices, even over basic matters such as when to have a drink or go for a walk. Children in residential care may have little say over what they wear, what they watch on television, when they go to bed. They are therefore less likely to believe that they can exert any control over the way their body is used by an abuser. The permitting of corporal punishment in institutions is an abuser's charter as indicated by one victim's evidence to the Beck Inquiry. When one of the residents tried to tell the police what was happening in the children's home, 'the Police came to Ratcliffe Road ... no one admitted ringing them and we all said we hadn't been hit. We daren't admit it because we wouldn't be believed and would get a worse beating' (Kirkwood, 1993).

Obedience and compliance to a variety of adults is expected. This means they are less likely to resist any adult in the setting including those who may be casual staff with no real authority over them. So malleable do they become, that they find themselves unable to object to older or stronger youngsters abusing them.

The experiences of children in residential care sometimes mirror those of adults in total institutions such as mental hospitals, military academies, prisons and monasteries. Here the system deprives inmates of dignity and any sense of real worth. Erving Goffman, in his study of institutionalization, wrote:

> Like the neophyte in many of these total institutions, the new inpatient finds himself cleanly stripped of many of his accustomed affirmations, satisfactions and defences, and is subjected to a rather full set of mortifying experiences: restriction of free movement, communal living, diffuse authority of a whole echelon of people, and so on.
>
> (*Goffman, 1968*)

Children in institutions are, to some degree, objectified by the system as they lose their special unique qualities and become part of the institution. It is already known that, during an assault, perpetrators view their victims as objects. A child who is already partly objectified is an easy target.

Some children with disabilities spend much of their time in institutions. They are a particularly vulnerable group. Their welfare is usually of concern to health professionals and this will be discussed further in Chapter 4. However, all children, whatever the setting, are susceptible because of the skill and dexterity of most perpetrators.

INCIDENCE AND PREVALENCE

The term 'incidence' relates to the number of new cases occurring in a specified period of time. Most incidence statistics are based on annual findings. The figures will be given as a number, such as 1500 per year, or a rate, for example 1 per 6000 children per year (Glaser and Frosh, 1993). Prevalence refers to the number of people experiencing child sexual abuse in existence in the population. This is usually expressed in percentages, such as 10% of all girls, or as a fraction, for example 1 in 10 of all girls.

It has been seen that child sexual abuse covers a wide range of activities, perpetrated by men, women or young people on children of either sex and of various ages. It is also an activity shrouded in secrecy and guilt. It is therefore difficult to give any accurate indication of either incidence or prevalence. However, there have been a considerable number of studies that help to give some idea of the size of the problem. For the purposes of busy health professionals, an exact figure is not needed. However, as with physical illnesses and disabilities, it is useful to know if this is a rare and unusual phenomenon unlikely to be met in a professional capacity, or a relatively common one which could well be encountered.

Until the 1970s the usually quoted figure was that given by Weinberg (1955), who indicated that incest was a one in a million occurrence. Given this statistic, it would not have been a major problem for most health professionals. But it is interesting to note that earlier prevalence studies had indicated a much higher rate of child sexual abuse. Salter (1988) provides a table summarizing all the main prevalence studies undertaken between 1926 and 1965. These sought information from adult populations about childhood experiences. It is interesting to note that, taking an average of all the studies, 28.5% of the populations surveyed remembered instances of being sexually abused as children. The studies examined and tabulated by Salter included subjects from the middle socioeconomic brackets, thereby dismissing the theory that this is a problem only to be found among the overcrowded poor or the eccentric aristocracy. The fact that, though available, these figures were largely ignored or dismissed is an indicator of the extent of denial that can occur in society.

Both Finkelhor *et al.* (1986) and Salter (1988) discuss and summarize the more recent prevalence rates. The figures vary considerably depending on the definitions of sexual abuse adopted by the researchers, the size and type of sample and other methodological variations. The range is from 6% to 62% of females and 5% to 16% of males. A collation of the 19 studies shows that an average of 21% of females and 8% of males were sexually abused during their childhood. It is noted that these rates, especially in relation to male subjects, are likely to be an under-estimate because of the inability or reluctance of some people to recall or admit to having had abusive experiences.

Many of the studies originate from America. The most extensive British study was undertaken by Baker and Duncan (1985). This analysis of the responses of 2019 men and women showed that 12% of women and 8% of men had been sexually abused as children. There was no significant correlation with social class or place of residence, indicating that victims come from all walks of life.

The importance of this varied research is that it repeatedly demonstrates that child sexual abuse is not a 'one in a million' occurrence. It is a problem that health professionals could well encounter at some time during their careers, regardless of the geographical area or socio-economic groups in which they work.

3

Perspectives on perpetrators

Effective intervention in abuse cases must focus primarily on the child victims. The safety and best interests of the child must be the first consideration of health professionals, even if their patient is someone other than the child, such as a non-abusing parent or a perpetrator. But effective intervention also requires an understanding of the issues. A clear appreciation of the role of the perpetrators is the primary and major requirement of health workers in the field of child sexual abuse. Only by becoming acquainted with the behaviour of sex offenders will the emotional impact on the children, survivors and co-victims be understood.

Men account for the overwhelming number of child abusers, both inside and outside the family. This has been found to be the case irrespective of the ways the figures were collected. Some retrospective, self-report studies (Finkelhor, 1979; Baker and Duncan, 1985) have gathered statistics from student or general populations; here respondents may or may not have been abused. Some researchers have concentrated on known survivors of child sexual abuse. Others have drawn on information given by offenders themselves (Abel, et al., 1987; Ballard et al., 1990). Yet other statistics are provided by governments, such as the Home Office figures on convictions for sexual offences. All these different sources consistently give a ratio of female to male abusers of about 1:30. This means that roughly 3% of all perpetrators are women.

The findings of Finkelhor, Williams and Burns (1988), researching child sexual abuse in day care settings, provides one exception to the general trend. This study indicated that 40% of the abusers were women, a ratio, women to men of

1:1.5. However, there are far more women than men employed in day care settings; estimates vary from between 10:1 to 100:1. Taking the lower ratio a quick mathematical calculation would still give a figure of only 4% of female abusers if the ratios were equal.

Some clinicians report that the number of women being referred for treatment as child sex offenders has increased from virtually none to about 8%. It is certain that more abuse by women is coming to light and that earlier figures may be an underestimate. However, even this increase is a long way from an equal ratio of female to male offenders. It appears that, with reference to sexual abuse, men still pose a far greater danger to children than women.

When a child is found to have been sexually assaulted and murdered the police invariably search for a man rather than a woman. The evident threat from some men has led to a number of 'Danger–Stranger' campaigns, aimed at protecting children, which emphasize the risks posed by men in contrast to the safety of women. This is somewhat misguided because, as Finkelhor, Williams and Burns (1988) found, there is substantial evidence that women can be child molesters.

In relation to child sexual abuse within families the emphasis has been on father–daughter incest. The incest laws in England and Wales accept that a grandfather can be guilty of this offence but excludes grandmothers. There are, however, survivors who disclose that female relatives, including grandmothers, have sexually abused them. The issue of female perpetrators is discussed in greater detail later in this chapter.

A number of reasons are advanced to explain why child sexual abusers seem to be predominantly male. The first is that many victims of female perpetrators do not disclose their abuse either as children or as adult survivors. Girls abused by women, it is argued, may fear they will be thought of as lesbian if they disclose the sex of their abuser. This point is raised, not as a condemnation of lesbianism, but as a reflection that in very many societies and cultures it is a stigmatizing label. Boys will not disclose abuse by women because this runs contrary to cultural expectations of male sexual dominance. A teen-age boy engaged in sex by an older women is expected to find the experience fulfilling and not a cause for complaint. While these arguments have some validity, the question has to be asked whether it is really harder for a girl to disclose that an aunt or sister has abused her rather than that her father has done so. Fearing the homosexual label, boys have similarly found it difficult to acknowledge that they have been abused by men, and yet they have managed to do so (MacVeigh, 1982; Ben, 1991).

Another theory is that women, in their mothering role, engage in sexually abusive activities that remain undetected. However, it is now known that sexual abuse is a compulsive activity. It would take a rare degree of control for a woman to confine abusive activities to those that mirror acceptable mothering, while avoiding those that leave the child feeling guilty, ashamed, exploited and bound by secrecy, especially once her children no longer needed intimate care. Jill bears witness to this inability of women to stop before a child realizes something is wrong. 'My mother started abusing me when I was about 5. She would take me into the bedroom and rub cream into my genitals. I dreaded her doing it. It went on when I was old enough to know it wasn't right' (Elliot, 1993).

One reason for the over-representation of male abusers could lie in the difference between male and female sexuality. There are obvious physiological differences between the sexes. Different hormones and hormone levels can affect behaviour. Furthermore, except where there is medical intervention, intercourse and procreation is not possible unless the male ultimately engages in overtly positive action, whether the female initiated contact or not.

It is likely that physiological and biological differences are emphasized by the socialization of the sexes. Small boys are presented with an image of manhood that is associated with taking control of situations and being powerful and dominant. Small boys in the Western world have any number of male role models through stories, cartoons and television programmes. The more traditional Robin Hood, cowboys and pirates vie with Fireman Sam, Captain Planet and Turtles. Role models available for small girls consist of young women needing rescue, preferably by a handsome prince, such as Cinderella, the Sleeping Beauty or Snow White. A few female characters like Heidi or Alice in Wonderland, do show a degree of independence, but female heroines exerting power and mastery are few and far between; Superwoman has not caught the popular imagination in the way that Batman, Superman or Spiderman have. Frequently female characters are portrayed as being responsible for looking after boys or menfolk – Wendy in Peter Pan and Sue, Sooty's companion, for example.

Traditional male attributes such as independence, competitiveness and emotional strength mean that boys are taught to suppress the expression of emotion, intimacy and dependence. This leaves many men with difficulties in forming close relationships, resulting in feelings of isolation and alienation (Gilgun and Connor, 1990). Such men find that sex is one way they can gain a sense of closeness without threatening their masculinity. Closeness with intimacy can mean that sex becomes a means of gratification without any regard to the feelings and needs of a partner. This leads to the objectification of the victim, which is one of the key features of child sexual abuse. There is a useful discussion of the various theories relating to male sexuality in Glaser and Frosh (1993).

In most societies children lack any real power. They may be seen in a negative light, as incomplete human beings, having to be dominated and controlled until they are able to control themselves. It is not unusual to hear adults refer to a child as 'it'. Women, however, are socialized to take care of children. Little girls are expected to look after their dolls and play 'nicely' with them. In this way they are taught to be caring of small figures and, maturing into womanhood, to regard childcare as important to their status. Boys and men are not trained to adopt a caring role and may find it easier to objectify children, seeing them as of no value unless they serve their needs.

These various theories help to explain why there are more male than female perpetrators of child sexual abuse, although they do not explain why one man becomes an abuser and another does not. To date this has not been satisfactorily explained. There have been attempts to draw up a profile of the typical offender, but as research and clinical experience provide more and more information, the profile of the child sexual abuser has become wider and more elusive.

PERPETRATOR PROFILES

The following profiles are largely extracted from studies of male offenders although, judging by what is rapidly being learnt of female ones, most of the features will also apply to women who abuse.

Perpetrators of child sexual abuse are drawn from all walks of life and every sector of society, even if their distribution is not found equally in each social and cultural group.

Occupation and socio-economic status

The unemployed and people from low-income backgrounds figure more prominently in child abuse statistics generally. People from lower socio-economic backgrounds are more likely to come under scrutiny and are less likely to be able to use money or influence to buy their way out of trouble. Furthermore, there is validity in the argument put forward below:

> Since the size of the wealthy classes in society is very small, even if there is uniform distribution of child sexual abuse across the social strata, lower class offenders would still be much more 'visible' because of the relatively much larger number involved.
>
> *(Li, West and Woodhouse, 1990)*

What is clear from the statistics is that every income group and social class is represented to a greater or lesser extent (Finkelhor *et al.*, 1986; Becker, 1991). It is therefore not possible to state that a particular person cannot be a perpetrator because he or she is too wealthy or from too high a class in society.

Similarly, although studies show that a proportion of offenders are unemployed a significant number are in employment. In a study of incest perpetrators Ballard *et al.* (1990) found that 72.5% were in employment at the time the abuse was discovered.

A wide range of occupations is represented. They include those in business, service industries, manual occupations and the professions. In the Great Ormond Street study (Bentovim and Boston, 1988), occupations represented were: professional; intermediate/managerial; clerical; skilled manual; partially skilled; and unskilled. Clinical experience indicates that a significant number of abusers choose jobs that bring them into association with children, such as working in paediatrics, teaching, social work, residential care, school caretaking and youth leadership.

Perpetrators may also volunteer for work that legitimizes their relationships with children, such as being a foster-parent, holiday play-scheme leader or amateur sports coach. It is worth emphasizing, however, that the majority of people volunteering for such work are not child molesters.

The stereotypical image of child sex abusers as uneducated, unemployed vagrants has been challenged and found wanting by recent research. Abel and his colleagues looked at a non-prison population of self-reported perpetrators and found that 'the majority of the participants had received a moderate amount of education, 40% finishing at least one year at college' (Abel *et al.*, 1987).

Culture and creed

Research has shown that perpetrators are not drawn from a narrow range of cultural groups. Although Caucasian groups figure more prominently in many studies, this could be a reflection of the larger numbers of people from this group in American and British populations. In the study by Abel *et al.* (1987), perpetrators were drawn not only from Caucasian backgrounds but also from Black, Hispanic, Oriental, American Indian and 'other' origins. In a comparison study of Afro-American and White-American women Gail Wyatt (1985) noted: '81% of women of both ethnic groups were abused by a perpetrator of their own ethnic group'. Perpetrators in that study also came from Hispanic and Asian groups. Another early American article on father–daughter incest found that Asian, Black, Caucasian and Native American were represented in roughly the same proportions as they were present in the general population (Julian and Mohr, 1979).

Perpetrators also have a range of religious affiliations. Mary de Young (1982) examined a group of 'paedophiles' and found an assortment of religious preferences including Protestant, Catholic and Jewish as well as atheist and agnostic. In the study by Abel and colleagues (1987) the religious orientation was varied: Catholic, Protestant, Jewish, Muslim, Eastern Orthodox, 'other' and no religious affiliation.

Some cultures and creeds may be under-represented because of a general denial that sexual abuse can occur in a particular cultural or religious group, or because people in authority from dominant white Western cultures hold erroneous beliefs about other cultures. Bandana Ahmad (1989) cites the example of a Punjabi girl who complained to her teachers of sexual abuse by her father. The school initially failed to take action to protect the pupil because the staff were 'anxious to check out whether "incest" was accepted in Punjabi culture!'.

Some offenders may try to justify their behaviour on cultural or religious grounds. This can lead to a failure on the part of child welfare agencies to recognize the abusive nature of their behaviour. An example of this is the man living in the UK, but originating from a Middle Eastern culture, who defended his abuse of his 12-year-old daughter on the grounds that in 'his country' girls of that age could marry. What he failed to acknowledge is that his country of origin also had strict laws against father–daughter incest, whatever the daughter's age.

It is possible that certain cultures and creeds have a greater inhibitive influence over people who are sexually attracted to children. However, it is not possible to say that someone cannot be a child sex abuser because he or she comes from a specific background or is of a particular religious persuasion.

Age

People of all ages can be perpetrators. In the study by Abel *et al.* (1987) the ages ranged from 10 to 79 years, with 67% falling in the 20-39 age bracket. Doyle (1987) found that the ages of the perpetrators at the time of disclosure were from 15 to 65 years, with a mean average of 38 years. This does not mean, however, that when a person reaches the age of 80 offending behaviour will automatically stop. As long as a person is capable of any form of sexual activity he or she is equally capable of abusive behaviour. Some perpetrators have used their image as a harmless, gentle, trustworthy grandfather-figure to lull children and parents alike into a false sense of security, and have then molested the children.

At the other end of the age range, children as young as two or three years old have engaged in sexually abusive activities against children who are in some way weaker and more vulnerable. Care has to be taken not to ascribe the same responsibility for their actions to young children as is legitimately apportioned to adult perpetrators. Very small children are often merely copying behaviour they have seen or been taught. On the other hand, to fail to recognize their behaviour as inherently abusive is equally potentially damaging to both their victims and the children themselves. This issue is more fully discussed later in this chapter.

Sexual orientation

All child sex abusers have to a greater or lesser extent a sexual orientation towards children. They may be drawn to children for physical reasons: small stature; smooth, soft skin; lack of pubic hair. They may be attracted for emotional reasons: non-threatening compliance; uncritical acceptance of sexual activity; easily dominated and terrorized.

Some perpetrators are attracted exclusively to children. As noted in the opening chapter, they are termed 'fixated paedophiles'. Others, 'regressed paedophiles' relate sexually to both adults and children. Groth and Oliveri (1989) have extended this categorization into three groups. The first is exclusively oriented towards children and is not interested in sex with adults – exclusive fixation. The second is primarily oriented towards children but, under certain circumstances, is sexually active with adults – non-exclusive fixation. The third group is primarily oriented towards adults but, when adult relationships become problematic, children are used as substitutes. Although abusers do not always fit neatly into one category or another, Groth and Oliveri's findings are useful because they have helped professionals move away from the assumption that a person who is 'happily married' or who appears to have successful sexual relationships with adults cannot be a child molester.

Salter (1988) distinguishes between offenders who are categorically sexually attracted to children, with deviant arousal patterns, and those without such patterns who are basically converting non-sexual problems into sexual behaviour. There appears to be validity in this, but fundamental to all child sex abusers is that they must have a degree of sexual orientation towards children. If they did not then they would express anger, stress or the need to control in emotional or physical terms. It may be some perpetrators are primarily motivated by the need for sexual gratification, and that desires in relation to power or stress-release are either secondary or non-existent. Other offenders have a mix of motives in which needs for domination or control are as important as sexual fulfilment.

Clinical experience and research have shown that people with a homosexual orientation are neither more nor less likely to abuse children than people with heterosexual orientation (Groth and Oliveri, 1989). Some homosexual men will abuse boys, some lesbian women will abuse girls; most will not. Similarly some heterosexual men will abuse both girls and boys, but may prefer one particular sex; the same is true of heterosexual women. Child sexual abuse is no excuse for homophobia.

A significant number of child sex abusers would seem to have totally inadequate sexual boundaries; they will use anybody or anything for sexual gratification. They will sexually relate to men, women or children, inside and outside the family, and to animals.

Alcohol and drug dependency

Alcohol is frequently used by perpetrators to excuse their behaviour – the 'I was drunk and didn't know what I was doing, m'lud' defence. Research indicates a link between alcohol and child molestation. Mary de Young (1982) found that although only two 'heterosexual paedophiles' in her sample were alcoholics, 20 (61%) committed their offences while under the influence of drink. While Ballard *et al.* (1990) considered that alcohol was a significant factor in less than a third of their sample, alcohol-dependence was a factor in 32.4% of the incestuous families studied by Julian and Mohr (1979). In a survey of adolescent offenders Becker (1991) found a statistical relationship between the use of alcohol and an increased number of victims. Summarizing the research evidence Finkelhor *et al.* (1986) concluded 'alcohol plays a role in the commission of offenses by some groups of sex abusers'.

It is doubtful that alcohol is a causal factor. It acts as a disinhibitor, rather than effecting a personality change. Child molesters have a sexual orientation towards children. The 'conscience' or internal inhibitors prevent some people with this orientation from engaging in sexual activities with children. However, alcohol helps lift the inhibitions, with the result that they commit an offence while under the influence of drink. People with no desire whatsoever for sexual relations with a child or very young person do not suddenly start molesting a juvenile after downing a few pints. Were this not the case there would be absolute mayhem on New Year's Eve in some parts of the UK!

The statistics show that drug dependency is not so prominent. In the study by Ballard *et al.* (1990) only 1.9% were habitual drug users and just over 3% used drugs occasionally. Bentovim and Boston (1988) identified drug abuse in 4% of families, although it was an unknown factor in most of the other families. Becker (1991) found that in the sample of young boys she studied drug use was low, despite the belief that drug taking is an activity prevalent among young people.

History of childhood abuse

Studies consistently show that many perpetrators were themselves subjected to some form of abuse as a child. Ballard *et al.* (1990) give figures of 52% physically abused and 53.5% sexually abused. In the Northern Ireland study (The Research Team, 1990) 26.8% of the sample had been sexually abused as children. Bentovim and Boston (1988) identified a history of sexual abuse in only 5% of the perpetrators, but in 80% this was not known or not applicable. Becker (1991) found that in the group of adolescent offenders there were statistically significant correlations between having been sexually or physically abused and having an increased number of victims. Matthews (1993) observed that of the 800 or so male offenders and 36 females she had encountered, one thing they all had in common was an abusive background: emotional, physical and/or sexual abuse was part of their childhood experiences.

The factors involved in the victim becoming a victimizer will be discussed more fully later in this section. It is, however, important to note that while many abused children become sexually abusive adults, not all do, by any means. Indeed, it may well be the minority that do. It must also be remembered that people who do not appear to have been significantly abused as children may become sex offenders.

Physical illness or psychiatric disorder

Perpetrators may well wish to excuse their behaviour by emphasizing a physical or mental illness. However, research shows that illness is rarely a significant factor. The Northern Ireland study (The Research Team, 1990) showed 5.7% and 11.1% of perpetrators suffering from physical and psychiatric illness respectively. Ballard *et al.* (1990) found that about 30% had only fair or poor health, with 15.4% having a psychiatric history. It is not, therefore, true to say that people who commit sexual offences against children 'must be mad'.

Personality factors

Child sex abusers do not always conform to the stereotypical image of people who are social misfits. A proportion of perpetrators would appear to have excellent personality functioning. However, the truth is that while not all can be easily identified as society's outcasts, child sex abusers have in common low self-esteem, difficulty in forming relationships and a sense of emotional isolation.

People with these personality traits have a number of ways of coping. Some evidently do not try to handle their problems and virtually opt out of society. They tend to be obvious losers. They are rarely family men or women and will therefore target vulnerable children they see in streets and playgrounds. They are often not attractive to many children, but may either assault a lone child in an opportunistic way or may befriend a youngster who is as lonely and unloved as they are. Although not all are 'old', this group tends to be the stereotypical 'dirty old men' children are warned about.

Also typical of those featured in the 'Danger–Stranger' campaigns are the loners who either live on their own or perhaps with their elderly mothers. Again, they are more likely to gain access to children in playgrounds or parks, although they may molest relatives such as nieces and nephews. They may befriend local children and, again, will tend to target the lonely, poorly-cared for youngsters. Such people will obviously lack social skills and be awkward in adult company. They may well be employed, but will either be serious, quiet, less than gregarious workmates or they will have jobs in which they do not have to work closely with other people. Their jobs may, however, give them access to children.

Other people will tend to mask their low self-esteem more effectively. Often they obtain jobs that give them power or a veneer of respectability. They will collect 'labels' that demonstrate to society that they are people to be highly regarded. Some become pillars of the local church, synagogue, humitarian society or temple. They may take social responsibilities very seriously, offering their services to charities or to their local community. Finkelhor, Williams and Burns (1988) found that the majority of the female perpetrators in their day care study were 'highly regarded in their communities as church and civic leaders, intelligent business women and generally law-abiding citizens'. They may be talented, attractive people. Many will be married with children and appear to have a happy family life. Jacqueline Spring (1987) talks of the family life her father imposed on his children: 'We were under orders to be a large, jolly, rambling family, interesting, fun to be with, bound for great things. And so we were. We were so good at it that we completely fooled everyone'. Invariably they have skills in relating to children. Above all, such perpetrators may be plausible, articulate and possess highly-polished social skills.

As already indicated many perpetrators are quiet, passive people. They will tend to emphasize their passivity in order to excuse their offending behaviour. They will say they were driven to abuse. If married they will put the blame on other family members, especially their spouses. Female perpetrators frequently maintain they would not have engaged in sexually abusive activities had their partner not persuaded or coerced them into doing so. To be fair to such women, a comment by Hilary Eldridge (1993) is worth noting: 'some operate in situations of extreme fear of a male offender. Their fears are real: we live in a male dominated society in which women are frequently abused, both sexually and physically, by men'. It is common to find perpetrators who blame their victims, insisting they were enticed, coerced or tricked into a sexual relationship.

Other perpetrators, who seem pleasant and engaging to the casual acquaintance, are really overbearing, aggressive and possessive. They are haunted by the idea of having to have power and control over situations. They often obtain jobs where their aggression is lauded, such as senior managerial positions in businesses or institutions where 'macho' management is valued. They may well be wealthy, gaining a fortune by aggressive, ruthless methods. They can also be very competitive at sports, games and competitions, determined to win and to do so aggressively.

PERSPECTIVES ON ABUSING BEHAVIOUR

The information gained through research and clinical observation about sexually abusing behaviour is, as with perpetrator profiles, largely based on material that male offenders have been willing to share in relation to themselves. To date there have been far too few female perpetrators together in one place at any one time for their behaviour to have been placed under the same scrutiny as that of men. The descriptions of abusing behaviour therefore refer to adult male perpetrators. 'Women and men behave differently, both in relation to their commission of non-sexual offences, and in relation to sexuality' (Eldridge, 1993). This means that female abusers may have different motives, attitudes and behaviour patterns. Nevertheless, the models provided in this section may be useful in gaining some understanding of female perpetrators. This is because what is described has its parallels in other forms of compulsive behaviours common to human beings in general. Slightly different models are used in understanding child and adolescent abusers because of their developmental immaturity.

One key to understanding sexually abusive behaviour is the concept of certain preconditions being required before a person commits an offence against a child. Finkelhor (1984) was the first to introduce the idea of four preconditions.

1. **Motivation to sexually abuse:** the offender must in some way want to abuse children. Various explanations as to why some people desire sex with children have been put forward. The reasons are likely to be complex and complicated. It is possible some people are born with a sexual orientation towards children. Recent research appears to be demonstrating the possibility of a genetic difference between heterosexual and homosexual men; it is not outside the bounds of scientific possibilities that there is a similar genetic difference in the case of paedophiles (Freund and Kuban, 1993). There is a chance that physiological functioning plays a part (Gaffney and Berlin, 1984). There is a link between sexual drive and hormones; it is already known that lower testosterone levels are related to a lower libido (Berlin, 1985). In others a preference for children may originate in their own childhood experiences. They may have had so disrupted an emotional development that sex with children feels more natural and gratifying than sexual relationships with adults. Some people may only achieve power and control through erotic activities with children. Yet others have never learnt to impose sexual boundaries and cannot distinguish between sex with adults, children or animals.

2. **Overcoming internal inhibitors:** some perpetrators overcome any internal inhibitors relatively easily and readily convince themselves that there is nothing wrong in having sex with children. Other people have strong internal inhibitors or a well-developed conscience. Given a strong conscience someone sexually attracted to children may not allow himself or herself to indulge in fantasies about this form of sex. On the other hand, many offenders manage to convince themselves that under certain circumstances sex with children is permissible.

3. **Overcoming external inhibitors:** perpetrators need to be able to indulge in sex with children relatively undisturbed, and most do not want to get caught. In some way they have to ensure that people able to protect their chosen victims are not in a position to defend them. Various strategies can be used to separate the child from his or her protectors, from choosing a child who has none to ensuring potential guardians are also involved in the activities.

One of the features of organized ritual abuse is that whole families, communities or day care centre staff are drawn into the ritualistic activities so that all the adults caring for the children feel either too guilty or too frightened to disclose what has been happening.

4. **Overcoming the child's resistance:** this can be achieved through a careful choice of a lonely child longing for attention. It may be through a gradual and gentle seduction, slowly and patiently winning the child's trust and confidence; or it may be through the use of brute force to make a child submit.

Cycles of offending behaviour

The cycles referred to in this context are recurrent, individual behaviours rather than the cyclical transmission of sexually abusive behaviour from one generation to the next.

Essential to understanding the behaviour of child sex offenders is an appreciation of the fact that they are not in some way inhuman. Monstrous as their behaviour sometimes seems, they are human beings and have behaviour patterns that they share with the rest of humanity. What is different is the way in which they think about children and their attitude to children's sexuality. These cognitive and attitudinal issues will be discussed later in this chapter.

Early studies of sex offenders by criminologists came to the conclusion that their offending was not repetitive. However this conflicted with the experience of clinicians working with perpetrators who believed that it was. Two researchers, Soothill and Gibbens, criticized the previous methodologies employed: 'the comparatively short follow-up favoured by criminologists may be seriously misleading with respect to certain sex offenders, and fails to reflect systematically what is a fairly familiar clinical experience' (1978). They also appreciated that account had to be taken of the period of risk; if a sex offender is in prison for five years, he is very unlikely to reoffend during that period. Soothill and Gibbens studied some 174 convicted male child sex abusers covering a time-span of up to 22 years, and found recidivism rates considerably greater than those of earlier studies. Even their figure of nearly 50% is likely to be an underestimate because a lot of sexual offences are never reported, and even when they are the lack of conclusive evidence leads to proportionally few convictions. It has now been accepted that sexually abusive behaviour can be described as addictive or compulsive. To understand sex offenders it is helpful to think of other compulsive behaviours. Health professionals are frequently involved with people who have difficulty controlling potentially damaging habits: smoking, drinking and eating disorders are three which spring readily to mind. Health professionals are only too familiar with the efforts of patients who are trying to abstain from some form of indulgence. Many manage to control the behaviour for a while, then they encounter a number of stresses and set-backs. To comfort themselves, or to help them survive a difficult period, they allow themselves 'just one packet of cigarettes', 'just one bottle of whisky' or to indulge in an eating binge. Some then give up all attempts to control their habit. Others feel remorse, responding with 'never again', convincing themselves it was a 'one-off', temporary relapse. Those in this group will then control their habit until another set of difficult circumstances arises. Given help and their own willpower and determination, people with addictive habits can control them fully, but they are never reliably 'cured' in the way that someone may be cured of a physical disease.

A similar process can be detected in many, although not all, child sexual abusers. This is called the cycle of offending behaviour and its stages are described below and illustrated in Figure 3.1. In common with all models based on stages, it must be remembered that people do not move smoothly from one to another. Sometimes there is back-tracking or a lengthy period of being stuck at a particular stage. Offenders may move quickly or slowly through them, for some the time-scale may be a matter of hours, for others the process takes years.

1. Sexual Arousal: as Finkelhor (1984) emphasized, perpetrators have to be sexually aroused by children, although in some cases not exclusively by them. People with non-sexual feelings towards children may abuse them physically or emotionally but will not do so sexually.
2. Distorted Thinking: perpetrators have cognitive and perceptional distortions that will eventually allow them to justify their behaviour, if only to themselves. These

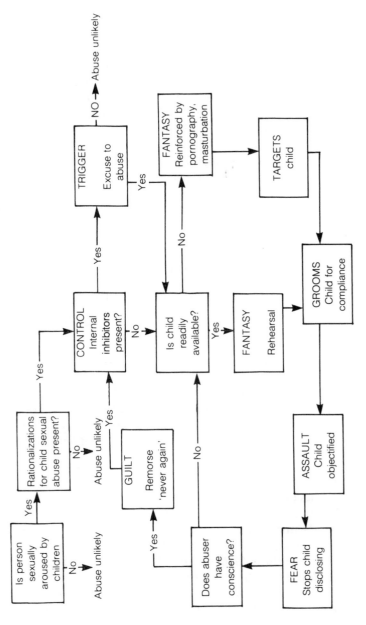

Figure 3.1 The dynamics of child sexual abuse.

distortions can vary, although all tend to deny the essential human dignity and worth of children.

Some of the distortions can be generally described as a belief that children benefit from sexual contact with adults. As one perpetrator stated, 'It seems to me to be beneficial to children to have a good relationship with an adult ... The relationship is stronger if there's a sexual element in it ... the child enjoys the sexual relationship, it doesn't prevent the child from growing up' (Li, West and Woodhouse, 1990).

Many perpetrators feel they are giving a child the love that he or she would not receive without them as another abuser stated:

> The major reason for a child to establish a loving relationship with an adult has got to be the lack of that facility in his own immediate environment. In other words, that outside adult provides something that is missing in that child's life.
>
> (*Li, West and Woodhouse, 1990*)

Another benefit to children is described by Bruce who abused peri-pubertal girls:

> My whole interest in this direction is a wish to give children around this stage of their sexual development sex education that I never had ... the majority of the teaching about sex needs to be done by the opposite sex, to teach them what the opposite sex's viewpoint is.
>
> (*Li, West and Woodhouse, 1990*)

Other perpetrators can see no wrong in what they are doing or integrate sexual activity with children into their religious beliefs or life philosophy. Tom stated: 'As far as I'm concerned I don't feel there's anything wrong with this, it's just sort of society and the way society works' (Li, West and Woodhouse, 1990). Another perpetrator believed, 'I think God's given – let me do this, particular thing [i.e. sex with children], one to satisfy me, not to let me suffer too much' (Li, West and Woodhouse, 1990).

Another view is that men have an inalienable right to sexual satisfaction. Women seemed to find one man unattractive and so he turned to children: 'I'm deprived, and I think to myself, why should I be deprived of my sex life, every animal, every human being has got a sex drive. If you can't get one, you're going after the other' (Li, West and Woodhouse, 1990). This attitude tends to be endorsed by many in Western society. In the 1980s a judge in the UK showed acceptance of an offender's defence that it was understandable that he turned to his 14-year-old step-daughter for sexual satisfaction since his wife was pregnant. Perpetrators will look for validation and confirmation of their views. They will also misinterpret the actions of children. They will perceive a young boy in swimming trunks on a beach not as enjoying the sunshine and splashing about in the sea but as wanting sex. A daughter undressing for the bath will be seen as disrobing because she wants sex, not because she is looking forward to a warm, relaxing soak. From time to time the judiciary can seem to be endorsing these distorted beliefs. In the UK in June 1993, Mr Justice Ian Starforth Hill commented that an 8-year-old girl victim was 'not entirely an angel', when giving a probation order to a 21-year-old male baby-sitter who had attempted to have sexual intercourse with her.

3. Control: a proportion of offenders have no internal inhibitions about having sexual relationships with children. They have overcome any compunctions a long time ago. Consequently, because they believe they are doing nothing wrong, they will simply fantasize about having sex with children until the opportunity arises for them to translate fantasy into reality.

   On the other hand, a substantial proportion feel that sexual relationships with children are inappropriate. Those who have a conscience may try to suppress their fantasies or convince themselves that, although they day-dream about having sex with children, they would never translate this into reality. Some people may have such strong internal inhibitions that, although they are sexually aroused by children and have a degree of distorted thinking, they nevertheless never allow themselves to act on their fantasies.

4. Triggers: for many people trying to control their fantasies the urge to engage in sexual activity with children becomes

overpowering. For some this is because they are under stress and no longer have the emotional strength to deny themselves an indulgence. (Dieters will no doubt recognize something of this feeling. Will-power tends to diminish when tiredness and exhaustion set in.) They may also have suffered a set-back or rejection, and believe no one loves them; so, full of self-pity, they seek solace in a child. Potential offenders can feel powerless and out of control in other areas of their lives and by controlling a child they can reassure themselves that they are still powerful. A few parents have felt they are losing control of their teenage children; by forcing them to have sex they are regaining parental authority.

Such people will then give themselves an excuse for the offence. Here alcohol and drugs have a role to play. These substances may not only serve as disinhibitors but also give perpetrators a way of avoiding responsibility for their actions: 'I was under the influence, m'lud'. I was not responsible for my actions. It was quite out of character'. Illness may serve a similar function: 'I was so depressed at the time, I didn't know what I was doing'. Another excuse involves blaming other people, especially the victim: 'By wearing red knickers she was asking for sex'.

Some perpetrators will use their own past victimization as an excuse.

EXAMPLE: Joe was sexually abused as a boy and still has dreams about his mistreatment. In his police statement he wrote: 'I know that nobody else has touched the girls but I can't remember doing it to them. Put it this way, I can't see my wife touching her. It must be down to me when I'm having these dreams ... I've had these dreams when Justina has been in the bed next to me but I don't think of her as my daughter when I'm dreaming.'

5. Fantasy: the absence or removal of internal inhibitors leads to an unrestrained indulgence in fantasies. Perpetrators may relive past assaults or imagine new situations. Their ideas are often enhanced by the use of pornography, especially with images of children. It has been suggested that pornography can help prevent sexual assaults by

providing a safe outlet for sexual urges. This is rather like saying that looking at pictures of chocolate will help a person stick to a diet, or that watching advertisements for beer, wines and spirits will help an alcoholic abstain. Child pornography is the 'oil in the engine of paedophilia' as Tim Tate (1990) accurately describes it in his definitive text on child pornography.

There is a huge and insidious child pornography market. By the late 1970s there were more than 260 child pornography magazines in the USA alone. Child pornography leads to sexual arousal and also reassures paedophiles that what they are doing is 'normal' in the sense that lots of other people are indulging in the use of children for sexual purposes.

At the same time it could be said that pornography is in the eye of the beholder. Some perpetrators are stimulated by material that is not usually identified as sexual. Mail order catalogues, for example, portraying children in swim wear or underclothes can arouse them. Some advertisements can be full of meaning for perpetrators. A notable example was the one for oranges showing children engaged in play alongside the slogan 'small ones are the juiciest'.

Perpetrators will usually masturbate while indulging in fantasies of sexually abusing children. In this way abusers will reward themselves. This fantasy-masturbation-orgasm-reward is a form of reinforcing behaviour. Behavioural psychologists have long understood that behaviour can be encouraged if it is rewarded. Perpetrators are, in effect, encouraging themselves at this point.

If the perpetrator does not have a readily available victim, the fantasy may focus on past victims or a fictitious one. When a particular child to target has been identified, the perpetrator may rehearse the abuse of the youngster in fantasy.

6. Targeting a child: perpetrators usually choose a particular child or small group of children. In some cases this is any child in the wrong place at the wrong time. The child may be of any age, of either sex and of any appearance or personality.

Many abusers have a preferred sex or age range. Bruce, quoted earlier in this chapter, preferred girls aged about 12 or 13 years. Jack, on the other hand, said, 'I think I am looking for a little extra pleasure with a young girl because her vagina is smaller and tighter. Most people believe that the youngest and freshest are the sweetest and of most value' [shades of the oranges advert?] (Li, West and Woodhouse, 1990). Russell, who had six convictions for indecent assaults on little girls, also had a target age. 'Always the same age group, 6 to 11: no younger and no older, outside those limits it didn't appeal to me at all' (Parker, 1970). Some offenders feel more comfortable with boys. Graham, convicted of buggery with boys commented, 'My liking for boys increased and once I'd recognized it as something unalterable in myself it didn't make me unhappy' (Parker, 1970).

Despite these statements, there is growing clinical evidence that if perpetrators cannot gain access to children of the preferred sex or age range they will migrate to other ages or the opposite sex. This is termed 'crossover'. While in treatment offenders who, for example, prefer boys will sometimes admit to having had sexual relations with girls. One did so to prevent himself and other people from thinking he was homosexual, until eventually he found boys much more satisfying.

In the USA there has been increasing concern that as older children are empowered to give evidence in court, perpetrators are targeting pre-school children. 'With the increasing awareness of the problem of sexual abuse and the increasing willingness to believe children's allegations, older children are risky targets. Therefore, pedophiles are choosing the younger victim, perhaps not out of preference but out of prudence' (Faller, 1990). Faller then gives an example in her research of a man who raped a teenage girl, then repeatedly asked for work in a day care centre. There he sexually abused at least 20 children, boys as well as girls, aged from 2 to 5. It is certainly a mistake to believe that if a person has only targeted children of a particular age and sex other children outside the target group are safe.

Perpetrators may have a preference in terms of personality or physical appearance: '''dark hair, brown eyes''

... "quiet, non-aggressive, leggy blondes'" (Budin and Johnson, 1989).

One teacher molested all the children in his class by putting his hands under their skirts or, in the case of little boys, up the legs of their shorts. In the days when physical chastisement was used he was able to use this as an excuse for touching children's bottoms. However, during the lunch-time break he chose a group of blonde, blue-eyed girls to perform extra 'jobs' for him.

Again, a perpetrator may not keep exclusively to his preferred group. Li, West and Woodhouse (1990) give the example of Daniel who was at first attracted to an 18-year-old, then a 16-year-old, followed by a 12-year-old.

> The 12-year-old had a 9-year-old sister, who actually had a much nicer personality ... She was fairly plump – I said I liked looking at a thin girl, but the plumpness doesn't deter me. I was very fond of the 9-year-old and by this time I started fantasising about her.

A particular type of behaviour may prove attractive, especially affability or a trusting approach. One abuser preferred 'vivaciousness, friendliness, proximity, close to me. No physical characteristics. I felt they would be victims willingly because they were being overly friendly with me' (Conte, Wolf and Smith, 1989). Another said he would select a child on the basis of 'the way the child would look at me, trustingly. The child who was teasing me, smiling at me, asking me to do favors' (Conte, Wolf and Smith, 1989). In contrast, another liked those who were 'comatose and unresponsive'(Budin and Johnson, 1989).

Other perpetrators select the obviously lonely, vulnerable child. 'I would probably pick the one who appeared more needy, the child hanging back from others or feeling picked on by brothers or sisters' (Conte, Wolf and Smith, 1989); 'any kid I could manipulate' (Budin and Johnson, 1989). Similarly, children may be selected because they have disabilities that restrict their opportunities to disclose.

> EXAMPLE: A man obtained a job as a residential care worker in a unit for children with severe physical

disabilities. He molested several of the youngsters including Winston, who had cerebral palsy which restricted his bodily movements. He could only communicate slowly through a word-board. But he was a very intelligent boy who had been provided with sex education and was therefore able to spell out words such as 'penis'. He was also aware of appropriate and inappropriate sexual activities. He was therefore able to tell trusted members of staff about the care worker's assaults.

Other children may be targeted because they provide the perpetrator with an opportunity to abuse them. For example, pupils playing truant from school are particularly vulnerable, especially when they believe they will be in trouble if they are caught truanting; they know they cannot disclose the abuse because this will mean admitting they were not in school.

Some victims are chosen by offenders, employed as teachers or sports coaches, because they have a talent which the perpetrator suggests could be enhanced by private tuition, thereby enabling him or her to be alone with the child. One school music teacher was a well-known choir master, member of the local orchestra and general pillar of society. He would select attractive, teenage girls who had a musical talent, befriend their parents and suggest the pupil came to his house for extra coaching. There he would rape her. So 'respectable' did he appear that when one of his victims tried to disclose the rape she was not believed and expelled from school.

Some perpetrators will restrict themselves to children outside their own family, others, conversely, will only abuse family members. A father may molest his daughters until they leave home and then refrain from sexual abuse until he has grandchildren available. However, there is ample evidence now to show that many perpetrators will abuse both family and non-family children. 'Most offenders targeted both children who were related to them and unrelated children' (Conte, Wolf and Smith, 1989). 'What determines whether [some] offenders molest children inside or outside of families is the availability of a child of the sex and age that is of interest' (Becker, 1991).

Perpetrators may also target institutions that provide ready access to children, seeking jobs in day care settings or residential establishments.

There are those who take advantage of families in need. They comb through the 'lonely hearts' columns of newspapers seeking out single mothers with children. They are aware that these women are eager to form new relationships. They frequently have an ability to enter the world of children, so seem to the unsuspecting mother to be the answer to all her problems – a person to support and love her and an ideal stepfather for her children.

EXAMPLE: Len befriended a woman who had been left in deep financial difficulties by her estranged husband. Len, who was a wealthy business man, solved all her money problems and set up in business with her, then moved in. Once in the household he had ready access to her teenage daughters, whom he sexually abused. The mother could not afford to reject Len because she was now firmly bound emotionally and financially to him.

On occasion, perpetrators have a child readily available, for instance a father who has a compliant daughter in his preferred age group. Here the target is obvious and the father would move rapidly on to the 'grooming' stage, which is discussed in the next section.

Similarly, in some forms of organized abuse all the available children are involved in sexually abusive activities, like the pre-school children attending a day care centre described by Finkelhor, Williams and Burns (1988). In such cases there is no need to target a particular child, although some children may be selected to suffer more intrusive abuse than others. What is important to note is that a child of any age, type, sex or size may become a target. Even tiny babies of a few days old have been victims.

7. Grooming: not all targeted children will eventually be abused. They may be able to protect themselves or may be protected by others. Having selected a child the perpetrator has to overcome both external inhibitors,

the people who could protect the potential victim, as well as the child's own resistance. In a few cases an offender assaults a youngster who is a complete stranger without any prior grooming behaviour. In such cases the victim, who is physically isolated, perhaps walking home alone, is subdued by force or fear.

Most offenders gain morTe satisfaction and feel safer if they have a child who is compliant. It is easier to convince themselves that they are doing no harm if the child is not struggling and appears to consent to the activity.

Perpetrators may have to begin by grooming the people who are in a position to protect the chosen victim. Within families this may mean isolating the child from the rest of the family:

EXAMPLE: One father was overly strict with all his children except the one daughter he had targeted. The other children were jealous and would bully her whenever possible. The father openly compared his wife unfavourably with his daughter, but would also complain to his wife about the girl's lying and dishonesty. Eventually these tactics alienated the mother from her daughter. The girl's only protector and companion was her father. When he tried to assault her sexually she pushed him away. He reciprocated by rejecting her and behaving punitively. She now had no one to protect her from the antagonism of her mother and siblings. She eventually had to beg her father for sexual attention in return for the restoration of his protection.

Some perpetrators involve the whole family in the activities, perhaps forcing the children to have sex with each other, thereby guaranteeing they all share a 'guilty' secret. Others ensure that the victims believe they alone are being abused and that by agreeing to the activities they are protecting their brothers and sisters. Offenders may encourage the non-abusing parent to engage in activities outside the home: 'I let her go out to work', 'I offered to baby-sit while she went to bingo on Thursdays'.

In cases of abuse outside the home, potential abusers are likely to befriend the parents. They may already have a label that generates trust. One medical consultant at a leading hospital raised money to enable children recovering from injury and illness to go away on holiday. While on holiday he molested them. Parents had naturally felt able to trust such an eminent and obviously caring medical man. Graham Gaskin (MacVeigh, 1982) recalled the activities of a man called Malcolm who first befriended, then sexually abused, him. Malcolm used to take boys camping and decided to hold a 'Boys' Aid Camp' reunion – all expenses paid.

> He had singled out these kids, all of whom were between 11 and 15 and good-looking, and listed them mentally as potential sex material for the future. He had no intention of luring them into his bed just then, but was merely casting a net like the one at Blatchwick which had eventually landed him me. The parents, all of whom were desperately poor, were glad to be able to give their kid a treat, and every one of them agreed to hand their boy over the following week.

Grooming tactics can vary a great deal depending on the circumstances. The process may take years or minutes. In some incest cases the fathers have groomed their offspring from babyhood but have waited until they reached adolescence before indulging in any overt sexual activities. At the other end of the spectrum, a stranger may notice the name of a young girl on a bracelet; because he is able to address her by her name, she is easily convinced that he is a friend of her parents. After a few moments' conversation he has gained her trust sufficiently to entice her into a car or a lonely part of a park.

Many grooming tactics are non-violent. A child may be bought presents or made to feel special. One 9-year-old victim explained that what distressed her most was that she had thought her mother's new boyfriend was buying her presents because he really liked her, 'but he only did it to keep me quiet', she added with disgust.

Many perpetrators are well able to enter the world of a child and engage in play. Non-sexual touching may desensitize youngsters to sexual touching which comes later. By the time the victims realize what is happening they feel that having allowed the activity to progress they are as guilty as the offender. Time and again intrusive behaviour will be dismissed by perpetrators as 'just a bit of horseplay'.

Some children are dependent on the perpetrator for love and affection. As in the case of the punitive father described above, his daughter had no option but to comply with his sexual advances. Children can become confused about the distinctions between love and sexual exploitation. Maya Angelou (1984) describes how, when she was about 8, her mother's boyfriend gently held her. 'He held me so softly that I wished he wouldn't ever let me go. I felt at home. From the way he was holding me I knew he'd never let me go or let anything bad ever happen to me.' She then began 'to feel lonely for Mr Freeman and the encasement in his big arms'. She therefore sat on his lap uninvited. Eventually he raped the trusting little girl.

Other forms of grooming are not so gentle. Sometimes intimidation and violence are used. Jacqueline Spring (1987), an incest survivor, describes her father's grooming. 'My father did not threaten me overtly, as far as I can remember ... For he did not beat me as he did David. The remotest threat of that possibility, together with its very occasional execution, was enough to make me let him do as he pleased.

8. The assault: in some cases the transition from grooming to assault is so gradual, so subtle that it is difficult to separate one stage from the next. This makes prosecution problematic because most legal systems demand a single identifiable offence, an attack, a distinct assault – not a process with no clear start or finish.

In other cases there is a clear assault. This may not involve contact, for example the child may be forced to have photographs taken with clothes removed posing in a sexual manner. More frequently there is contact.

The one consistent feature at this stage is the objectification of the victim. In trying to understand how her father could have sexually abused her, Spring (1987) reflected:

When I read about concentration camps, I am drawn again and again to speculate on what made men and women able to live comfortably in the midst of such devastation without seeming to have any feeling for the suffering they were inflicting, or allowing to be inflicted, upon fellow human beings. The answer of course is, that it was only possible for them because they did not see the prisoners as fellow human beings.

Child sex abusers deny the essential humanity of their victims at the time of the assault. Often they will avoid looking at the child's face. Not infrequently they cover the victim's face with a towel or clothing. Anal abuse has the added merit for perpetrators that they can approach the youngster from the back. Not infrequently they make the victim bend over, thereby averting the child's face.

Professionals who were aware of this were not surprised that there was an increased rate of diagnosis of child sexual abuse when doctors used reflex anal dilatation in Leeds and Cleveland (Hobbs and Wynne, 1986; Butler-Sloss, 1988; Campbell, 1988; Wyatt and Higgs, 1991). Anal abuse of children is probably far more common than most people care to believe.

Perpetrators lose sight of the identity of their victims during the abuse. Joe, who had abused his daughter, claimed he did so while 'dreaming'. He commented: 'I don't think of her as my daughter when I'm dreaming'. Perpetrators sometimes use the word 'it' when talking of the children they abuse: 'You can pick the child up and you can cuddle it, and you can do a lot more with it' (Li, West and Woodhouse, 1990).

Perpetrators either do not care about, or block from their minds, any pain and suffering they are causing. Angelou (1984) describes her experience:

> Then there was the pain. A breaking and entering when even the senses are torn apart. The act of rape on a 8-year-old body is a matter of the needle giving because the camel can't. The child gives, because the body can, and the mind of the violator cannot.

It is this objectification of the child that is so dangerous and can lead to the death or serious injury of the victim. A screaming or resisting youngster becomes just a 'thing' that has to be subdued even if that involves extreme violence, strangulation or suffocation. The observation of Mezey *et al.* (1991), reporting on community group treatment of child sex offenders, is apposite.

Generally, the men were unable to see these children as having separate personalities, with their own needs, feeling and wishes. The children were either narcissistically identified with as extensions of themselves or were simply 'objects' . . . In the course of treatment, men spoke of twisting children's arms behind their backs or stuffing their hands or handkerchiefs inside their mouths, along with routine threats of physical violence. Although initially shocked by one offender's preoccupation with killing a victim, most men reluctantly recognized their own potential to act in a similar way for sadistic reasons or out of sheer panic.

9. Fear: after the assault most perpetrators are fearful of being caught. They therefore have to 'groom ' the child again, this time to prevent disclosure. As before, a wide range of strategies is used.

Persuasive tactics include giving money or presents. Having accepted these the child is now an accomplice. Older children may be made to feel they have been prostituted. Victims may be promised something they have set their hearts on as long as they do not tell. Others are made to feel special, 'this is our special secret, it's just between you and me'. Children often believe that it is a point of honour to keep secrets.

Perpetrators may capitalize on a child's feelings of discomfort or guilt. 'It was all your fault, look what you made me do', 'You wanted me to play that game with you, you started it', 'What did you expect me to do when you wear such provocative clothes'. Children on the receiving end of such comments might well fear that they, rather than the abuser, will be punished for the activities.

Threats are likely to be used, although these can take the form of a subtle manipulation of the emotions rather than violent intimidation. The simple comment 'and who is going to believe you?' may be sufficient to prevent a disclosure, especially if the perpetrator is a 'pillar of society'. Time and again in the Leicestershire Inquiry, youngsters commented: 'I didn't think anyone would believe me'; 'I was fearful of Frank Beck and thought no one would believe me' (Kirkwood, 1993). Other menaces may reflect the reality of the situation, 'If you tell, you will have to leave home', 'I will be sent to prison', 'Your mother will become ill'. The perpetrator puts all the responsibility for the consequences of disclosure on to the child.

Violent intimidation is not infrequently used. Sylvia Fraser (1989) recalled the tactics her father used when she said she would tell her mother. He first threatened to throw away all her toys, then to send her to an orphanage where she would be spanked every night and given only bread and water. Finally, he guaranteed her silence by indicating he would kill her cat. The man who raped Maya Angelou (1984) threatened to kill her if she screamed out and to kill her brother if she told anyone about the assault.

10. Guilt: perpetrators who have no conscience about what they have done will simply need to assure themselves that they are safe from disclosure. If they are frightened of getting caught then it may be some time before they will assault a child again. Most will enjoy reliving the assault in fantasy until they can find a new opportunity to abuse a child. For some this may only mean waiting until their wife has gone out the following evening or until the neighbour's child they are molesting comes back from school. Other perpetrators may have to wait longer to target and groom a new victim.

A proportion of abusers feels not only a degree of fear but also remorse about what they have done. They may react by angrily blaming the youngster. 'You whore, look what you have done'. They might subsequently reject and ignore their victim.

Alternatively, they will become very caring of the child, promising the sexual assault will never happen again. They vow to themselves that under no circumstances will they repeat the offence. However, the continuation of a fantasy life is hard to resist. Their already low self-esteem is further damaged by guilt. They will be all the more vulnerable to temptation when a new trigger arises. Control may be re-established for a while, but the likelihood is that without help they will eventually find an excuse to reoffend and so the whole circle starts again. How far they have to target and groom again depends on the availabilty of a particular child. Whatever the time-scale, the perpetrator is bound up in a cyclical pattern of behaviour that can only be controlled by a total commitment to change on the part of the offender, alongside skilled external assistance.

Matthews (1993) gives a description of Helen, a woman who appears to have the pattern of behaviour just described.

> Fantasies of sexually abusing children cropped up. She fought the impulses, shamed and hated herself for having the thoughts, felt the fantasies come back, heaped more hatred and shame on herself and finally acted on the impulses. She repeated this cycle six times over the next five years. One child revealed the abuse and an investigation was conducted. Helen steadfastly denied the abuse and no charges were brought. The last victim was her own daughter.

FEMALE PERPETRATORS

Research and clinical experience relate overwhelmingly to adult male perpetrators. Fewer female offenders come to the notice of health professionals. Despite the growing number of biographies written by adult survivors, the vast majority describes sexual abuse by men. This is true even where the survivors are male, such as Graham Gaskin (MacVeigh, 1982) and Ben (1991). Nevertheless, there are accounts of sexual abuse perpetrated by women. Kathy Evert has given an account of being physically and sexually abused by her mother, although she was also abused by a male friend of the family (Evert and Bijerk, 1987). Some descriptions of female abuse are given by Bain and Sanders (1990). Michelle Elliot and co-authors (1993) have produced a series of narratives given by both boys and girls who were abused by women.

It is difficult to draw any firm conclusions from the research because the numbers involved in each study are quite small: Wolfe (1985) had a sample of 12 women; McCarty (1986) studied 26 incestuous mothers; Chasnoff *et al.* (1986) examined three mothers; Krug (1989) based his research on eight cases of mother–son incest; Matthews, Matthews and Speltz (1989) looked at 16 women and followed up with a study of 37 women (Matthews, 1993); Finkelhor, Williams and Burns (1988) found 147 female perpetrators in their study of day centres, although only 22 were included in the in-depth study. Two more recent studies have covered larger samples; one by Elliot (1993) included 127, while ChildLine had 780 reported cases over the year 1990/1 (Harrison, 1993).

Another problem is that samples are not necessarily comparable. Brown, Hull and Panesis (1984) studied 20 cases of women who used force at some stage during the sexual assault. Matthews (1993) had a sample in which the women used less force than the men. Finkelhor, Williams and Burns (1988) focused on women in the day care setting, whereas McCarty (1986) and Krug (1989) specifically examined offenders in mother–child incest cases. In the study by Chasnoff *et al.* (1986) the subjects were all mothers of infants.

This leads inevitably to some discrepancies. Finkelhor, Williams and Burns (1988) found that several of the female abusers coerced others into being their associates. No woman in the Matthew's 1993 study did so. Elliot (1993) found that in three-quarters of the cases the female abusers acted alone, and the ChildLine cases revealed that the father was frequently absent. On the other hand, Matthews (1989; 1993) includes as one of three major subgroups women who are always coerced by men.

Conclusions can, nevertheless, be drawn from the various studies. Firstly there seem to be many similarities between male and female perpetrators: they are drawn from every sector of society; they are just as likely to be 'church and civic leaders, intelligent business women and generally law-abiding citizens' (Finkelhor, Williams and Burns, 1988) as they are to be poor, uneducated or social outcasts. They can be any age from pre-adolescent girls to grandmothers in their 70s. They may have a preferred sex or age of target child but both girls and boys from babyhood to late teenage can be abused by women. McCarty (1986) found that in her sample the offenders, as in the case of male perpetrators, lacked any consistent sense of intimate attachment and encountered relationship problems, while a similar observation was made by Matthews (1993).

Women's sexuality is the subject of controversial debate and their sexual fantasies are still relatively unexplored. However, there are no indications that female perpetrators are exempt from the cycle of abusing behaviour described in the previous section. One woman, Diane, who had been accused by her sons, aged 8 and 12 years, of sexually abusing them, was asked to give a verbal pen-picture of her family members. When she described the adults there was no sexual content. But trying to describe her children she immediately talked about their sexuality, their masturbation and sexual activities. The account of Helen cited by Matthews(1993) at the end of the previous section is a further illustration of the cycle of behaviour.

Some attempts have been made to classify female perpetrators. Matthews, Matthews and Spetz (1989) identified three different typologies: the teacher/lover; the predisposed; the male coerced.

1. Teacher/lover: she tends to be involved with pre-pubescent and adolescent boys whom she claims she is introducing to sex. This is very similar to fathers who assert that they are gently teaching their teenage daughters the 'facts-of-life' or to Bruce who wanted to give girls the sex education he never had.
2. Predisposed: Diane, described above, would fall into the predisposed category because she came from a family in which sexual abuse was endemic. The women in this group have probably been sexually abused for a long period when small and then sexually abuse their own children. There are of course many male offenders who have had a similar history of childhood abuse.
3. Male-coerced: this group is the equivalent of the very passive male perpetrators. However, women who engage jointly in abuse with a male partner and do so only with a degree of persuasion, seem to feature more regularly than men being coerced into abuse by women.

These three typologies do not account for all female perpetrators. The day centre study by Finkelhor, Williams and Burns (1988) identifies additional types. The first are women who, offending in conjunction with other adults, act as initiator and use persuasion and loyalty. The second are women who participate in multiple-perpetrator situations but act in a subordinate role to other women, such as their mothers or female friends. The third type identified might be included in Matthews' 'predisposed' category. This is the lone woman who seems to be severely psychologically disturbed and abuses very young children.

One myth asserts that abuse by female perpetrators is less serious and more gentle than abuse by men. This view is echoed by the comment of Mathis (1972) 'What harm can be done without a penis?' Yet the suffering that can be caused by women to their victims can be every bit as great as that caused by men. When remembering the abuse by her mother Evert (1987) recalled 'Sometimes when she touched me – put her fingers in me – it hurt both emotionally and physically'. Gillian, another victim, recalled that when she was about 5 years old her mother 'took the hairbrush from the dressing-table and rammed its handle into my vagina – I have a lasting memory of the fury on her face. The pain was enormous' (Elliot, 1993).

Another myth about female offenders is that they are less responsible for their actions than men in equivalent positions. For example, a young boy disclosed that his 15-year-old brother had been sexually abused by their great-aunt. One professional argued that because the woman had a drink and drugs problem she was incapable of knowing what she was doing and had been assaulted by the boy. This is similar to the view once held that promiscuous teenage girls seduced their inebriated fathers. This is no longer accepted as tenable, the adult male is held accountable for his actions and so similarly the great-aunt was responsible for hers. Nevertheless, there are some instances of very powerful teenage youths using physical force or weapons to rape their older sisters, mothers and grandmothers and in such cases the allocation of blame and responsibility becomes less clear cut.

It is possible that some of these myths and attitudes to women as offenders affect the reporting, investigation and management of cases in which the perpetrator is female. Experience shows that when a woman is accused there is either general disbelief and the allegations are quickly dismissed, or there is a harsh, overly condemning, punitive response. Neither extreme helps either victim or perpetrator.

A source of increasing concern is that the notice being paid to female sexual abusers diverts attention away from the apparently far greater problem of male sex offenders. There is the danger that any attempt to examine the contribution of male power and domination as a key factor in relation to the sexual exploitation of children will be deemed invalid. However, Simon Hackett (1993) refutes this with the argument:

> Abuse does not occcur in a vacuum, but in a society of power inequalities. If individual women are perpetrating abuse, they do so within systems (communities, establishments, families and so on) where men hold the power and ensure that children are made vulnerable.

CHILD AND ADOLESCENT ABUSERS

There has been increasing recognition that children can be sexually victimized by other children. Youngsters of barely 2 years old have been described as 'perpetrators'.

It is necessary to draw distinctions between various forms of activity and the age of abusers. As defined in Chapter 1, sexual abuse occurs whenever one person with power abuses it in order to fulfil his or her own sexual needs. With very young children there is an argument for saying that they are not true abusers because, while they may be overpowering another child in some way, the activities they are engaging in are only sexual in the view of adults. Any sexual arousal is incidental, the dominant child is simply acting out his or her own experiences. Very young children who engage in sexual activities with weaker, more vulnerable children do so because they have themselves been sexualized. They should not be viewed in the same light as adult offenders and should not be labelled 'sex abuser'. This does not, however, mean that their behaviour should be allowed to continue or be condoned. Both the sexualized child and his or her victim will need attention and help.

Youngsters in the latency period may be more aware of the inappropriate nature of their activities than are pre-school children, but again they cannot be viewed in the same light as adult offenders. Recalling Finkelhor's (1984) preconditions, the first two – sexual orientation and internal inhibitors – do not really apply to children. Youngsters learn to recognize that certain bodily sensations are pleasurable and show some signs of arousal such as penile erection. But this does not have the same significance as it would for an adolescent or adult. Sexual orientation is an unreal concept when applied to children. Similarly, children are not expected to have developed internal inhibitions to the same level as adults. Nevertheless, children who coerce weaker youngsters into sexual activities must be prevented from doing so again; and as they are likely to have learnt such activities from an adult or older child, they will need help for their own victimization.

Adults caring for sexualized children must be responsible for stopping an assault by becoming effective external inhibitors, not by the use of punitive methods but by addressing abusive behaviour and by providing adequate help and supervision. All too often adults finding children engaged in sexual activities believe that a good spanking will stop the problem. Unfortunately it is more likely to perpetuate it, as Cantwell (1988) noted in one case: 'This form of punishment seems to have preserved silence among the victims, protecting the perpetrator for years. The victims were afraid that they would be spanked'. There is no place whatsoever for corporal punishment when children's sexual behaviour is an issue.

Adolescents may well be motivated by curiosity. One feature of this stage is experimentation without serious thought to the long-term consequences. It is also a period of rapid physical and emotional change and of sexual development. It is therefore hardly surprising that some experimentation is sexual and that some young people use any available person for this exploration. Nevertheless, this behaviour is abusive if it exploits the vulnerability of other youngsters who are unable to give informed consent. Whatever the motivation of the abuser, the experience and consequences for the victim can be very distressing. But in cases of misdirected experimentation the adolescents may 'grow out' of their offending behaviour.

However, an increasing number of studies and clinical experience demonstrate that sexual abuse by adolescents is by no means always a case of inappropriately focused curiosity. Abusive behaviour may reflect a need to exert power and control in a sexual manner, and this will not diminish as the youngster gets older. Research (Abel *et al.*, 1983; Ryan *et al.*,

1987; Cantwell, 1988; Becker, 1991) and clinical experience have revealed that many perpetrators start abusing in childhood or early adolescence and may have had fantasies about sexually abusive activities some years before carrying out an assault. At the age of 12 Bruce attempted intercourse and partially penetrated a 10-year-old neighbour. By the time he was 36 years old he could comment, 'My repeated reliving of that experience in daydreams and masturbation fantasies must have contributed to my paedophilia' (Li, West and Woodhouse, 1990).

Gail Ryan (1989) comments on the significance of the age range of 6 to 12 years. 'Many teenage offenders report first practising offender behaviors and experiencing offender thinking during that same span (6–12 years old)'.

Some adult perpetrators cannot remember an age at which they did not feel sexually attracted to children. George had been in prison for offences against pubescent girls. 'Paedophilic feelings do not arise. They exist already. Girls fascinated me before my fourth birthday. They still do 50 and a half years later . . . No decision had to be made, I was already ''girlified'' (Li, West and Woodhouse, 1990).

Many sexually abusing adolescents are found to have been sexually abused themselves. The figure is 48% in the study by Pierce and Pierce (1990). In Mary de Young's early study (1982) two of the four 'adolescent paedophiles' were the victims of incest. Knopp (1985) comments that data from adolescent treatment programmes show that 60% to 100% of the offenders indicate they experienced some form of early sexual victimization. Others have suffered from other types of distress or abuse in early life. In the study by Pierce and Pierce (1990) 63% had been physically abused and 70% had been neglected. Two came from families in which children had died from neglect.

Many young people demonstrate a cycle of offending behaviour that is similar to that shown by adult perpetrators (Ryan, 1989). However, its pattern is expressed slightly differently from that of adults. All children have experiences that make them feel helpless, powerless and out of control. Many, perhaps most, can cope with these because they also have positive experiences that give them a growing sense of autonomy, competence and confidence. Some youngsters, however, endure either so many damaging incidents or such traumatizing ordeals that these outweigh more positive experiences. They are frequently made to feel 'small' and are eventually haunted by their feelings of helplessness. At a certain point they find themselves in a situation which reminds them of their lack of control and powerlessness. This is called the 'trigger' (Ryan, 1989) and can be similar to the trigger for some adult perpetrators. They then feel bad about themselves, victimized and self-pitying. They need to gain control of the situation to help them feel better. This may be coupled with anger emanating from a sense of loss and injustice. They fantasize about situations in which they are powerful. At this stage their negative feelings could lead to other types of aggressive behaviour, such as mugging or arson, but when they have been sexually victimized or are sexually preoccupied then their offending behaviour is likely to take the form of sexual abuse.

Some victims of sexual abuse have described how they started to fantasize about 'turning the tables' and sexually assaulting the perpetrator – coming out of the encounter 'on top'. The original perpetrator becomes, in fantasy, the victim and is reduced in size. In actuality, the only people smaller or weaker than the young person are likely to be other children, although the frail elderly might be too. If the adolescent is to translate fantasy into reality then the obvious victims are children or occasionally a vulnerable elderly person.

At the same time the adolescents might have received messages that, in effect, give them permission to act out their fantasies. They may have been told by the perpetrator that the abuse was not serious and would do them no harm. Boys in particular may have tried to tell someone about their victimization only to find it dismissed as horseplay, a bit of messing about. If their molester was an older girl or woman they may be told to think themselves 'lucky'. They are taught to minimize sexual abuse and so are able to deny that they are doing any real harm by assaulting a weaker child. The feelings of powerlessness underpinning their behaviour mean they can shift responsibility for it on to someone else. They abuse to gain control and yet use their inability to control past events as an excuse to blame other people for their present behaviour.

They are now set to act out their fantasies. They often derive pleasure in outwitting others and manipulating a situation.

There is a process similar to the targeting and grooming found in the adult cycle. Among siblings it can start as a game. One survivor, abused by her brother, recalled: 'It started when I was 3 ... and it lasted until I was 12. And what my brother would do is he would say to me, "Do you want to play doctor?" ... He was 12' (Armstrong, 1978).

After the assault, the youthful abuser, afraid of being caught, will groom the victim to prevent disclosure. Perhaps lacking some of the skills of the adult perpetrator, younger people more often use threats of intimidation and violence. On occasion they panic and kill the victim. There is a trickle

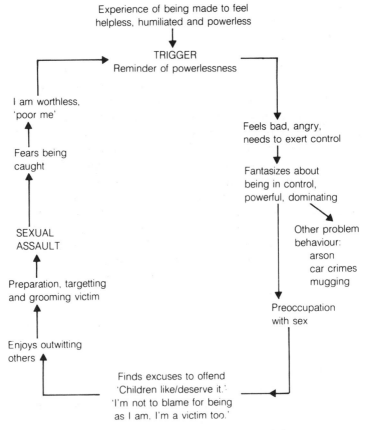

Figure 3.2 Adolescent abuser's cycle of offending behaviour

of cases each year in which a child's body is found and a teenager charged with the homicide.

Increased feelings of guilt serve to reinforce the offenders' low self-esteem; the fear of being caught adds to the 'poor me' syndrome (Ryan, 1989); and so the cycle re-starts – sooner or later they will offend again (Figure 3.2). Sometimes the sense of power derived from the assault was eminently satisfying and despite the risks it is an experience that young abusers wish to repeat as soon as another opportunity presents itself.

It is worth repeating that the apparently easy options of ignoring the abusive behaviour of children and young people or hitting them is only running the risk of creating very much more serious problems in the future. A section of Chapter 7 is devoted to a discussion of more adequate responses to adult, adolescent and child offenders.

It may be apt to close this chapter with the words of Peter Seven (1991) who, referring to sex offenders wrote: 'We should recognize the self-worth of those offenders as individuals who, whilst they may have committed wicked, vile crimes are not in themselves worthless or vile'.

4

Victim perspectives

The term 'victim' can be used in relation to a number of different people involved in a case of child sexual abuse. The primary victim is the child who is directly subjected to sexually abusive activities. However, non-abusing parents, other children and family members who are not directly abused can be regarded as 'co-victims'. They are subjected to targeting and grooming processes by the perpetrator. It will be remembered from the previous chapter that abusers have to overcome 'external inhibitors', usually parents, siblings and friends of the target child. The term 'secondary victim' can apply to the victim's acquaintances and relatives, who are not directly groomed or manipulated by the perpetrator but who nonetheless suffer as a result of his or her activities. Professionals can sometimes become co-victims but are more often secondary victims. This chapter will discuss the difficulties and dilemmas of each of these groups.

PERSPECTIVE OF ABUSED CHILDREN

This section will examine the perspective of the primary victim, the child who is directly sexually exploited by one or more offenders.

Understanding these children is far from easy because the skill and manipulation of their abusers render them unable to appreciate fully what has happened to them. As adult survivors they still cannot have total comprehension of their experiences. They will never therefore be in a position to convey precisely their ordeals, motivation and perspectives to other people.

Health professionals are often perplexed by the responses of victims. It is now known that the overwhelming majority of sexually molested children has enormous difficulty disclosing the abuse. Sometimes they will go to great lengths to shield their offenders, for whom they express considerable affection. When children manage to disclose, they will often retract what they have said during the investigation. Some children who are sexually abused in their own home will resist removal and will want to return to the family at the earliest opportunity.

An understanding of sexually abused children can be increased by examining the parallels with other people who are in a distressing or terrifying situation from which there is no obvious escape. Of particular relevance are three groups that have been the subjects of recent study: patients that are aware they have a terminal illness; concentration camp prisoners; and hostages, including kidnap victims.

A number of comparisons between abused children and camp prisoners or hostages have been made. Paul Celan (1971) evoked the image of a mother destroying her infant with 'black milk of dawn' when he described German death camps. Bruno Bettleheim (1979), a camp survivor and child psychiatrist, drew clear parallels between Nazi concentration camp survivors and abused children. Jacqueline Spring (1987) tried to comprehend her own experience of incest by reflecting on issues relating to concentration camps. Papers have been written comparing the various groups of victims, which include camp prisoners, hostages, subjects of totalitarian states and battered spouses (Fillimore, 1981; Doyle, 1985; 1990).

Frozen fright

If a fire breaks out in a roomful of people they will usually scream, panic and make for the nearest exit. If there is an obvious and easy escape route people will take it. In the same way some sexually assaulted children will have no hesitation in disclosing to a protective figure. This usually means they have not been 'successfully' groomed by the perpetrator, or they have been convinced, maybe by a preventive campaign such as those run by Kidscape (Elliot, 1986), that they have the right to receive protection against such abusive behaviour and should 'tell' if molested.

On the other hand, if a group of people is trapped with no means of escape, they will not scream and run. Instead they will freeze. Martin Symonds (1980) called this initial response 'frozen fright'. Similarly, health professionals may be familiar with patients who, when first told they have a terminal illness, seem stunned or unmoved, unable to take in the information they are being given.

Frozen fright is not simply a stunned paralysis. The victims are apparently calm, quiet and obedient. Symonds spent over 20 years interviewing the victims of violent crime and explained that frozen fright, 'superficially appears to be a cooperative and friendly behavior that confuses even the victim, the criminal, the family and friends of the victim, the police, and society in general' (Symonds, 1980).

This initial quiet, compliant phase explains why so many perpetrators are able to claim that their victims must have liked the sexual activities. If children feel trapped in an abusive situation they will find it hard to scream and resist. At the age of 9, Graham Gaskin was abused at boarding school by a housemaster, while he was ill in bed. He recalls that the master came into his room:

> As we chatted in this stilted fashion he slipped a hand under the sheet. I tried to ignore it, but after a minute it came into my pyjama jacket and stroked ticklingly over my belly. By now both of us had stopped talking. His hand came into my flies and took hold of the little tassel of flesh there. We remained silent while he held it.
>
> *(MacVeigh, 1982)*

There are positive reasons for this initial reaction. A compliant response is very often safer than histrionic crying, panic or aggressive challenge, all of which may lead the abusers to use further violence to gain control. A fight or flight response, when neither will effect an escape, will merely use up energy that could be saved until a realistic opportunity to escape presents itself. As Symonds (1980) noted, 'the victims focus all their energy on survival, exclusively concentrating on the terrorist'. At the same time they feel isolated, helpless and powerless. For many years child protection workers have recognised 'frozen watchfulness' in physically abused children. This is present in the form of extreme compliance in cases of sexual molestation. Symonds himself first became aware of the 'cooperative behaviour of frozen fright' when interviewing an 8-year-old incest victim.

Compliance can also be gained through psychological contrast. This is a well-known tactic and is sometimes used by law-enforcement agencies to gain confessions to crimes. In a captive or abuse situation the abuser is sometimes kind and friendly, at other times cruel and threatening. In *The Gulag Archipelago* Alexander Solzhenitsyn (1974) describes this tactic. 'The interrogator would be extremely friendly ... suddenly he would brandish a paperweight and shout', or, as a variation, 'two interrogators would take turns. One would shout and bully, others would be friendly, almost gentle'. A hostage-taker described the same tactic, 'One would be the bad guy and the other one would be the soft-spoken good guy'. (Knuston, 1980).

In many cases of child sexual abuse, the perpetrator befriends the victim and is gentle and kind, only to become overpowering and threatening on other occasions. In some siutations – a family home or an institution – one parent or member of staff is cruel and abusive while another, perhaps in an attempt to compensate for the mistreatment, is kind and gentle. Finkelhor, Williams and Burns (1988) describe this in the day care setting. A young woman became friends with an older, strong, independent woman. Both worked as teachers in a day care centre. Both were sexually abusive, but while her friend was aggressive the younger woman 'often "comforted" the children, letting them suck her breasts and taking the role of the "good guy" in counterpoint to the co-perpetrator'. If psychological contrast can induce compliance in adults, how much more effective is it with children who are being taught from their earliest years to be compliant and obedient to people who seem older and wiser?

Denial

A feature of the early response phase to a frightening situation is either complete denial of the situation or a dismissal of its importance. Health professionals may be familiar with the work of Elizabeth Kubler-Ross, who did research into the reactions of terminally ill patients. She noticed the early denial in patients when told of their prognosis. 'When this initial feeling of numbness begins to disappear and he can collect himself again, man's usual response is "No, it cannot be me"' (Kubler-Ross, 1970, p. 37).

Illustrating the denial of the seriousness of the situation, a passenger on the hijacked Lufthansa flight 181 said of the initial reaction of his fellow hostages: 'funnily enough nobody seemed afraid. Perhaps everyone felt as I did that it was too much like a gangster movie to be taken seriously ... I thought we were involved with desperadoes out for a high ransom and that the whole affair would be over in a couple of hours' (Dobson and Payne, 1977). In a similar way, sexually assaulted children may deny the reality of what is happening and minimize the attack or dismiss it as unimportant.

Some victims remain in a state of denial. Again Kubler-Ross gives examples of patients who never accept the prognosis and deny their illness to the extent that they refuse appropriate treatment. This can happen to sexually abused children. Sylvia Fraser, an incest victim, had to protect herself from the devastating experience of her father's abuse.

I created a secret accomplice for my daddy by splitting my personality in two. Thus, somewhere around the age of 7, I acquired another self with memories and experiences separate from mine, whose existence was unknown to me. My loss of memory was retroactive. I did not remember my daddy ever having touched me sexually.

(*Fraser, 1989*)

Short-term denial can be a useful cushion against an unpleasant experience. It can give the victim time to muster other emotional resources. Longer-term denial, however, can have adverse effects. In the terminally ill patient it can mean palliative treatment is rejected. In hostages it can mean prolonged hostility towards the law enforcement agencies who rescued them. In abused children it can lead to the development of dual or multiple personalities. It may sometimes result in victims becoming victimizers as they grow up, having convinced themselves that, just as the abuse they suffered was not damaging, so their own sexual activities with children will do no harm.

Fear and anger

In her study, Kubler-Ross noted: 'When the first stage of denial cannot be maintained any longer, it is replaced by feelings of anger, rage, envy and resentment' (1970). In addition to these bitter emotions, patients and victims alike also experience fear as they realize the danger and enormity of their situation. These strong, turbulent feelings of anger and fear have to be expressed somehow. For victims it can be too uncomfortable and too dangerous to direct them against their abusers. This will result, on occasion, in their being turned against an anonymous 'outside world'. They are often directed against the very people who are trying to protect or rescue the victim.

Doctors, nurses, physiotherapists and occupational therapists are only too aware that they can become the targets of anger from patients who feel they are facing a bleak future because of accident or disease. Similarly, after liberation from concentration camps some long-term prisoners expressed anger and hatred against American and English journalists who had tried to help them and publish their plight.

This projection is also seen in hostage situations. In Stockholm on 23rd August, 1973 a gunman, later joined by a fellow criminal, held four bank employees hostage. 'Contrary to what had been expected, it was found that the victims feared the police more than they feared the robbers. In a telephone call to Prime Minister Olaf Palme, one of the hostages expressed the typical feelings of the group when she said, ''The robbers are protecting us from the police''' (Strenz 1980). This redirection of fear and anger away from the victimizers is one of the features of what, in the wake of this particular bank siege, has been termed the 'Stockholm syndrome'. It is a psychological phenomenon that is seen in many terror or victim situations. Its hallmark is the bond that develops between captor and captive, between abuser and abused.

A similar projection of fear and anger on to the very people who could help is seen in sexually abused children. Fraser recalls how her favourite teacher held her back after school to ask her why she had been hostile towards her:

'Why have you been so mean all year? You seem to have developed such a chip on your shoulder. It's as if you've decided not to trust anyone any more.' I shift my gaze to the exit through which the last students are shoving, wretched to have caused this suffering, appalled to have possessed such power, resentful to be called to account. 'If you'll give me some explanation, I'll try to understand. Why do you hate me so?' . . . Miss Buchanan is staring at me, waiting for some response. My tongue lies frozen in my mouth.

(Fraser, 1989)

The fear and anger against possible rescuers has a basis in reality. A man taken hostage by the South Moluccans in a terrorist incident in The Netherlands in the 1970s recalls how he realized that if the anti-terrorist forces stormed the train it could mean the deaths of hostages and terrorists alike (Strenz, 1980; Ochberg, 1978). Sexually abused children have been physically abused, and some have been killed, by the perpetrator during investigations in order to silence them. The investigative and legal systems themselves are often abusive. Furthermore, the concept of the dangerous professional who makes the situation worse for the child is now acknowledged (Dale *et al.*, 1986; Department of Health 1988).

Positive bonds and introjection

The external projection of fear and anger unites the victims and victimizers in a common bond that often becomes a positive one. The reason lies in the human spirit. The will to survive leads people to retain hope and seek out signs to support it. Health professionals will be familiar with terminally ill patients and their relatives who are over-optimistic about the possibility of a cure being found in time or about the progress of an illness when a patient is in a prolonged state of remission. Each positive sign is seen as confirming their optimistic view of the benign nature of the illness or a hopeful outcome, in defiance of the doctors' less sanguine prognosis.

In a similar way, victims of mistreatment hope their abusers are not as bad as they seem. Hostages are more likely to survive if their captors are, at heart, good people. Consequently, they search for confirmatory signs of goodness. Solzhenitsyn (1974) remarked on how precious the warmth in the concentration camp gaoler's 'good morning' became.

Every time an abuser shows some act of kindness – allowing hostages to have a drink, giving an exploited child a present – the victims see it as confirmation of their abusers' goodness. When asked how he gained control over his target one perpetrator said, 'by buying her presents, letting her stay at her girl-friends, letting her have favors, buying her things that I didn't buy other kids' (Conte, Wolf and Smith, 1989).

This can be the beginning of introjection. A simple logic is at play. If the abuser is good then their values, beliefs and actions must also contain some merit. The victim searches for that goodness. During the Second World War some long-term German concentration camp prisoners accepted Nazi politics and attempted to copy SS uniforms (Bettleheim, 1979). Hostages have adopted the values of terrorists. Publishing heiress Patty Hearst was a notable example, as she joined forces with her kidnappers and robbed banks with them.

This process explains, in part, why the majority of citizens of a tyrannical dictator or oppressive totalitarian regime come to accept the principles and norms of their rulers. Similarly, sexually abused children may come to harbour the same distorted views as their abusers. They arrive at the belief that they deserved the abuse or asked for it. They can eventually become convinced that there is nothing wrong in sexually exploiting children.

Adults and older children in the power of a victimizer might become as dependent as a baby. Infants will love the person who is able to protect them from unknown threats from an anonymous outside world. Similarly, adults and older children can feel the affection of dependency in relation to their abusers. Parents who abuse tend to keep their families isolated and in fear of an unfamiliar menacing world outside. For sex abusers, children's silence can be assured by telling them to be **careful** not to tell – implying some unknown danger if they divulge the secret.

The emotional bond between victim and victimizer is made all the more positive by the sense of gratitude felt by the victim for any acts of kindness. It can also be created by a threat that is not carried out, in particular the threat to life. 'The victim perceives that the terrorist, who has the power of life and death over him, is letting him live – profound and persistent attitudinal and behavioral changes occur. He now sees the criminal as the "good guy"' (Symonds, 1980).

If adults, who have their own values and principles, can become emotionally bonded in a positive way to their captors – sometimes in the space of a few hours – how much more vulnerable are children who have only very hazy and ill-formed views? The time scale of this process does not have to be great. A detective held for just over three hours by a criminal gang was interviewed two months later and maintained 'what a good guy the [gang] leader was' (Symonds, 1980).

According to Strenz (1980), although the time spent in captivity is not a significant factor, the nature of the contact with the abusers is important. Victims who have nothing but negative contact do not show affection, while those having some positive contact do. This has relevance for sexually abused children because the grooming process is very often an attempt by the perpetrator to establish a positive relationship with the youngster. A target child who has been violently and brutally attacked by a stranger or an indifferent acquaintance is less likely to protect and defend the abuser than one who has been patiently 'wooed' with presents, treats and declarations of affection by an apparently 'loving' friend or relative.

Depression and despair

After being held captive for very many hours the passengers of the hijacked Lufthansa flight 181 began to despair, they had 'reached the stage known to psychiatrists who specialise in terrorism as "switching off". This comes about with tiredness, when the body breaks down through lack of exercise and the use of too much adrenalin. Everything feels hopeless' (Dobson and Payne, 1977).

Health professionals will be aware of patients who become depressed as their sense of helplessness and loss becomes overwhelming. One of the causes of depression is anger projected inwards. Along with depression comes a host of negative feelings turned against the self.

There is, in addition, a straightforward logic that entraps victims. If the offender is good, then it is they (the abused) who must be bad. In some way they must have deserved to suffer. It is their fault if they feel distressed. The perpetrator is good, so either the activities are not really as bad as they seem or they, the victims, have caused the perpetrator to do something wrong.

> They [the hostages] have convinced themselves that the abductor's show of force was necessary to take control of the situation, that perhaps their resistance precipitated the abductor's show of force. Self-blame on the part of the victims is very evident in these situations.
>
> *(Strenz, 1980)*

Adults, who may have been held captive for a relatively short period of their lives, may show feelings of guilt, self-blame, shame and loss of self-esteem. Children are all the more vulnerable to being made to feel negative about themselves because they are naturally inclined to feel responsible for events and have a fragile, poorly-developed sense of self-esteem.

Acceptance and integration

Children who are in this helpless, hopeless state of despair are unlikely to seek rescue. Instead they accept the abuse, seeing it as their burden to bear. In extreme cases of constant, severe abuse they will have reached a state of numbness similar to that experienced by some concentration camp prisoners.

Some terminally ill patients show a resigned helplessness, a sense of 'what's the use' (Kubler-Ross, 1970). Others reach a state of acceptance, which, although not a happy state, is one free of fear and despair. This is also true of some sexually abused children. It is a constructive stage for the ill patient who is able to die in peace and with dignity. Acceptance may also be useful for the adult hostage or prisoner who can at least exist without the pain of terror.

It is not, however, a useful state for sexually abused children. To grow up unable to feel happy is to be robbed of a precious birthright. Neither resigned helplessness, numbness nor acceptance is an appropriate state for a child. Youngsters who have reached this stage might well be emotionally disadvantaged as adults. They may have become totally dependent on their abusers. Some children who have been maltreated by their parents live with them until they die, a number of incestuous siblings have remained life-long partners: all are unable to free themselves from the emotional ties formed by abuse. In other cases victims, dependent on the perpetrator, have found a substitute in the form of partners who are themselves abusive.

Finally, sexually abused children may not only accept their victimization but identify with the abuser so closely that they integrate their beliefs and attitudes with those of the perpetrator and become the next generation of abusive adults.

A proportion of victims does not experience these stages and feelings in the order described. As with all attempts to categorize human responses it is important to recognize that human beings do not clearly move from one stage to the next. They may move forwards and backwards emerging from a state of anger into one of despair only to retreat back into anger. Some, like Fraser (1989), stay in an almost permanent state of denial, with feelings of anger and self-disgust overlaying the denial.

Similarly, abused children can experience just one or two of the stages described above. For example, by no means do all sexually exploited children have an affection for their abusers. Ben, at the age of 14, was anally raped by his uncle, on whom he depended for a job. He was regularly abused for the next three years and wrote, 'I hated that bastard and everything concerned with him' (Ben, 1991). This did not stop him from experiencing despair and negative feelings about himself. After evenings enjoying himself in the company of friends, Ben knew that when he was on his own, 'the loneliness and sadness and misery would return. The guilt, filthy feelings and hopelessness would be my companions again' (Ben, 1991).

Not all children integrate the values of the perpetrator with their own. Many do not become abusers themselves, nor do they collude with and condone other child sex abusers. As parents, many do all in their power to avoid subjecting their children to similar experiences. As a child, Alan was subjected to sexual spankings; as an adult he is able to state firmly:

> Although I have four children I have never once hit them or allowed the women I was with to hit them. I have no doubt this is because of my own experience . . . because my own 'abuse' was linked with spanking, I have never struck my children (although I've spanked women and men).
>
> (*Elliot, 1993*)

Only a proportion remains dependent on their abuser or finds partners who are abusive. Many victims deliberately reject child sexual abuse and ensure they find partners who are not abusers. Sarah was sexually, physically and emotionally abused by her father. She nearly married a similar man but 'she realised when she had recovered from the broken engagement she did not want to marry a bully' (Doyle, 1990). Her eventual husband was like her grandfather, 'the one good man who could love in a giving way'. Jacqueline Spring, a victim of incest, wrote in a letter addressed to her father: 'I met and married a man of goodwill. As unlike you as I could find' (Spring, 1987).

CHILDREN WITH ADDED DISADVANTAGES

Some youngsters deserve special consideration because they are placed in a position where they are particularly vulnerable or have difficulties over and above those of other children.

Black, Asian and ethnic minority children

Some black and Asian children and those from ethnic minorities may already have problems with self-esteem before they encounter abuse. If their community is despised and ridiculed, they will personally share this denigration. In addition, a proportion of black children, especially those cared for by white people, is brought up to have negative attitudes towards other black people. Jocelyn Maxime (1986) writes: 'Thus the physical realization of self as "black", which is not perceived to be good and right, becomes terrifying to many of these black children.'

These youngsters may also have problems in a society whose language uses black in a derogatory fashion to indicate something undesirable such as 'black sheep' or 'blackmail', and which values things that are golden or white, equating the latter colour with purity.

EXAMPLE: Alice is of dual heritage (mixed race) and has dark skin and black–brown eyes. She was sexually abused by a member of her family. She was already aware that, being seen as black, in school plays she was never chosen to be an angel or Mary or the May Queen. She was always a poor shepherd, a 'baddy' or member of the crowd. Fellow pupils had asked her why her skin, being a deep brown, was so dirty. Her view of herself as dirty and defiled by the abuse was further compounded by a society that favours blond, blue-eyed little girls – giving the message in subtle ways that black, dark-haired ones are poor, dirty or 'bad'. As a child she would scrub her skin until it bled in an attempt to make herself, in her words, 'clean and white'.

Once black and Asian children become aware of racism, those abused by a member of their own ethnic group may be reluctant to disclose because they fear it will give ammunition to racists. Charmaine, aged 12, whose parents were from the West Indies, wrote: 'I couldn't tell about my dad because I loved him and didn't want to get him into trouble and I thought white people would make racist comments' (Rouf, 1991a).

Kadj Rouf's father was from Bangladesh and she was brought up in the UK as a Muslim (Rouf, 1990). She describes, through poetry, the reaction of her father's family when her father's incestuous behaviour was disclosed:

A blood bond with my family dissolved.
Untouchable, Unweddable. Liar.
These names replaced beloved grand-daughter, niece, cousin.

Her mother was white and British but she fared no better with her mother's family:

Here in my other home,
Through deep black eyes I saw hatred.
I listened to open hostility **and** the quiet comments
Of those who didn't realise that I wasn't quite one of them.

(Rouf, 1991b)

Black and Asian children, those from other minority ethnic groups or those of dual heritage have additional problems with which to contend. They have added perspectives that require an appreciative and understanding response.

⚡ Children with physical or learning disadvantages

Health professionals may encounter proportionally more children with physical or learning disadvantages/disabilities than some other professional groups. The sexual abuse of these children is therefore an important issue for health workers.

Some children suffer particular disadvantages due to their physical or mental condition and may, in consequence, be rendered more vulnerable to sexual abuse.

Sense of value and worth

Just as Western society tends to value people, especially girls, with light skin, blonde hair and blue eyes, so it also tends to value people who are healthy, wealthy and wise. This is well expressed by Sandra Walmsley (1989) who writes: 'In a society which sets store by intellect, physical attractivess and earning capacity, people who fall short of the norm in any of these ways are not able to develop a sense of self worth.'

Discussing the plight of deaf children Margaret Kennedy (1990) writes: 'If identity brings strength we now have a major difficulty. The Deaf child has crossed from one culture to another which views "Deaf" as deficient/pathological. The Deaf child is placed in a position of inferiority and begins to take on this view of himself as "fundamentally deficient".'

Due to their experience of discrimination, many people with disabilities may be lacking in self-esteem and confidence, which makes them more malleable and less able to assert themselves or express their wishes. A sense of rejection and unworthiness increases children's desire to please. Such youngsters can be all too eager in their response to attention and signs of affection. They will not want to resist an apparently caring abuser for fear of losing his or her love. They can feel they have no right to protest when assaulted. In addition, they might fear that no one will believe them or think them worth helping if they do disclose. As sexual abuse can damage the self-esteem, it is therefore all the more devastating for people who already have a poor self-image.

Children with disabilities can have a host of negative feelings because of their physical or mental limitations and experience of discrimination, which are compounded if they are also the victims of abuse (Kennedy, 1990).

- There is guilt and self-blame:
  because of disability – 'I cause my parents a lot of trouble';
  because of abuse – 'I caused this to happen, all this trouble is my fault'.
- There is a sense of rejection and failure:
  because of disability – 'I am not as good as other people';
  because of abuse – 'I am only good enough for this, as I'm worse than other children'.
- There is anxiety and fear:
  because of disability – 'I may make a mistake, appear stupid, fail';
  because of abuse – 'I may be found out. It may happen again'.
- There is bitterness and anger:
  because of disability – 'Why was I made like this? Why did this happen?'
  because of abuse – 'Why did he do it to me? Why did this happen to me?'
- There is confusion and frustration:
  because of disability – 'I don't understand. How can I cope?'
  because of abuse – 'I don't understand what happened. How can I stop it?'

These overwhelming doubly negative feelings mean that these youngsters can reach the stages of despair and acceptance rapidly. They are therefore less likely to resist or seek help.

Issues of control

Children with disabilities may not achieve complete independence until quite late in life, if ever. Those unable to walk or move limbs will need help in intimate situations such as toileting and bathing. Those with severe learning disabilities 'may find it difficult to distinguish between different sorts of touch when most or all body care is attended to by other people' (Brown and Craft, 1989). People with visual impairments may have to be touched and physically guided as a supplement to verbal communication, and for people with both visual and hearing impairments touch becomes an essential part of communication.

For these reasons children with a range of disabilities have less control over who touches them, so are more easily groomed and desensitized. All children have some difficulty drawing the line between appropriate and inappropriate touching; these youngsters have even greater difficulty.

When they recognize a behaviour as abusive they may find it harder to convince other people of this. In the case of a severely handicapped 12-year-old boy the perpetrator maintained that on a couple of occasions he had 'accidentally' touched the boy's penis when helping him to change his clothes.

Generally, children with disabilities have less control over their lives, with fewer opportunities to decide when they eat or drink, watch the television, go out, play, go to bed. If they cannot manage these tasks for themselves they have to wait for a carer to help them. They are dependent on their good-will and so have to be accommodating and obedient. They can feel that they have very little choice over what happens to them and simply have to accept their treatment, if not with gratitude, then at least without complaint.

Self-protection

Overprotection is a feature of the lives of many children with physical and mental disadvantages. This can mean that they do not learn self-protection strategies. They are never allowed to become 'street-wise'. They may not be made aware of danger signs or of behaviours that could be misinterpreted by potential abusers. For example, a visually impaired girl may not learn through unconscious example to sit with her legs together, and so may sit with them apart. She is then seen by an abuser as sitting provocatively and being sexually inviting.

With so much else to master, the formal sex education of children with disabilities is sometimes neglected and they can lack access to informal ways such as chatting with peers or borrowing relevant books from friends. Some carers, denying the sexuality of their charges, withhold information on sexual matters. This means that a proportion of children with disabilities does not understand how they are being exploited and cannot, therefore, raise a voice in protest.

Just as children are generally taught kerb drill and water safety, they should have accurate sexual education and instruction on how to protect themselves from sexual exploitation. Children with disabilities are no exception. Some of the standard prevention programmes may have to be adapted before the materials can be used by those with visual impairments or very severe learning difficulties. But it can be done.

Communication

For children with disabilities, communication difficulties are substantially increased. Speech therapists may have a key role in helping many articulate their experiences. For others the alternative is disclosure through a word-board or by signing, which require determination, persistence and patience. Sometimes victims have to know how to spell words, such as 'vagina', if they are to make their meaning clear.

Children with severe hearing impairments exemplify some of the problems:

> The 4-year-old prelingual, profoundly deaf child whose communication consists only of pointing, shouting and much pulling and pushing may achieve her objective in obtaining a drink of lemonade. It will not, however, be enough to determine whether she has been sexually abused, and if so, how she is feeling about it.
>
> *(Kennedy, 1989)*

Victims, with or without hearing or speech impairments, will communicate non-verbally through their behaviour. Here again, children with disabilities may be at a disadvantage. If they lack muscular control they are unlikely to have a very wide non-verbal repertoire. A distressed demeanour may be ascribed to problems in coping with their disabilities. 'Problem behaviour is too often accepted as normal for people with mental handicaps, so that symptoms which may signal alarm in a child or young person without handicaps are perceived as an inevitable consequence of the handicap' (Walmsley, 1989).

Isolation

When youngsters attempt to communicate their distress they depend on the skill and training of their carers to recognize that sexual abuse is the issue and to respond appropriately. Uninformed adults may feel that it is in the best interests of the child to ignore the matter and let him or her forget it, on the basis of 'least said, soonest mended'. Carers may become overprotective, thereby making the child even more dependent and isolated. Unable to accept what they are being told, some parents may deny what has happened, choosing to believe that the victim is mistaken or having fantasies, and that any injuries are self-inflicted. They will cling to all the myths about disabled children and abuse, such as 'people feel sorry for them so would not exploit them' or 'they are not attractive as sexual objects' (Marchant, 1991).

While most children are encouraged to keep telling trusted adults until eventually someone helps, those with disabilities are usually more isolated, less mobile, less independent and have fewer people with whom they can communicate. If they are not believed or helped by the first adult to whom they disclose, then they may have no one else to turn to.

Sexual abuse itself increases feelings of isolation, 'I am the only person who has been used like this'. Compounding the situation, children with disabilities can be made to feel different from others because of their physical or mental condition. They may have been ridiculed or bullied by their contemporaries and dismissed or patronized by adults. It is hard for children who are dependent and have to be supervised by adults to have many peer friendships. In consequence, those who are abused are doubly set apart and isolated. 'I am not like everyone else, I am different, I'm not as good'. Isolation and its attendant loneliness in turn make them more vulnerable because they are eager for attention and friendship.

Children with substitute carers

Children living with substitute carers also have special problems and needs. Whatever the care situation many will already feel guilt and rejection. They believe, albeit subconsciously, that their natural parents no longer care for them because of some deficiency in their nature or behaviour. 'If I had been really loveable mum would not have left me'. 'If I hadn't been so naughty dad might not have died'. If they are then sexually abused by a substitute carer this reinforces the low opinion they have of themselves as rejected, bad and unworthy.

Feeling different from their peers is common to many children with substitute parents. If they are sexually abused in care then their feeling of being different and set apart from others is increased. They become all the more isolated, which in turn increases their vulnerability.

Sometimes youngsters who have felt rejected by at least one natural parent will respond eagerly to any show of interest and affection. They will want to please to avoid being rejected again. Children who have been adopted may be vulnerable in this respect, although those whose adoptive parents have done their best to enhance self-esteem and confidence are less likely to be at risk.

Research (Finkelhor *et al.* 1986; La Fontaine, 1990) has indicated that the presence of a non-biological father in the family is a risk factor. These are 'stepfather families' although the term includes ones in which the mother's partner is not her legal husband. There are a number of reasons put forward for this added risk factor. One possibility is that potential perpetrators may target families in which a mother is struggling to bring up her offspring on her own. Another is that youngsters whose own fathers appear to have rejected them may be especially keen to please a new 'dad'. An alternative reason for the high proportion of cases of non-biological fathers coming to light might be that children who have had loving parenting will know the difference between their own dad's behaviour and that of their stepfather. At the same time they feel little loyalty towards their step-parent and are all the more willing and able to draw attention to his inappropriate conduct.

Children taken into care because they were sexually abused are particularly vulnerable. Youngsters who have been sexualized are pliable in the hands of potential abusers who justify their actions on the grounds that the target child was provocative and wanted sexual relations. Victims may not attempt to protect themselves in the belief that they are 'soiled goods', fit for nothing else except sex. For some youngsters sex is the only type of 'affection' they have known, can hope for, or understand.

Foster care can present its own risks (Faller, 1990). Some people offering themselves as foster-parents do so in order to procure children for sexual exploitation, although they may not be aware of their own motivation. Frank Beck, sentenced to life imprisonment for serious sexual offences against children and the subject of the Kirkwood Inquiry (1993), as a single male applied to be a foster-parent. One consultant psychiatrist who supported his application wrote:

> It is quite clear that Frank has an excellent knowledge of children and an unusual ability to relate effectively with them so that he is a constructive and nurturant guardian. He also shows excellent common sense in the kinds of control he applies to children and is well experienced in managing the special problems of adolescents . . . he is without doubt responsible sexually and would not under any circumstances take advantage of a minor within his care.
>
> (*Kirkwood, 1993*)

Children placed in care are vulnerable. Their attempts to disclose abuse are often interpreted as false allegations, the result of the transfer of angry feelings from the natural parents who failed them on to the foster-parents. Disturbed behaviour is interpreted as a symptom of background problems rather than a sign of present abuse.

Some victims are not sexually abused in their foster home but are rejected when, while there, they divulge previous sexual abuse. Their carers are unable to cope with the disclosure and fear that the child will make false allegations against them. They may worry that their own offspring will be at risk from the victim. Some are unable to cope with the foster-child's pain, particularly if they were themselves sexually abused and have not resolved dormant emotional problems.

The issues for children in residential care were highlighted in Chapter 2. These youngsters are particularly vulnerable because of the negative feelings and helplessness that abuse evokes, which is compounded by the equally negative effects of institutionalization.

SIBLINGS OF ABUSED CHILDREN

The siblings of sexually abused children sometimes have significant difficulties to face that are all too easily overlooked. In a number of families all the children are primary victims because all are directly assaulted. Sometimes children are jointly abused. In other situations, every child in the family is abused separately in a way that means the victims do not realize that their brothers and sisters are also being mistreated. Often it is only when they are older and one of them talks of their experiences that the others find out the truth.

Cases in which all the children are jointly abused may take the form of organized or ritual abuse. In others, the family has few boundaries. The distinction between child and adult is blurred. There is a family culture of sexual abuse stretching back through several generations. The children have very little sense of what is, and is not appropriate contact and sexual conduct; lacking this knowledge they may well abuse each other.

They may also prove very difficult to 'rescue' as the family system is powerful with a tradition of keeping secrets and fending off curious outsiders. In the shadow of the Stockholm syndrome, the children may remain very loyal to their parents. They will have been exposed to the family belief system from their earliest years and will have absorbed its values. This bodes ill for them as adults as they are likely to have few internal inhibitions about sexual relations between children and adults. If removed from the family, they may present considerable risks to other youngsters in their foster or residential home. The power of the family system is such that unless they are removed at a very early age they may be drawn back to the family once old enough to leave care.

In some cases, when siblings are forced against their will to abuse each other they are aware the activities are wrong and abusive but are unable to resist the power of the perpetrators. The sense of guilt and powerlessness of the coerced children is overwhelming. There are parallels with concentration camps where prisoners were forced to beat or kill their fellow prisoners. It effectively silences the children because those forced to act will not disclose for fear of punishment and blame, while those on whom the acts were performed may be reluctant to cause trouble for the coerced siblings.

Where the molester has abused one child at a time there are several possible outcomes. Sometimes each youngster is made to feel that he or she must submit to the abuse in order to protect the other children in the family. In this way the perpetrators make the victim responsible for the fate of the whole family. They will also give the children the impression that they made a positive choice to agree to the activities and are therefore as 'guilty' as the abusers. Those youngsters who make a sacrifice for what they believe is the greater good can feel overwhelmed by a sense of betrayal, shame and uselessness if they find that they did not, after all, manage to protect their brothers and sisters.

In some families, children who think their siblings are not being abused may be resentful and envious. The perpetrator may incite these feelings by comparing each victim unfavourably with his or her brothers and sisters. Here the perpetrator is adopting a policy of 'divide and rule'. Sarah, who was sexually abused by her father, commented:

> I remember truly hating my sister. My father used to say to me: 'Why can't you be like your sister, she's gregarious, has lots of friends and is cheerful? You are just a sour puss'. I was jealous of her. I did not realize he said the same to her about me, making her jealous as well . . . I now only have a superficial relationship with my sister.
>
> (*Doyle, 1990*)

The effects of the Stockholm syndrome may mean that some of the children in the family feel intense loyalty towards, and affection for, the perpetrator. If one of the victims discloses, other siblings – despite the fact that they have been abused too – can be very angry and rejecting of the one who disclosed.

In other cases, there may be only one primary victim, although children living in the same household as the victim and the perpetrator at the time of the abuse are co-victims. They will have been groomed so that they will not or cannot protect their brother or sister. This grooming can take several forms, with a number of different repercussions.

Siblings, if not molested, can be physically abused and intimidated. This creates feelings of isolation and helplessness.

It sometimes produces an 'everyone for him/herself' philosophy so that the primary victim is left to fend alone. An alternative effect is to make the siblings despise themselves because they know that their brother or sister is being sexually exploited but they are powerless to help. They may live in constant fear that they will be the next ones to be molested.

Isolating the primary victim by favouring him or her is another grooming tactic. This creates feelings of jealousy in the siblings who may believe, once they know about the abuse, that the victim deserved to be mistreated. They will not attempt to help someone they feel merits exploitation and are unlikely to disclose on their sibling's behalf. Gail Berry (1975) cites the example of Janet, whose older sister had been sexually abused by their father. 'It became clear that Janet's jealousy was a screen for an intense, unconscious envy of the sister's incestuous relationship with her father'.

Grooming tactics can have a profound negative impact on the self-esteem of non-abused siblings. Failing to understand the dynamics of the situation and the suffering endured by the victim, they feel unworthy of the perpetrator's attentions. They must be unattractive or undesirable. In one primary school the teacher targeted and molested blonde, blue-eyed girls. Leonie, a black girl, recalls feeling 'unattractive' because she was not among the pretty, fair-haired favourites of the teacher.

Another tactic is to remove any siblings who might attempt to protect the primary victim. Perpetrators can achieve permanent removal from the home by making life there intolerable for older brothers and sisters, who therefore leave. They might manipulate both family and welfare services so that an unwanted sibling is removed from the household. In other cases, siblings are encouraged to keep out of the way.

> EXAMPLE: Hugh was keen on music. His father arranged for him to have regular piano and guitar lessons in the evenings. His mother was persuaded to drive him to the lessons. During their absence he sexually assaulted Hugh's twin sister. Later, when Hugh found out, he gave up music. He felt guilty believing that his love of music had in some way caused his sister's suffering.

Siblings are secondary victims when they are not in sufficiently close proximity to the perpetrator to be directly groomed and manipulated, but nevertheless suffer from the inevitable 'ripple effect' of child sexual abuse. Examples of this are abuse by a stranger outside the family or, alternatively, in the home when the siblings were not family members, maybe before they were born.

The effect of any sexual abuse on families is to cast a shadow, sometimes with an atmosphere of mistrust and fear. Non-abused children may be overprotected and lose much of their independence as the parents restrict their activities in an attempt to keep them safe. There might also be an irrational, but nevertheless pervasive, sense of guilt and shame which the non-abused children do not understand but feel all the same. Similarly, there could be an ambience of secrecy, especially if siblings are not told about the abuse. In addition, as can happen when one child has a serious illness or disability, secondary victims come to regard themselves as less important or valuable because of the attention paid to the primary victim.

NON-ABUSING PARENTS

Parents of abused children can be placed somewhere on a continuum from, at one end, knowing nothing about the abuse but on finding out immediately taking protective action to, at the other end, being a perpetrator or active co-perpetrator. In between are parents who may have known there was 'something wrong' but did not realize sexual abuse was the problem. Some may have suspected abuse or even known what was happening but tried to convince themselves that nothing untoward was going on.

The phrase 'non-abusing parents' refers to those who either know nothing about the abuse or are aware of a problem but cannot allow themselves to recognize that it is sexual abuse. It tends to relate to the mother in cases where the father-figure has committed the assault. However, fathers are also non-abusing parents in cases where the offender is the mother or some other person.

The needs and feelings of non-abusing fathers have been somewhat overlooked in the literature on child sexual abuse.

Health professionals may well have their primary contact with these fathers, especially if they have a health problem. Indeed they may not have been able to protect their child because of their medical condition, a fact that the perpetrator will have used to his or her own advantage. Non-abusing parents will have been groomed by the perpetrator so that they are unable to protect the victim. In some instances the parents will be alienated and isolated from their child. In others the parents will have been encouraged to trust the perpetrator. One illustration is the case of the eminent doctor taking ill and injured children on holiday in order to abuse them with impunity. When abuse occurs in the home the non-abusing parent may have been encouraged to go out while the perpetrator baby-sits. Alternatively, the offender will have seized opportunities presented by any parental limitations, examples include physical disability preventing the parent from moving quickly around the house or the effects of sleeping pills making a potential protector too sleepy to know what is happening.

When parents find out about the abuse their first reaction may be one of shock and numbness. 'One mother reports being immobilized and unable to react when she walked into the room where a neighbor's girl, considerably older than her child, was performing oral sex on her daughter' (Hagans and Case, 1990). If the assault was not witnessed there is sometimes denial on the part of the parents. They may refuse to believe their child or think that he or she is mistaken. They would rather substitute what they would like to have heard for what they really did hear.

Having accepted the truth, the parents are likely to feel angry. This may be particularly painful for non-abusing fathers if the perpetrator is another man who he trusted. The father has a sense of betrayal by one of his own sex and of being outwitted and duped by another man. Sometimes the perpetrator's grooming is so effective that the parents cannot feel angry with the offender and therefore project their rage on to other people. They blame the victim for having apparently colluded in the abuse or 'allowed' it to continue: 'Why did you keep going to Scouts when you knew the scoutmaster was doing that to you?' They may hold their other children responsible: 'I told you not to let your little sister out of your sight'. They may rail against anonymous figures, the helping agencies or society generally: 'It's the fault of all these do-gooders, they let these child molesters off too lightly'. Their anger can be turned against themselves, resulting in feelings of guilt and shame. One father felt that he had colluded with the perpetrator because he used to give his daughter a lift to the friend's house where, unknown to him, she was abused. Another father later suffered considerable remorse because, unaware of the situation, he had insisted his reluctant son return to his boarding school where he was being sodomized by his housemaster.

Parents can become depressed with feeling of helplessness and isolation. Some break down in tears whenever they see the victim. They may withdraw from their abused child, unable to give support to either spouse or offspring. Abuse can reactivate memories of parents' own childhood exploitation, leaving little emotional energy for their unfortunate offspring.

Alternatively, parents may suppress and deny their own needs and feelings in order to give their attention to the victimized child. Some parents, however, cope with their own emotions and provide excellent support. Finkelhor, Williams and Burns (1988) noted that, in cases of molestation while in day care, children whose parents helped them cope with their victimization had fewer distressing symptoms: 'According to both therapists and investigators, the parents can play a critical role in lessening the impact of the abuse on their children and helping them to adjust over time.'

Parents whose partner is the perpetrator have to cope with a greater number of impact issues than those whose partner is not implicated. This is usually the victim's mother and therefore throughout this section it is the mother that is referred to. However, if the roles are reversed the impact issues could as easily relate to the non-abusing father.

Firstly, there is the impact on the mother's emotions and self-image. There is a sense of loss and grief as well as one of failure as a mother, wife and woman. She may have been made to feel responsible by the perpetrator, victim or investigating professionals. She might believe that she was sexually inadequate, otherwise why did her partner have to look elsewhere for satisfaction? If sexually abused herself she might not only relive her own molestation but have an added sense of failure: 'I vowed it would **never** happen to my children'. On a practical level, if the perpetrator leaves home, there could be a loss of income and adult support.

The mother may feel confused with regard to her partner as she recognizes his positive, lovable qualities and yet senses disgust, betrayal and anger at having been 'conned' by him. She questions whether she can ever trust men or her own judgement of them again. She has to ask herself what sort of woman she is to have made such a poor choice of partner. Sometimes she will have been so effectively groomed by the perpetrator that she is unable to accept that he could possibly be guilty of the offences. Alternatively, if she is aware of his guilt, she will accept his excuses and minimizing. She may have too much to lose emotionally and materially if she recognizes the extent of his offending behaviour.

The perpetrator's grooming may also have been so forceful that the mother disbelieves or blames the child. He might have isolated and alienated the mother from the victim. Sometimes, she does not know whom to believe and is divided in her loyalty between the partner she loves and the child she also loves. She might have to make a painful choice between forcing her partner to leave home or having her children removed.

When a mother accepts that her child has been abused she has to cope with a sense of failure as a mother. She may also not know how best to help, especially if the victim turns his or her anger against her.

Many mothers have responsibilities for their other children. They might worry in case they too have been abused and fear that they will be removed from the home. She will wonder how best to support her other children and explain to them what has happened. She could feel her younger offspring will be 'corrupted' or lose their innocence if they are told. On the other hand if not told they may learn about what happened from someone else. The children are often jealous and blame or bully the victim. She will have to contend with these sibling tensions and conflicts.

Mothers are often left to struggle with the extended family and the community response. Sometimes the offender's family defends him and censures her. Occasionally, her own relatives blame her for 'allowing' the abuse to happen or for marrying 'that man' against family advice. If it becomes public knowledge she will have to cope with, at best, community curiosity and gossip, and, at worst, blame, derision, ostracism and possibly verbal or physical abuse. The news media can intrude insensitively on her grief and privacy. If it has not become common knowledge, the mother lives in constant fear of being 'found out'. She will have to lie and make up explanations. She is likely to withdraw and become isolated and lonely as she tries to maintain the guilty family secret.

HELPING PROFESSIONALS AS VICTIMS

Professionals who are already working with cases of physical and emotional mistreatment can find, sometimes to their surprise, that having to respond to cases of child sexual abuse can have a profound impact on them. This is partly because everyone is gradually desensitized to the physical and emotional cruelty to children. Desensitization, familiar to many health workers, is a process by which aversion to a particular subject or object can gradually be reduced by increased exposure to it. From infancy, youngsters are regaled with stories in which children suffer at the hands of various adults. Cinderella is perhaps one of the most popular examples in Western society. Modern stories, such as Roald Dahl's *James and the Giant Peach*, also incorporate themes of cruelty or neglect. As a result the physical and emotional mistreatment of children, while still distressing and unacceptable, is no longer unimaginable or even unfamiliar to people at large.

In contrast, there may be sexual innuendo in folk tales but there are very few popular stories for children explicitly about sexual abuse. The story of Saint Dymphna, the princess desired by her father, is one of the few exceptions. There is no gradual introduction to the idea of child sexual abuse so it is hardly surprising that society in general, and some professionals in particular, should deny its existence or, as happened in Cleveland, its extent and nature.

Sexual abuse touches on matters that, despite more liberal attitudes, are still very personal and private. Many people have sexual desires and fantasies that they would either not share or share only with their closest acquaintances. Sex is rarely a topic that adults can contemplate and discuss without any doubts, embarrassment or guilt whatsoever.

Furthermore, sexual arousal is not completely voluntary. Professionals have found that discussions of sexual abuse have caused sexual arousal. The manifestation of this arousal can be obvious and immediate in male workers if they experience an erection. Some male therapists have become temporarily impotent as they generalize their attempts to control and suppress their arousal. Other professionals have reported that their libido became depressed once they had made the association between sex and the suffering of the children with whom they were working.

Involvement in child sexual abuse cases can therefore affect a professional's sexuality and extend beyond this to his or her marriage or partnership and family relationships.

A number of helping professionals were themselves sexually abused as children (Wilson, 1987). For some this is an experience they have to come to terms with and which they can use to the benefit of victims because of their level of understanding and sensitivity. For other professionals it reactivates long-suppressed memories and can be a devastating ordeal.

Although training in this area can be a help, some teaching strategies are themselves designed, either deliberately or inadvertently, to awaken any repressed memories. Unless conducted with extreme care training can have a devastating effect on former victims by reviving long-forgotten experiences and emotions in a context where they cannot be dealt with appropriately (Doyle, 1986).

There is a further discussion of the issues for professionals who are also survivors in Chapter 8.

Health professionals may themselves be co-victims because they have been groomed and manipulated by the perpetrator. Those such as health visitors or family doctors may have known the family for some time before the abuse came to light.

EXAMPLE: Mrs A was increasingly disabled by a degenerative disease. She was married with three children, Betty aged 11, Carl aged 7 and Donna aged 3. The family doctor, health visitor and community nurse visited regularly. Mr A presented a very concerned, caring father and husband. He was a religious man and was much admired and supported by the local church. He seemed totally devoted to his family. He gave up his job and took over the care of his wife and children when Mrs A became incapable of looking after the home.

Mr A expressed worries about his children because Betty was evidently a tense, nervous child who was bed-wetting and eating very little. Carl was usually withdrawn and unhappy but in school he could be defiant, boisterous and a bully to younger children. Donna was quiet, but otherwise making good progress. Mr A suggested that the older children's distressed behaviour was due to his wife's illness and increasing incapacity. The health professionals were inclined to agree.

It came as a complete shock to them when Betty told her teacher her father had tried to have intercourse with her. Mr A explained that he had been unable to have sex with his wife and on one occasion was tempted to use Betty as a substitute. He regretted his lapse and vowed it would never happen again. The health professionals felt a degree of sympathy for this man, whom they felt had been pushed beyond the bounds of endurance, and had, under considerable stress, done something that was 'out of character'.

But a thorough investigation revealed that not only had he been abusing Betty prior to the onset of his wife's illness, but he had also regularly sodomized Carl. The health professionals, who could hardly believe the extent of the abuse, felt overwhelmed by anger, confusion and a sense of betrayal at having been 'conned' by this man who had for so long elicited their admiration, support and sympathy.

Not only will helping professionals feel used and betrayed, they may also feel guilty and responsible because they believe that they failed to pick up the signs of something that may have been going on metaphorically 'under their very noses'. Sometimes they have a sense of having added to the child's suffering. For example, teachers or school nurses may have dealt unsympathetically with a challenging pupil only to learn that the child was being systematically sexually abused. This can lead to regret, guilt and a wish that they had been kinder and more perceptive.

5

Recognizing and responding

Health professionals will naturally want to feel able to intervene effectively when they come across a case of child sexual abuse. This chapter examines some of the problems inherent in recognizing the signs of abuse. It will also indicate how a disclosure by a child might be facilitated.

PHYSICAL SIGNS AND SYMPTOMS

Diagnosing child sexual abuse is complicated by several factors. Although there are recognizable signs and symptoms, many sexually abusive activities cause no physical signs or only very transitory ones, such as reddening of the skin or mucosa. It can also be very difficult for health professionals to recognize what is normal and what is abnormal. Although doctors are taught to perform a complete examination of all patients, in practice most do not routinely inspect the anus and genitalia of children. It would be unethical to subject them to uncomfortable examinations just to gain medical experience. Doctors therefore do not know with absolute certainty what is normal, part of the 'wear and tear' of everyday life, and what is a sign of abuse.

Signs of acute damage to the genitalia might have occurred accidentally or be evidence of physical rather than sexual, abuse. For example, Darryn Clarke was barely 4 years old when he was burnt and battered to death by his mother's cohabitee, Charles Courtney. At the subsequent inquiry (DHSS, 1979) verbal evidence, supported by medical findings, was given that

'Charles Courtney had tied the child's penis and inserted a cork in his anus in order to stop him being incontinent'.

Reddening, soreness (erythema) and abrasions of the penis or vaginal or anal area may be indicative of masturbation, vulvar, intercrural or other 'simulated' intercourse, or full anal or vaginal penetration. It could, however, be due to a child scratching because of some other condition such as worms or allergy. There are other misleading signs, such as lichen sclerosis et atrophicus, which most frequently affects the penis or vulva and can cause alarming subepidermal haemorrhages after minor trauma such as wiping after toileting (Bays and Chadwick, 1993).

Despite these problems there are physical signs that should alert health professionals to the possibility of sexual abuse.

Indicators relating to the genitalia

As well as abrasions and erythema, there may also be bruises, or lacerations of the penis, labia, vagina and hymen. Flattening of the labia could be due to pressure from a hand or penis, although it could be caused by nappies or tight clothing. Vulvar intercourse may cause lacerations to the posterior fourchette, which can result in scarring in this area or in small perihymenal scars.

In pre-pubescent girls damage to the hymen is significant. An undisturbed hymen could be between 2 mm and 10 mm, although in the very young girl it should be no more than 3–5 mm. It should be smooth with a circular or crescent-shaped opening and a smooth regular margin (Bamford and Roberts, 1989). Lacerations to the hymen are most often found at the 6 o'clock position, but may occur between the 3 o'clock and 9 o'clock positions. They may extend to the posterior fourchette and even the perineum.

Penetration tends to give rise to bumps, scarring and thickening of the hymenal tissue with rounded, redundant hymenal remnants that sometimes adhere laterally and distort the opening to the vagina or extend into it (Durfee, Heger and Woodling, 1986).

Other signs of vaginal penetration may be spasms of the pubococcygeal muscle or ready relaxation of this muscle if the child is touched lateral to the vulva. There may be bleeding or discharges from the vagina. Forced penetration may cause internal injuries and the abdomen may be tender.

Assuming the exclusion of genital disease, a damaged hymen in pre-pubescent girls must be regarded with concern because, although self-injury or accidental injury could be the cause, these are unusual. The hymen is an internal structure and it is therefore unlikely that vigorous activity such as horse-riding or gymnastics would cause any hymenal trauma (contrary to popular belief) although sudden splits could cause mid-line lacerations of genital structures (Paul, 1977). Straddle accidents, such as falling onto a bicycle, a large solid toy or an open cupboard door, will result in injury to anterior or lateral structures rather than the interior vaginal introitus (Enos, Conrath and Byer, 1986; Hobbes and Wynne, 1987; Heger, 1991). Research by Herman-Giddens and Frothingham (1987) and Pokorny and Kozinetz (1988) found that accidents involving the genitals did not cause hymenal injury, although other researchers indicated that falling on a sharp, penetrating object could do so (Unuigbe and Giwa-Osagie, 1988).

There has been a widely-held belief that tampons could cause damage in pubescent girls, although this has been refuted since some of the earliest studies in the 1940s and continues to be disproved (Bays and Chadwick, 1993). The insertion of other foreign objects into body orifices is also unlikely to cause genital injuries (Hyman *et al.*, 1990). Finally, research indicates that vigorous masturbation will not cause hymenal trauma (Woodling and Kossoris, 1981; Hobbs and Wynne, 1987; Tipton, 1989).

On the other hand, not all hymenal abnormalities are indicative of sexual abuse. It is worth noting that the hymen is occasionally congenitally absent and in other instances it can be cribriform, that is naturally perforated.

Indicators relating to the anal area

Bruising and lacerations to the anus are possible signs of anal abuse. In addition, recent anal penetration will also result in the swelling of the anal verge which may become rounded and smooth. There will be small tears and fissures (these should not be confused with folds in the anal canal). Occasionally, there will be obvious tearing and bleeding of the anus. Forceful anal intercourse, as in the case of vaginal penetration, may result in internal injuries and tenderness to the abdomen.

Signs of anal penetration may have disappeared completely in 50% of cases within three weeks of the last incident (Durfee, Heger and Woodling, 1986). However, signs of non-recent anal penetration may include scarring extending out from the anus, especially in the 6 o'clock position. Healing fissures may leave skin tags. Anal ridges and folds may thicken and become distorted. There may be genital warts, although these are not always transmitted sexually; Heger (1991) provides an illustration of a 2-year-old girl who acquired these at birth through her mother.

In a study of 161 girls and 106 boys aged 2 months to 11 years, screened to exclude sexual abuse victims (McCann *et al.*, 1989), there was a high incidence of perianal soft tissue changes. But there were no abrasions, haematomas, fissures or haemorrhoids. None of the boys, and only 18 girls, had anal skin tags or folds. Outside the mid-line there were no skin tags/folds and only four instances of possible scars between the 12 and 2 o'clock positions.

Chronic anal abuse may lead to dilation and/or reflex dilation of the anal canal. If the internal sphincter is unable to remain closed the external sphincter relaxes after a short time (between 10 and 30 seconds) of gentle separation of the buttocks. This allows the anus to open or gape. It may already be open and therefore will close and open again. For any significance to be attached to this the rectum has to be empty because the internal anal sphincter can be relaxed by faeces in the lower rectum (Bamford and Roberts, 1989).

In the study by McCann *et al.*, (1989) a high proportion showed anal dilatation when a stool was present in the rectal ampulla. However, a dilatation of 20 mm without the presence of the stool was very unusual. Marked irregularity of the anal orifice was rare. The authors recognized that they may not have excluded all abused children; indeed, the mother of one boy with anal dilatation of greater than 20 mm expressed concern about the child's behaviour since the arrival of a male lodger.

A substantial degree of anal dilatation and conspicuous irregularity of the anal orifice is therefore a possible significant indicator of abuse (Hobbs and Wynne, 1986), although other explanations have been offered such as forceful separation of the buttocks, constipation, especially chronic constipation, and threadworms (Butler-Sloss, 1988). Disease and congenital abnormality have also been suggested. Most other explanations can be accounted for by further medical investigation.

Oral indications

Signs of oral abuse are rare. There may be petechial bruising on the palate or a torn frenulum in a small child. Venereal disease might be present, resulting in oral sores.

Associated injuries

Injuries in other areas of the child's body can corroborate the victim's allegations. Finger-tip bruising may show where a child has been forcibly held. Rope burns on ankles and wrists reveal where a youngster has been tied up. If extreme violence has been used there may be fractures, burns and extensive bodily bruising.

In some cases children have been drugged, leaving marks where they have been injected or producing associated complications. 'Injections given to one 6-year-old girl caused a strep infection and subsequent osteomyelitis with physical impairment. Another child was repeatedly treated for infected "mosquito bites". . . later identified as injection marks' (Snow and Sorenson, 1990).

Pregnancy

Pregnancy may be the result of sexual abuse. Girls who seem unable to say who the father is are a cause for concern.

> EXAMPLE: A quiet 15-year-old lived alone with her invalid father and elder brother and was known not to go out at weekends or after school because she looked after her father. On finding that she was pregnant she insisted that the baby's father was a boy she had met on holiday the previous August. The baby was not born until the following September. She was adamant that she had had a 13-month pregnancy.

Forensic signs

Forensic investigation may reveal evidence of abuse. Semen on any part of a girl or a pre-pubertal boy, blood of a different group from the victim, and another person's hair in the vagina, anus or associated areas are all clear signs of sexual abuse. Lubricants in the vagina or anus are also highly suggestive of abuse.

Sexually transmitted diseases

The possibility of sexual abuse should always be considered when sexually transmitted disease is found. Soreness of, or discharge from, the vagina should be investigated. Babies can be infected *in utero* or at birth. It is now accepted that the manifestation of disease a significant time after the birth is likely to be due to sexual abuse, although this was not always the case. As late as the 1970s it was thought that venereal disease could be transmitted to children by non-sexual means. A high incidence in the Yuit communities was cited as evidence that it was transmitted non-sexually. This was later challenged by Sheila Thompson (1988) who worked for many years with the Yuit Eskimos.

Over recent years views have varied. In an article on sexually transmitted diseases Carol Baker (1978) recommended: 'All suspected cases of sexual misuse, which would include all cases of children with sexually transmitted diseases acquired by means other than birth-canal contamination, should be reported to a child protection agency'. In contrast, the following year Frewen and Bannatyne (1979) maintained:

> There are two main viewpoints concerning the mode of transmission of gonococcal infection in this age group [2–10 years] – sexual abuse or nonsexual acquisition of infection from intimate contact with contaminated bedding, underwear, toilet seats, etc. . . We agree that the majority of cases were associated with either an infected bedmate or a family member and association with sexual abuse as determined by history was not a prominent factor'.

A year later, however, Wald *et al.* advised that 'the presence of genital infection in the young pre-pubertal girl must be assumed to be due to sexual abuse until proven otherwise' (1980).

A more recent comment is made by Heger (1991):

> Children as well as adults can contract sexually transmitted diseases but they can only do so as a result of sexual contact or via the birth process . . . In the United Kingdom it has been standard practice for sexually transmitted disease clinics to report the statistics nationally. Each year the statistics included a certain number of children. Unfortunately this group of clinicians have identified a disease without understanding or recognising what these statistics really mean.

Particular diseases, notably gonorrhoea, chlamydia, trichomonas vaginalis and syphilis are almost certainly evidence of sexual contact if perinatal acquisition is excluded. On the other hand, recent research (Ingram *et al.*, 1992a: Ingram *et al.*, 1992b) has shown that certain infections, such as Gardnerella vaginalis, ureaplasma urealyticum and large colony mycoplasma colonization in the genital tract in girls, can occur through sources other than sexual molestation, such as infected towels.

Recently, infection with the HIV virus has been added to the list of indicators of abuse. The virus has not been known to be transmitted through saliva, urine, faeces, vomit, tears, sweat or general skin contact. Children are therefore unlikely to be infected by kissing, cuddling or using the toilet. It is transmitted in blood, semen, vaginal fluid, breast milk and skin grafts. There are evident risks for children who are subjected to vaginal, anal or oral penetration, especially by perpetrators who lack sexual boundaries and have multiple partners. Youngsters engaged in prostitution or involved in sex rings are also at increased risk. However, studies, particularly from America (Gellert, 1990; Bennetts, Brown and Sloan, 1992), indicate that cases of infection of children through sexual abuse are currently comparatively rare. This may not remain the case in the future.

Recent research (Zierler *et al.*, 1991; Allers and Benjack, 1991; Allers *et al.*, 1993) and clinical experience are showing that a proportion of child sexual abuse survivors, including adolescents, is at increased risk of HIV infection. There seems to be a number of reasons, including the promiscuity and sexual impulsiveness of some former victims, increased substance abuse and revictimizing sexual relationships. Kaliski *et al.* (1990) suggest that in abused adolescents another factor is that they become depressed and suicidal and see contracting AIDS as a way of escaping their misery. This means that more molested young people could be found to have the HIV virus. If, as is believed, there is a connection between a history of abuse and sexually offending behaviour, this, combined with the connection between a history of abuse and increased exposure to HIV, may result in an increased risk to younger children in those instances when victims become victimizers.

Other conditions

Stress or feelings of guilt might lead children to present with physical symptoms for which no medical cause can be found. Unexplained recurrent stomach aches or difficulty in swallowing (in cases of oral abuse) are typical. Occasionally the psychological trauma is so great that it leads to hysterical paralysis and other forms of conversion hysteria. Maya Angelou was raped when she was 8 years old. Subsequently her attacker was murdered and she thought it was her fault. 'I could feel the evilness flowing through my body and waiting, pent up, to rush off my tongue if I tried to open my mouth. I clamped my teeth shut, I'd hold it in' (Angelou, 1984). She remained mute for the next five years.

UNCOMMON SEXUAL BEHAVIOUR

Abnormal sexual behaviours can be used to identify possible sexual victimization, but they have to be distinguished from unexceptional ones. A number of studies have tried to determine normal child sexual activities (Sgroi, Bunk and Wabrek, 1988; Waterman, 1986). It has to recognized that behaviour that is normal in one culture may be considered abnormal in another. Within Western cultures there appear to be certain sexual behaviours common to most children in certain age groups. Children suffering from physical or learning disabilities may be at increased risk of sexual abuse because behaviour that might be seen as 'abnormal', and therefore worthy of investigation in most children, may be dismissed in their case.

The word 'sexual' also requires qualification. Apparent 'sexual' behaviours do not have the same implications and connotations for children as they do for adults. A little girl inspecting a small boy's genitals is more likely to be satisfying her curiosity than any sexual passion or desire. Children do, however, obtain physical pleasure from stimulation to their genital areas. They can therefore be introduced to overt sexual behaviour, which they can emulate and desire. When this happens they are said to be 'sexualized' or 'eroticized' (Yates, 1982).

It is common for children to masturbate. Babies old enough to have discovered their genitals will do so openly. Toddlers and older children in most cultures are inhibited by adult disapproval from masturbating in public, but the majority will continue to do so in private. Occasionally, distressed older children will comfort themselves by masturbating regularly and openly despite adult censure.

In general, children will want to look at other people's bodies. For pre-pubertal children this is to satisfy curiosity. Children may take furtive peeps at adult bodies. However, they are most likely to engage in games with peers that involve undressing such as 'doctors and nurses' or 'strip poker'.

As youngsters reach adolescence the sight of naked bodies becomes increasingly sexually arousing. They may be interested in looking at those of their own sex in order to ensure that they are 'normal' or to identify a body image to which they can aspire. They may be fascinated by photographs, pictures and films portraying naked bodies.

The desire to touch other people is common. With peers, children will enjoy games or dares that enable them to touch or kiss each other. By adolescence the touching becomes more serious as the majority begins the task of forming intimate relationships. This is usually a peer activity. 'It is our observation that it is very unusual for preadolescents and especially for adolescent boys and girls to meet their social needs with younger children' (Sgroi, Bunk and Wabrek, 1988).

Uncommon sexual behaviour may not be conclusive evidence of sexual victimization, but it is a possible warning sign and further information should be gathered. It is difficult for health professionals to define what is uncommon. What, for example, is meant by 'excessive' masturbation? Here it is worth trusting the opinion of people who spend a lot of time with a wide spectrum of children. Health visitors and school nurses are two groups that are likely to see children day-in, day-out over a number of years. They begin to know what is common for children of a certain age in the particular area or culture in which they work. Their concerns about a child who is behaving differently from the rest in a community are probably well-founded.

Excessive masturbation

This tends to be a compulsive activity that the child cannot restrict to private moments. He or she engages in it regularly, openly or semi-openly and does not stop despite adults' attempts to warn, punish or distract the youngster. The child may be isolated. Masturbation serves as a comfort and relieves stress. An older child who has been sexualized may find this the only way of releasing feelings. This is one way that abused children can establish control over their own bodies and so may be a necessary activity.

In a study of sexually abused boys Sebold (1987) noted: 'younger males in particular may masturbate publicly or report excessive preoccupation with masturbation'. Conversely, because of possible homophobia, the youngster may see masturbation as a homosexual act and therefore repulsive. 'Even though the child may masturbate, he will often emphatically deny such behaviour and continue to act repulsed by even the thought of such an action'.

Age-inappropriate knowledge

Children may demonstrate knowledge of, and interest in, sexual behaviour that is more detailed and advanced than most youngsters of the same age. Pre-school children may be curious about the differences between boys and girls, and may have started to ask questions about where babies come from. They are generally not interested in, nor knowledgeable about, intercourse.

EXAMPLE: A 4-year-old girl picked up two small girl dolls and put them together, face-to-face, in a squirming, kissing movement. She then took all their clothes off, put one doll on top of the other and moved it against the other rhythmically. Next, she picked up a boy doll, making it knock the doll off the top. She placed him on top of the remaining girl doll and repeated the rhythmical movements. She later disclosed that she had been sexually abused by both her mother and her uncle.

Children usually have limited sexual vocabularies and even if they can repeat words they are often unaware of the true meaning. In a sample of 3- to 6-year-old children, only 14% of the girls had a name for the vagina (McFarlane *et al.*, 1986). In contrast, the 4-year-old described above had at least two words for the female genitals, 'fanny' and 'dilly'. Children who have a sexual vocabulary, particularly one that is derogatory and debasing, and who can apply words correctly when their peers are unable to do so, are a cause for concern, although account has to be taken of cultural differences and individual circumstances. Associated with this is the fact that a proportion of abuse victims become preoccupied with sexual thoughts and use a lot of sexual terms and language in every day speech.

It has been claimed that children gain advanced sexual knowledge from seeing films and television. They certainly acquire some ideas and a wider vocabulary but these media will not teach them how to perform sexually explicit acts. Most television programmes and films rely on an adult audience understanding certain signals, such as heavy breathing or a rhythmical heaving of the shoulders, the implications of which are beyond the comprehension of most 6-year-olds. After all, children do not learn to cook from watching meals being prepared in various 'soaps' or other popular programmes.

Children who manage to gain accurate sexual knowledge by being repeatedly exposed to explicit and detailed sex in pornographic films are being abused because they are being exposed to sexual activities to which they have not given informed consent.

Health professionals need to be alert to adolescents who have no interest in sexual matters and seem overly ingenuous.

They could be trying to conceal too much sexual knowledge. Helen was abused from the age of 5 by her elder brother. 'My fellow pupils used to jeer at me because I was regarded as naïve about sexual matters. The others would gather in little groups to read the "juicy bits" of various salacious novels. I did not join in because I was frightened I might "let something slip" and show that I knew too much' (Doyle, 1990).

Promiscuity

This can be a sign of sexual abuse in the pre-adolescent or adolescent person. 'Promiscuous' is a term used to refer to young people who have less well-defined sexual boundaries than those of their peers, and who will engage indiscriminately in consenting intercourse with frequent changes of partners. This has to be measured against the common behaviour of other youngsters of the same age and cultural setting. 'In the old culture, what might have been viewed as promiscuity by modern American culture was an accepted way of life among the Eskimo' (Thompson, 1988).

Children who have been abused may have been made to believe they are only acceptable to other people on sexual terms. Their lack of trust and self-esteem is such that they are unable to sustain intimate relationships. They therefore constantly seek attention and affection by the only way they know – by offering a sexual affiliation. In the absence of an ability to develop a relationship beyond the physical, it disintegrates and the youngsters move on to new partnerships.

Some young women describe themselves as 'promiscuous' when their sexual activity compared to that of their peers would not be seen as excessive. This demonstrates that they have a negative and judgemental attitude towards their own behaviour (Fromuth, 1986).

Health professionals should also be aware of the implications of the opposite extreme. An adolescent that has no apparent interest in sex and avoids sexual contact with peers may also be the victim of sexual abuse. Helen commented: 'I also didn't have boy-friends because I could not abide the feeling of being experimented upon by an inexperienced youth' (Doyle, 1990).

Sexually abusive behaviour

This refers to children or adolescents who are found to be sexually assaulting other weaker or younger children. In very small children the phrase 'abusive behaviour' is not entirely appropriate, as discussed in Chapter 3. The 2-year-old girl lying on a large stuffed teddy simulating intercourse, who then mounts a 20-month-old boy in much the same way, is probably motivated by the acting out and mimicking of behaviour. She has undoubtedly learnt the behaviour from someone else and is more than likely to be a victim of sexual abuse.

Older children and adolescents, again described in Chapter 3, may abuse a weaker child in order to redress their feelings of powerlessness, caused by their own victimization. Children acting in a sexual way towards other children, using their dominance to coerce others, are again very likely to be victims themselves.

Inappropriate sexual advances

Victims sometimes behave towards adults or more powerful children in a sexual fashion. A very young child may spontaneously sit on the knee of any man in the vicinity and try to rub his penis. A pre-pubescent girl may dress, look and behave in a way that would be sexually alluring in an 18-year-old. These youngsters expect a sexual response from adults and become confused or even angry if one is not forthcoming. They have been taught that the way to gain affection and attention from adults is by giving sexual favours.

The other extreme is the child who flinches from any form of physical contact with older people fearing that it might be sexual. Alternatively they may seem comfortable with one sex, but are frightened of the opposite sex.

Some sexually abused boys try to dissociate themselves from homosexuality to such an extent that they become homophobic and totally reject any sort of affectionate gesture or display from other males.

A sexually abused male spends a significant amount of time anxiously attempting to convince his peers that he is not gay ... The sexually abused adolescent male may also go to great lengths to put down and dissociate himself from anyone whom he perceives as weird or as having homosexual inclinations.

(Sebold, 1987)

Prostitution

Some children are enticed or forced into prostitution by adults, but others engage in this activity apparently on their own initiative. There may be a connection between male prostitution and early sexual abuse. A similar link can be found in female prostitutes. As one adolescent girl, abused by her mother's boyfriend and then her own father, commented, 'men took what they wanted from me for free, well now they can pay me for it'.

GENERAL BEHAVIOURAL SIGNS

Sexually abused children are often in a state of distress and loss. They will therefore show behavioural problems common to distressed youngsters in general.

Extremes of behaviour

Children may be very quiet as though trying to negate their presence, wanting to avoid attention. 'I know about trying to hide myself in a crowded classroom, in a crowded family, so that I won't be seen and brought forward for interrogation, ridicule, punishment, disgrace' (Spring, 1987).

They may behave very well and work hard at school. Helen recalled feeling, 'I had done something so wicked that I deserved a dreadful punishment. I tried to be good and work hard in order to avoid any punishment. I could not bear being given a bad conduct mark at school as it only served to confirm how dreadful I was' (Doyle, 1990). Some may be timid and tearful and can become the target of school bullies.

At the other extreme is the noisy, naughty child who constantly challenges authority and seems to invite punishment. Some are evidently full of anger and become aggressive, physically and verbally bullying others. Some are not particularly badly behaved but seek attention by being boisterous and vociferous.

It is not unusual for sexually abused children to fail at school and truant. Marie, an abuse victim, explained: 'You can't concentrate at school while wondering what will happen when you get home' (Doyle, 1990).

These extremes may co-exist within one child. A volatile youngster can be compliant and well behaved at one moment and noisy and aggressive the next. Sudden behavioural changes can be significant. One boy who had been quite talkative and outgoing became quiet and withdrawn after a male baby-sitter had anally penetrated him.

Regression

Under stress people often retreat into earlier coping behaviours or forget more recent learning. For this reason older sexually abused children may become incontinent or unusually dependent. Their speech can sound infantile, while some resort to dummies, thumb-sucking and bottles. A proportion, despite having average intelligence, may make very little progress educationally, preferring to play games, read books or use material designed for a younger age group.

Sexually abused boys sometimes spend more time with younger children than with their peers (Sebold, 1987). It is important to determine whether this is associated with regression or with the desire to attain a sense of power by dominating weaker youngsters.

On occasion, child victims and adult survivors seem to be compelled to return to the age at which the abuse first started. This is discussed in more detail in Chapters 6 and 8.

Terrors and fears

Nightmares and terrors are a possible manifestation of stress. Foster-parents have found their young charges clinging to one end of the bed at night, shouting out in terror. Victims, by day or night, can be haunted by seemingly inexplicable fears. This affects their behaviour, for example, a child might refuse to walk down a particular path or wear certain clothes. 'A 10-year-old boy constantly became panicked around swimming pools, although he did not have fears related to water. Later it was discovered that he had been molested while swimming'

(Sebold, 1987). A certain type of person – a bearded man, a woman wearing spectacles – may engender fear. Anxiety can be raised in abused youngsters by the behaviour of other people. They could, for example, fear being closeted alone with an adult. They may 'freeze' if touched. 'Many therapists noted that . . . touching tends to elicit a rigid and uncomfortable physical response' (Sebold, 1987). Victims may express their fears in ways that adults find disturbing. A 4-year-old involved in satanic rituals became totally absorbed while methodically cutting up rag dolls. She would attempt to strangle other children, at the same time expressing fears of being cut up or strangled herself.

Escapist behaviours

On occasion, abused youngsters will retreat into a world of their own, becoming cut off and difficult to relate to. They appear over-absorbed in books or films, living constantly in a fantasy world. However, anyone with a teenage son or daughter will no doubt agree that aspects of this behaviour are common in the average non-abused adolescent. This is only a significant sign if it is prolonged or combined with other indicators.

Another psychological escape is to split off the child who is being abused from the 'real' self. The child compartmentalizes his or her life, thereby becoming asymptomatic. A vivid description of this is given by Sylvia Fraser (1989) in her autobiography. This is a form of dissociation. Symptoms of a dissociative disorder in children include fugue states, amnesia and feelings of depersonalization. It can be a forerunner to multiple personality disorder. It has been connected to the post-traumatic stress syndrome (McElroy, 1992).

Children may literally run away and continue to run away. Stiffman (1989) found that of 291 runaway youths aged 12 to 18 (207 girls and 84 boys), nearly half (141) had been either physically or sexually abused. Eventually, for a proportion, their running away becomes compulsive, as if they were trying to escape from themselves. They may keep running even when dangers presented by the perpetrator are removed.

Some children, especially adolescents, attempt the ultimate escape – suicide. Marie recalled her sister's actions:

Pauline told me that our father had sexually abused her . . .
Not long after this conversation Pauline ate 100 aspirins in
front of me. I didn't realise what was happening. I thought
she was eating crumbly white cheese. She tried to commit
suicide six times after this.

(Doyle, 1990)

 Destructive behaviour

Among the most destructive behaviours are self-harming ones.
Suicide, the ultimate self-harm, has already been mentioned.
Behaviours that fall short of suicide include self-cutting and
burning or reckless drug misuse. Youngsters with medical
conditions such as epilepsy, diabetes or asthma sometimes
become careless about their medication and the management
of their illnesses. Taking risks related to the HIV virus has been
seen as indicative of sexual abuse by Kaliski *et al.* (1990) and
Allers *et al.* (1993).

Eating disorders, including anorexia nervosa and bulimia
nervosa, are potentially harmful and have been associated with
sexual abuse (Oppenheimer, 1985; Oppenheimer *et al.*, 1985;
Palmer *et al.*, 1990; Miller, McCluskey-Fawcett and Irving,
1993). Children subjected to oral abuse may develop psycho-
somatic problems with eating and swallowing.

Fire-raising seems to be related to child sexual abuse in males
(Sebold, 1987). The reasons are unclear, but it could be a way
of drawing attention to distress. It does not seem to be so
common in female victims.

OTHER PEOPLE'S BEHAVIOUR

Chapter 3 gave a description of the behaviour of perpetrators
in targeting and grooming both victims and potential protectors. Health professionals may be alerted to potential
problems through the behaviour of adults, rather than of
children.

Vigilance is required if an adult singles out a child or small
number of children for special treatment, such as showing extra
affection, giving costly presents or selecting some children
for more rigorous or punitive treatment. This may become

apparent not just in the family situation but also in institutions, such as schools and hospitals, or in group activities, playschemes or youth clubs.

EXAMPLE: A 14-year-old girl who had been her father's 'favourite' disclosed that he had been sexually abusing her. The case conference (in its wisdom) accepted the father's explanation that the girl had 'seduced' him. She was removed from home and the father stayed. A few months later the social worker noticed that not only was the 10-year-old sister becoming increasingly withdrawn and tearful, but her father was buying her expensive presents, something he had not done when her elder sister was at home.

Parents and carers who are preoccupied with their children's genitals or their sexual behaviour and development should give cause for concern. Here the judgement of the experienced health professional is of considerable value. Health visitors, for example, who spend years discussing children's development with parents, will recognize when discussions with a particular parent seem out of the ordinary.

OBSTACLES TO DISCLOSURE

Sexual abuse victims have many obstacles to overcome before they can seek help. That some children manage to disclose is almost more surprising than the fact that many do not.

Entrapment and accommodation

Chapter 4 demonstrated how victims can become trapped in a situation, feeling grateful loyalty to their abusers and fearful and mistrustful of potential 'rescuers'.

The state of denial may cause victims to forget their abuse or dismiss it as unimportant. Sylvia Fraser's account (1989) provides an excellent example of a child who could not disclose because she had denied and split off the abusive activities of her father.

Victims may be too angry and fearful to seek help. Non-parental perpetrators may make children angry with, and fearful of, their parents, thereby ensuring the youngsters cannot confide in them.

Children in a state of gratitude and hope may have convinced themselves that the perpetrator is really so good that he or she will not abuse them again and if abuse does reoccur it is because they (the victims) have deserved it.

Youngsters who have reached the stage of desolation and despair will not feel worthy of help and will be too depressed and guilt-laden to seek or hope for rescue.

Ultimately, children in a state of acceptance will see no wrong in the activities and therefore no need to disclose or, alternatively, will have decided it is their lot in life to put up with it, a state described by Ronald Summit (1983) as the 'accommodation syndrome'.

In intrafamilial abuse children have a natural loyalty towards relatives. Condemning members of their family means condemning themselves, because part of an individual's identity is derived from the community or group to which he or she belongs. There are additional problems in this area for black youngsters in a predominantly white society, which, they fear, is all too ready to make negative judgements on the black community.

Fear

Children have very many fears to overcome before they can disclose.

Fear for others Chapter 3 described how perpetrators groom to prevent disclosure, maybe using overt threats, maybe using more subtle methods. Children abused by a non-relative sometimes do not tell their parents because they do not want to worry and upset them. Victims who have the closest and most loving relationships with their parents can be the least likely to disclose. Children may have considerable anxiety about the well-being and fate of other people if they tell.

Fear for themselves They may fear for themselves, including being punished and cast out, because they believe they have done something wrong. The perpetrator may have been one of the few people to have shown them affection and they fear the loss of that affection. They may worry that they will not be believed and be branded a liar. The perpetrator may have threatened them with harm if they tell: 'I . . . took an overdose sufficient to get me into hospital . . . A doctor asked me if

I had been sexually assaulted . . . but I daren't tell him in case I was sent back' (Kirkwood,1993).

Communication problems

Absent or limited verbal skills Disclosure depends on verbal skills, which makes it difficult for children with communication problems or who cannot yet speak well, to do so. Babies have a great ability to demonstrate their needs and feelings in the present, but they cannot give a history of what has happened in the past. Other children have restricted or absent verbal skills, such as those with physical and learning disabilities that impede speech, or those with emotional impediments to clear speech. Youngsters who only speak a minority language and require an interpreter will have a restricted choice of people in whom to confide.

Lack of vocabulary and misunderstanding Children who have very good verbal skills will still encounter considerable communication problems. Few children are able to use the medical terminology for the genitals and other 'private' parts of the body. A 16-year-old studying biology may be able to tell the school nurse that her uncle attempted to penetrate her vagina, in which case the allegations will be clear. Most children cannot precisely describe what happened because they lack the vocabulary needed to explain what happened. They may have to make up words: 'he gooed on me, 'he put his wee-pee in my mouth'. They may have to transfer words they know to this new context: 'he put his sausage in me', 'she put her finger in my button hole'. They may use very vague generic words 'it' 'his thing'. One word is sometimes used for several parts of the body. 'Dad hurt my bottom' or 'he kissed me on the cheek' may not sound significant until it is revealed that 'bottom' is the child's word for vagina and the 'cheek' is the buttock.

Children may only have family words for the genitals and soon learn that these are not words to use with other adults. Youngsters also learn that they may be punished or at least meet with disapproval if they talk about 'private matters'. One teacher, on reading a teenage girl's essay in which she attempted to disclose her father's abuse, wrote: 'I do not expect to have to mark such disgusting material'.

Youngsters with restricted speech may be taught to communicate general matters adequately. But without any sex education they have no way of describing what has happened to them. Some languages do not have words for intimate body parts and activities even if an interpreter is available. Sometimes children from an ethnic group with a minority language tell a trusted adult within their community but the adult is unable to seek help because of language barriers.

Shame and guilt

Sexual abuse inevitably involves parts of the body that are associated with a degree of shame and embarrassment. From the earliest days, children are so often shamed into mastering bladder and sphincter control. The parts of the body involved in these functions also happen to be the primary sites for sexual activity. They become associated in the minds of children with 'dirty' lavatorial jokes, whoopee cushions and the like, all of which are part of the child's sub-culture, only rarely to be shared with adults.

Children harbouring a guilty secret will feel increased shame if they reveal it, embarrassed that other people now know about their 'rude' activities. They feel guilty about betraying a secret. The grooming process itself is designed to ensure that victims feel so guilty and responsible that they will not disclose.

A feature of the accommodation syndrome is that the victims are made to feel responsible for maintaining the well-being of other people – the perpetrator, their family, other children. Disclosure would mean they are too 'selfish' or too 'weak' to shoulder their responsibilities.

Power and control

The feeling of control is associated with the sense of responsibility. To some extent the victim who is keeping a secret and helping to protect the family is in a position of power and control. Children may have been able to contain the perpetrator's activities – 'you can do anything to me as long as you do not touch my little sister'. Many older children are aware that if they disclose they will no longer have control over the situation.

Children are usually aware, consciously or otherwise, that the perpetrator is powerful and it is therefore only worth divulging information to someone who is more powerful. 'It was clear to me that nobody believed me. Frank Beck had recruited weak members of staff, whom he was able to persuade to his philosophy. He is a very plausible man' (Kirkwood, 1993).

They may not tell their mother because they sense her lack of power. Sarah, sexually abused by her father, recalled: 'I always thought of her as my father's first victim and myself as second. I was distressed by the way I had to witness his treatment of my mother. He would constantly undermine her' (Doyle, 1990).

READINESS TO DISCLOSE

Despite all the impediments a number of children do manage to approach a trusted adult or tell another child, who in turn tells an adult.

Heather Bacon (1991) identifies three different groups of children:

- Group 1: these youngsters give a 'clear alerting statement which starts off the formal investigation, "giving permission" for an adult to intervene' (Bacon, 1991). Suzanne Sgroi similarly refers to 'purposeful disclosure' that is the result of 'a conscious decision by a participant to break the secret' (Sgroi, 1982). Some younger children do not have the inhibitions or accommodation of an older child and given the opportunity will spontaneously complain. Older youngsters may decide for a variety of reasons that the activities have to stop whatever the cost. Some girls, for example, are prompted by the fear of pregnancy.
- Group 2: children in this group are identified by the medical and/or behavioural indicators discussed at the beginning of the chapter, or by being the sibling or friend of another child whose vitimization has been recognized. A sensitive and enabling approach to these youngsters may help them to disclose.
- Group 3: these children may, like those in Group 2, be identified by other signs or by association with another

recognized victim. They, however, are unable to disclose. They may be in a profound state of denial like Sylvia Fraser (1989). They may be too fearful or constrained by a process similar to the 'Stockholm syndrome' to disclose, or they may be too young or suffering from too severe a disability. Some children are simply not ready to let go of their secret. Finally, for some the benefits of the abuse might outweigh the disadvantages. Whatever the case these children will not say what has happened to them. There is nothing that adults, however sensitive, caring and skilled can do to elicit a disclosure.

FACILITATING DISCLOSURE

Health professionals can be in a position to facilitate disclosure in a variety of situations. Health visitors, for example, often form close relationships with mothers, who are then able to share their suspicions. School nurses may be told by the victim or by a schoolfriend. Occupational therapists and physiotherapists may be told by patients they are helping.

This section will deal primarily with revelations from the victims themselves, but additional guidance will be given for situations in which acquaintances disclose on behalf of a child. Disclosures from adult survivors about their own abuse will be discussed in the final chapter.

Creating openings

Children may try to create their own openings. How successful they are will depend very much on the awareness and sensitivity of the health professionals the victims have chosen to tell.

Youngsters sometimes start with an oblique comment: 'I don't like my brother', 'I am afraid of going home that way', 'My class teacher makes me feel funny'. To a health professional they may complain about a physical problem: 'I keep having tummy aches', 'I'm always feeling sick', 'My bottom hurts'. They may ask a question about a physical condition or the 'facts of life': 'What is intercourse?', 'Has my period started? I sometimes bleed', 'Can children get AIDS?'

It is important not to dismiss such comments and questions. A facilitating query, giving the child a measure of control, is the preferred response: 'Do you want to tell me why you don't like your brother, is he upsetting you?' asked with real interest and concern – not a mocking 'So what's so wrong with your big brother?'

A health professional is in an ideal position to ask about a physical problem: 'Where does your tummy hurt?' 'How often are you sick?' Similarly most health professionals can discuss physical conditions and 'the facts of life' without embarrassment. In response to a query, a brief factual explanation of intercourse, menstruation or AIDS can be provided, followed by a caring question: 'You seemed a little anxious, do you want to tell me why you are interested in AIDS?' By showing a willingness to provide information without embarrassment or becoming angry, health professionals are reassuring the victims that they are ready to discuss intimate matters. It also gives the children time to decide whether to trust them and whether to say anything more.

Some youngsters are direct: 'I have something really important to tell you', 'I have a secret I want to tell you'. It is essential to establish as soon as possible that they will be listened to, but that some secrets cannot be kept: 'I cannot promise to keep everything you tell me secret, because maybe you or somebody else will need help. We'd then have to find someone who could give you the right type of help'. The issue of confidentiality is always a problem. If children are told it cannot be guaranteed then they may be silenced and the chance to help will be lost. On the other hand, if they are allowed to carry on talking in the belief that no one else will know, they will feel betrayed if the adult then has to make a referral to investigative agencies.

It can be useful to find out why the youngster wants a particular secret kept. It may be possible to allay fears: 'Little boys can't be turned into frogs', or, 'We do not need to tell your boy-friend, although you may decide to tell him yourself later. At the moment only professional people and your parents need to be told'.

Occasionally fears may not be easily allayed: 'He told me I would be taken into care'. Here honesty expressed as positively as possible is the best policy, 'Some children who have had difficult experiences at home do have to leave, although it is not their fault, but we try to help children stay at home if they can'.

In a few instances the opening gambit is very explicit or shocking: 'I don't like her, she puts her finger in my dilly', or, 'Can I look at your cunt?' The key here is not to convey shock or anger, but to seek clarification. This can often be achieved by echoing the child: 'She puts her finger in your dilly does she?', or, 'You want to look at my cunt?', said calmly. The youngster may then volunteer more information: 'Yes, she hurts me between the legs', or, 'My dad says my cunt is pretty'. The advantage of echoing is that it avoids leading questions and it also demonstrates to the child that he or she will not be punished or rejected for using 'rude' words.

Some children are unable to say anything directly but may write poems or letters or draw or paint. Occupational therapists, in particular, may identify an abused child through explicit writing or art work. Here again a punitive, shocked response is inappropriate; instead a general inquiry is advisable: 'Would you like to tell me about these drawings?', 'Would you like to tell me some more stories about yourself?'

Health professionals can try to create an opening for children, especially where medical or behavioural signs have been observed. 'With some of the children in Cleveland, a neutral comment such as "it looks as though something has been happening to your bottom" was sometimes responded to by a disclosure of abuse' (Wyatt and Higgs, 1991). Sensitive comments on a child's behaviour can be made: 'You seem to be very quiet nowadays, is anything worrying you?'

Openings can only be created in the right environment. If a child is trying to disclose, the health professional may have to create appropriate surroundings by finding a quiet room free of distractions where they can talk without fear of being overheard. However, care has to be taken to ensure that victims do not feel trapped and fearful of being abused, thereby recreating the abusive scenario. This means that children need to be invited into a secure room, but also told that they can leave at any time. It is sometimes appropriate to leave the door slightly ajar giving youngsters permission to close it if they want to. Another option is to choose a room where the conversation cannot be overheard, but where glass in the door or a window means that a child does not feel so 'closed in'.

Children need to feel relaxed and comfortable. Many disclosures are made with both adult and child sitting on the floor or on floor cushions. Adolescents may be more comfortable in a chair over a cup of tea. Formal settings are best avoided. Sufficient time is needed. This means professionals may have to miss meetings or find colleagues to cover. If time is at a premium, perhaps with a clinic full of patients, as much time as possible has to be spared with the reassurance of a follow-up appointment as soon as possible.

RESPONDING TO DISCLOSURE

Encouragement to continue talking should be given in order to gain sufficient information to make a decision about whether the matter needs to be reported to the statutory investigative agencies. Additionally, victims need an opportunity to unburden themselves and to be given positive feedback and reassurances.

There is a fine balance to be made by the non-investigative health professional between gaining enough information to pass on to investigators and avoiding eliciting so much information that the child is unwilling to repeat everything to an investigator later. It is necessary to obtain clarification of what has happened without being too preoccupied about gaining precise details.

In order to explain what has happened, children may have to be helped to find a vocabulary for intimate activities and body parts. When they talk about 'it' or use an unfamiliar word for the private parts it may be useful to look at a drawing of the body or use a doll so that the child can point to the parts. It is vital to ensure that the youngster means what the adult assumes is meant. A small child or one with a speech impediment may in fact be trying to say 'funny' not 'fanny'. The word 'bottom' is used by some girls to describe both the anal area and the vagina.

When children have clarified what they mean they can be asked if they are happy using a particular word. Some will be comfortable with their own words and they should be allowed to use these. Others have no words or may not like to use their own, in which case the adult can give them a choice of options: 'Doctors and nurses call it a penis, but a lot of people say ''willie'' and I know some families here use the word ''winkie'' which would you like us to use?' A few may still be unable to choose in which case the adult makes a decision: 'Some children I know call it willie, so shall we do the same?'

It is important to enable children to unburden themselves but not to force them to disclose. Clumsy questioning can lead to the formation of the wrong impression. This means that leading questions should be avoided and open questions used most of the time. This means avoiding 'Did he put his fingers in your vagina?', to which the child could give a vague 'yes', not understanding the question but wishing to please an adult who seems to want to help. Instead, the child who says his father 'touched' him could be asked, 'How did he touch you?', or simply, 'Would you like to tell me more about what he did to you?' Open questions usually start with words like 'how' 'what' 'where' 'who' 'why'. Leading or closed questions usually only require the answer 'yes' or 'no'.

Leading questions may also make inaccurate suggestions or emphasize aspects that were unimportant. For example, an adult, assuming that the father was the perpetrator, may ask, 'Did your dad give you that bruise by holding your leg?' The child answers 'yes', although her grandfather caused the bruise that way, because in her anxiety to give an account of what happened she did not realize that the adult said 'dad' not 'grand-dad'.

The difficulty over defining precisely what is and what is not a leading question is often a legal conundrum (Jones and McQuiston, 1988; Vizard, 1991). However, non-investigating professionals simply need to ensure that the way they ask questions does not result in their reaching the wrong conclusions.

One of the best ways of encouraging a child to continue with his or her account is by repeating what has just been said with a gentle question mark in the voice, the echoing mentioned earlier in this section. Questioning may be something like:

Child: 'He put his hand on me.'
Adult: 'He put his hand on you?'
Child: 'Yes, on my fanny.'
Adult: 'On your fanny?'
Child: 'Yes.'
Adult: 'Can you point to the fanny on this doll?'

Inducements such as sweets should never be given. Although there is little evidence that children can be bribed to make or embroider allegations of sexual abuse, inducements can throw doubt on the child's story. Even comments like 'good boy, you are being clever telling me this' during the disclosure can be seen as an inducement.

In order to ensure misinterpretations are not being made it is important to gain clarification. Much of the time this is verbal: 'Did you say Mummy or Mandy?', or, 'Is it your first Daddy or your second Daddy that you mean?' At other times, as mentioned, children can demonstrate with ordinary dolls and figures. They can be asked to show, model or draw what they mean.

It is worth restating that non-investigating professionals need not ask detailed questions about events, that can come later. Instead they should be endeavouring to make disclosure a positive experience so that children will not mind talking to the investigators.

Belief

The assertion that children divulging sexual abuse should be believed is controversial. However, they are likely to be telling the truth. They should be given the same degree of belief as is given to adults when they claim a crime has been committed. Drivers may declare their car has been stolen when in reality they have forgotten where it was parked or are obscuring the fact that they were involved in a 'hit and run' accident. But the police do not start with the premise that drivers are universally forgetful or dishonest. They believe a car is stolen until they find evidence to show this is not the case. So children should be assumed to be telling the truth until and unless an investigation proves they are not doing so.

Sigmund Freud, unable to cope with the histories of sexual abuse he obtained from distressed young people, developed the theory that girls fantasized about sex with their fathers and boys with their mothers (Olafson, Corwin and Summit, 1993). It is now known from accounts of survivors, admissions by perpetrators and an increased understanding of the medical signs of sexual interference, that children do not make up elaborate fantasies about sex with adults unless they have already been victimized and have facts to embellish.

Some 'experts' have maintained that children frequently fabricate stories. During the Cleveland Inquiry one mother believed her child, especially since her husband was a Schedule 1 offender, previously suspected of abusing children. The local MP, Stuart Bell, dismissed both the mother's judgement and the strong indicators against her husband, saying: 'The bairn's been told to say she was abused' (Butler-Sloss, 1988). Evidence given to the Cleveland Inquiry by Dr Underwager indicated that in the USA 65% of all reports are unfounded (Butler-Sloss, 1988). What he did not add, however, was that in the USA all professionals must, by law, report all suspicions of abuse to the authorities. 'Not surprisingly, this legal compulsion leads to professionals erring on the side of caution' (Davies and Westcott, 1991). Discounting a large number of reports is in no way an indication of how many children's allegations are proved to be fabrications.

A BBC survey showed that 53% of respondents agreed that children lied about abuse (La Fontaine, 1990). However, children have many disincentives and few inducements to lie about being sexually abused. Talking about these matters with an adult is embarrassing and difficult for most youngsters. The previous section explained how they often struggle to find an appropriate vocabulary and fear punishment for being 'rude'. One girl, raped by her teacher, was expelled for lying when she tried to disclose. By this example, other victimized pupils were effectively silenced and only felt able to disclose once they had left school. Eventually, many years later, the teacher went to prison on 12 counts of rape against young adolescent schoolgirls.

Adults have acknowledged that in their childhood they made up stories about 'strangers' approaching them, no doubt to add a little excitement to life. But they only offered vague details, both about the perpetrator and the abuse. This is very different from those children who complain about somebody they know, perhaps depend on and maybe love very much. Children can, very rarely, accuse the wrong person in an attempt to stop the abuse without getting the real perpetrator into trouble. On the whole, research is demonstrating that fictitious allegations by the young are extremely rare and when they do occur there is usually a discernible reason (La Fontaine, 1990; Toth and Elias, 1991).

It is important to let children know their story is accepted. A BBC survey showed that nearly a quarter of the respondents claiming to have been abused did not tell anyone because they thought they would not be believed (La Fontaine, 1990).

Sometimes the way in which children disclose and what they say leaves no room for doubt. In these cases they can be reassured: 'I believe you'. In other cases where belief may be less certain, it is appropriate to say: 'What you are telling me is very important'. In one case, a professional worker who knew the child gave a totally inappropriate response: 'We know what you're like, you're always making up stories, I've never known such a little liar'. Fortunately, a collegaue was on hand and sent the professional off to get a cup of tea while continuing to reassure and listen to the boy. The youngster, though sometimes unreliable, in this instance gave the police information that led to the uncovering of a neighbourhood sex ring.

Acknowledgement of child's feelings

At this stage health professionals are not attempting to give the victim therapy to solve all his or her emotional problems. Nevertheless, as well as determining whether to refer on, an important task is to help the child feel as comfortable as possible about his or her feelings and about making the disclosure.

As the story unfolds, instead of trying to get fine details out of the child it is worth asking, 'How did you feel about that?', or, 'What did you feel when he did that?' While some children can be emotionally numb or so concerned to tell their story that this sort of interjection is unhelpful, many will be relieved to be given the opportunity to talk about their feelings.

When children express anger it is appropriate to acknowledge their right to do so. However, anger against themselves can be gently challenged: 'Do you really believe you were silly to do that? Don't you think lots of other children would have done it too?' Some youngsters use strong language to express their feelings. This is not the time to teach the rights and wrongs of swearing. Their language must be accepted without shock or admonishment. The strength of their feelings should be acknowledged: 'I guess what he did really upset you'.

Some become distressed and tearful. They often need a little space and understanding before continuing. 'I can see you are finding this hard, I understand. There's no hurry. Carry on when you want to', or, 'It's okay to cry, it's natural to be upset about this'.

Other children remain very calm, matter-of-fact and detached as though they were describing a rather boring day at school. This does not mean they are lying or have no feelings. It demonstrates how in control of their emotions they have learnt to be in order to keep their secret. They have had to maintain an appearance of calm 'normality' and they continue to do so even when talking about what has happened.

It is essential not to assume feelings, attributing to children emotions they may not have. For example, 'You must really hate your brother after all he has done to you' may only serve to confirm for a girl, who loves her brother despite his behaviour, that she is abnormal and different from other girls.

Victims can be reassured that they are not the only young people to have been sexually abused. In the case of professionals who have suffered childhood abuse themselves, it is unlikely to be appropriate to share this, at this stage. On the other hand, if children ask directly then the simple truth without elaboration or details is usually the best policy, followed by a generalization, then a return to focusing back on the child: 'Yes, I was, when I was about the same age as you are. You know, there are quite a few people who have had a similar experience to yours. Is there anything else that you are worried about?', or, 'Like you, I've had a few bad experiences, quite a lot of people do. Is there anything else you want to tell me about your experience?' Health professionals who were sexually abused as children need to prepare themselves for the possiblity of being asked directly.

Control of own feelings

Hearing children reveal what has happened can be a devastating experience; it is nearly always harrowing, even for a hardened professional investigator. Health professionals may be more resilient than most because they are used to coping with all manner of human tragedies. Nevertheless, what a particular child says or does might hit a raw nerve.

Adults must seem strong but sympathetic. They cannot afford to break down in tears in front of a distressed child. On the other hand, remaining very distant and detached can give the impression of rejection or disinterest in what is being related. Health professionals again have an advantage because their job so often demands that they walk the tightrope between under- and over-reacting, between under- and over-involvement.

Anger may be felt, but not expressed. Animosity against the child is obviously totally unacceptable. Resentment against parents who have failed to protect or believe, as well as against the perpetrator, is understandable but must not be expressed in front of the child. Irritation may be felt against fellow professionals that have acted inappropriately, but this should not be commented upon except perhaps to say to the victim, 'I guess that might have caused some problems for you'. Youngsters may mistake anger directed against someone else for annoyance with them. Alternatively they may feel no resentment towards their parents or the perpetrator and become worried and confused by the adult's fury. Professionals dealing with disclosures must remain concerned but calm.

Giving comfort

Words of comfort are to be given whenever possible. These include assurances that the child is not to blame for either the abuse itself or any of the consequences of telling. They also need to know they are not responsible for the well-being of other children. It can be acknowledged that by disclosing they may be helping others, but it is ultimately the task of adults to protect children. They cannot, however, be absolved from responsibility if they have in turn abused or bullied another child, unless they were forced to do so by the abuser.

Physical comforting in terms of cuddling or holding victimized children, has to be exercised with care. Some people who work with children have a 'no touch' rule. One play therapist explains: 'I do not initiate touch as I feel the child must control that choice' (Cattanach, 1992). Some children will be very ill at ease with any physical contact, fearing that any touching is the start of grooming or an assault. They need a lot of space and definitely do not want to be physically consoled.

On the other hand, many victims feel they are literally untouchable and that the avoidance of contact on the adult's part is simply confirmation of their view of themselves. Children sometimes nestle up to the adult and obviously want physical comfort, in which case a gentle arm round the shoulders might be appropriate. With children who do not make their feelings clear it may be useful to give a light touch of the hand or arm or, with older ones, to offer a handshake at the end of the discussion.

Preparation for the next step

A decision inevitably has to be made about referring the matter on to the investigating agencies. Normally, when a child describes anything that could be construed as sexual abuse the matter should be referred on. Sometimes a youngster complaining about 'having been hurt' leads to uncertainty about whether the allegation is one of sexual or physical abuse. However, in either case a child protection agency will need to be informed.

Those disclosing have to be reminded that although good secrets, for example birthday presents or surprise parties, can be kept, those that make children uncomfortable should be told to people who can help. Health professionals involved in a disclosure have to explain that the matter must be referred on: 'I think more help might be needed than I can give on my own. I will have to talk to some other adults who quite often help children'.

It may be necessary to prepare for the fact that the police have to be involved: 'Sometimes people break the law and the police have to be told. You have done nothing wrong but I think that your uncle might have'.

Children need to be assured that whatever happens subsequently is not their fault, unless they have themselves abused another child. 'It is not your fault if the police see your daddy'. Older children can be helped to understand by drawing parallels. 'If your dad drove the car too fast and crashed it, would the crash be your fault if you were the passenger and enjoying the high speeds?' They can be encouraged to think of their own examples and the more appropriate the examples they give, the greater the certainty that they have understood they are not responsible. Younger children, or those unable to understand analogies, just have to be reassured several times that whatever happens they are not to blame.

Youngsters who have managed to disclose are to be thanked for sharing their secret and congratulated on their courage for speaking out. They deserve to be told that they have done the right thing by telling. An acknowledgement can be given that revealing abuse is a hard thing to do and that some victims are never able to do so.

Finally, it is worth bearing in mind that each person who sees a youngster that has disclosed abuse will have an important part to play in conveying certain essential points. One person reassuring a child will have an impact, but several people giving the same encouraging message will have an even greater effect. This is all the more true if those concerned are important to the youngster and/or are in a position of authority.

In summary, victims of abuse need to be told by as many people as possible:

- you are believed;
- you are not to blame for the abuse or for its consequences;
- you have a right to be angry;
- you are not the only person this has happened to;
- you were right to tell;
- you are a lovely, normal child who has had to cope with difficult experiences.

The perpetrator will have conveyed the opposite messages. Failure to grasp the opportunity of contradicting the perpetrator is, in effect, to empower the abuser.

ALTERNATIVE INFORMANTS

Disclosures from other children

Sexually abused children often initially confide in a friend of their own age. They may well want their friend to tell an adult; in other instances they simply need to unburden themselves.

Friends may be so worried that they tell, intentionally or inadvertently, a trusted adult, who could be a health professional such as a school nurse.

As in the case of victims, child informants who want what they say kept secret have to be told that good secrets can be kept but if it becomes obvious that they or another child needs help then the secret has to be shared with those who can best give assistance.

The first problem facing health professionals is to determine whether or not the informant is in fact the victim and is talking about him or herself. Alternatively, the other child might be a victim as well as the informant. Children who are themselves being molested may first test the reactions of adults by disclosing abuse of another.

> EXAMPLE: Mrs B was pregnant with her fourth child and being visited by the midwife. The eldest boy in the family, Jack, told the midwife that Mr B was abusing his younger sister, Francesca. The midwife reported the allegations and after investigations Francesca was taken into care. Jack, his younger brother and the new baby, all boys, were left at home with Mr and Mrs B. A few years later Jack, now 17, told the social worker involved, 'You know what I said happened to my sister, well it happened to me too'.

Initially child informants should be encouraged to talk about the youngster that is being abused. The adult should take the opportunity to explain that the victim is not to blame and need not feel guilty or ashamed. These messages will help encourage further revelations should the informants have been abused too.

They should be given the opportunity to describe how they are feeling. Again this may elicit a comment reflecting on their own abuse, such as 'I'm really sad, it's so hard to trust anybody', in which case the adult can pick up this possible cue: 'Has anyone done anything to you to make you feel this way?' In all cases it is as well to ask child informants, using great care and sensitivity, 'Has anything like this happened to you?'

Another major problem facing child informants is that they may be blamed for the consequences of disclosure. Even if the victim wanted the friend or sibling to disclose, the informant may become a convenient scapegoat. Often the consequences of disclosure seem disruptive at best and catastrophic at worst: a perpetrator commits suicide; a mother goes into hospital; a family has to leave its home; all the children in a family are taken into care. It is all too easy for youngsters who thought they were helping to end up feeling they have caused all the subsequent problems. Health professionals must tell child informants, just as they tell victims, that it was right to tell and the abuser is the only one to blame for any consequences. Investigating professionals, the informant's parents, the police and social workers should also reinforce this message.

Disclosures from non-abusing parents

Many disclosures come from non-abusing parents. Either their children confide in them directly or the parents pick up clues and strongly suspect that abuse is occurring. In a study by Mannarino and Cohen (1986), in 56% of the cases 'the formal abuse complaint was filed by the child's mother'.

A disclosure might be explicit and direct. A pregnant woman told her midwife: 'I have found out that my husband has been interfering with his nieces and I am worried about the baby when he or she is the same age'. One mother, seeking advice from her health visitor, explained that her eldest daughter had claimed her father had abused her, which the mother thought might well be the case because she had heard suspicious noises from the girl's bedroom.

At other times the disclosure might be more tentative: 'What do you think of these people who molest children?', or, 'There is something wrong with my son, I think he needs help'. Here a facilitating question can be asked: 'Are you worried about people who molest children?', or, 'Would you like to tell me about the problems you are having with your son?'

Parents who are certain or strongly suspect that their children are being sexually abused will be very distressed even if they seem calm. Their emotions have to be addressed. At an appropriate stage they should be asked, 'How are you feeling about all this?' Many parents, who have taken all reasonable precautions to protect their children, feel guilty, blaming themselves for what happened. Others may be very punitive towards the victim. Some direct their anger against other people they feel should have been protecting their children.

The message that the perpetrator is the only person to blame can be given unless the perpetrator is another child or an adult with diminished responsibility. In such cases, parents have to be helped to understand that sometimes trying to cast blame is an unproductive use of their efforts.

The issue of confidentiality has again to be dealt with. If there are strong indicators that a child has been abused within the family then the matter must be referred for investigation. The parents should be informed of this and told that confidentiality cannot be guaranteed if children seem to be at risk. In cases of non-family abuse parents should be encouraged to approach the police themselves. They may be reluctant to do so but an explanation of the compulsive nature of child molestation and dangers to other children may be persuasive. In cases of abuse within the family the allegations must be referred for investigation. In all instances health professionals have a duty to discuss the matter with their line-managers and colleagues in the local child protection agencies.

Some parents may have been victims themselves, a matter they disclose, or which becomes evident, as they discuss their fears for their own child. The response to adults abused as children is discussed in the final chapter.

Disclosures from perpetrators

Some perpetrators disclose inadvertently. One man recovering from a sports injury happily told his physiotherapist that he had taken some 'lovely pictures' of children. When he showed them to her they were explicitly pornographic. His judgement and thinking was so distorted that he could no longer see there was anything wrong with his activities.

On occasion perpetrators gain sexual arousal from describing their activities. They talk about them to a health professional in the mistaken belief that medical confidentiality is absolute.

Others are motivated by a wish to be helped. They believe that they have a medical or psychiatric problem that is causing them to abuse: 'too many sex hormones'; 'a queer bit of my brain'. They therefore turn to a health professional in the hope of gaining medical treatment and sympathy.

Whatever the case, health professionals have to make it clear to abusers that confidentiality cannot be maintained if it seems that the welfare of children is at risk. This may stop the perpetrator from any further disclosure but it is the only course of action to take once it is realized that the abuser is possibly making an admission. If, whether accidentally or purposefully, perpetrators give health professionals details of offences then they have a duty to discuss their evidence with colleagues from child protection agencies, which will probably include the police.

Disclosures from other adults

There is a variety of other adults who disclose on behalf of a child. Sometimes they are close relatives, such as grand-parents. In some instances, like this, health professionals, who usually work with elderly people and have very little contact with children, find they are having to deal somewhat unexpectedly with the issue of child sexual abuse. Again, the message about not being able to maintain absolute confiden-tiality has to be given.

The closer a relative is to a child the more distressed, and possibly guilty or angry, they are likely to feel. In cases of abuse within the family grandparents can find themselves divided between protecting their grandchildren and exposing their own son or daughter as a child molester.

Quite a few referrals come to the notice of health profes-sionals through the parents of the friends of victims. A girl tells her best friend who then confides in her own mother, who in turn confides in a health professional. The possibility of the friend being held to blame needs to be discussed with her mother, who can then give her daughter the support and emotional protection she will need during the investigation.

Finally, it seems useful to rephrase the advice given in the *Memorandum of Good Practice* (Home Office, 1992). The guidance relates to statements from children, but has a wider applica-tion to possible disclosures from adults as well. There are four principles, which are adapted and restated below:

- Listen first, rather than firing direct questions, although occasional open questions may be useful in helping the person continue, to clarify or to demonstrate interest and understanding.

- Never stop a person who is freely recalling significant events, although a perpetrator may need to be reminded of the legal consequences of any admission.
- Make a note of the discussion, taking care to record the exact time, where it took place and who was present as well as what was said.
- Record carefully, and in detail, all subsequent events up to the time of any court proceedings or until the matter appears to be resolved.

6

Investigation and beyond

A substantial part of this section is devoted to the investigative process because, although most health professionals will never have a role that is central to a detailed investigation, it is useful for them to know how suspected cases are managed. Enhanced understanding of the processes should ensure that they give appropriate information to those more directly involved and will equip them to provide support and help to anyone, patient or colleague, who may be depending on them.

Before an investigation, any health professional who has been alerted to a possible case of child sexual abuse must, unless a completely independent practitioner, consult their agency procedures. In the UK, the USA and much of Europe courses of action are prescribed for each professional group.

Occasionally, the evidence is so tentative that health workers are reluctant to invoke an investigation. In such cases careful observations and records must be kept. In addition, concerns must be shared with supervisors and/or local specialists, and additional information should be gathered from other colleagues that may know the children involved. A health visitor, for example, could consult the family doctor plus perhaps the school nurse responsible for the schools attended by older children in the family.

When there are distinct medical or behavioural indicators or a disclosure a referral must be made to the appropriate investigative agencies. In the UK these are the police, social services and the National Society for the Prevention of Cruelty to Children (NSPCC, in England, Wales and Northern Ireland) or the Royal Scottish Society for the Prevention of Cruelty to Children (RSSPCC in Scotland). Reporting is mandatory in the USA; in the UK and much of Europe it is not, but health professionals who fail to report a probable case of abuse for investigation are putting both the welfare of children and their own careers in jeopardy.

A number of health professionals, such as police surgeons, have a formal role to play in investigations, while a range of other health professionals find they have a peripheral role. Whatever their part, health professionals should be aware that the perpetrator may well have committed a crime for which the police will be seeking evidence. If offenders are warned of an impending inquiry they are likely to destroy any evidence – clothes, lubricants, ropes, films, photographs. They will also do everything in their power to silence any witnesses. Children, who could be the only witnesses, are easily silenced by persuasion or intimidation.

INTERVIEWING CHILD WITNESSES

Social workers and some health professionals will conduct exploratory or information-gathering interviews with children when, despite signs of possible abuse, it is very likely that there is an alternative explanation. The term 'disclosure interview' should be avoided as this presupposes that there is something to disclose.

Interviews will be clearly and formally identified as 'investigative' when there are strong indicators that abuse has occurred. Non-investigating health professionals will not be expected to formally interview child witnesses, but someone whom the child trusts may be asked to remain as a support during the process.

The main focus of the rest of this section is on investigative interviews, but it is not intended as instructions on how to conduct an investigative interview; there are already detailed works on this (Glaser and Frosh, 1988; Jones and McQuiston, 1988; Home Office, 1992). Instead it is a review of the process to enable health professionals taking a peripheral role to understand what is happening and distinguish good from bad practice. It should also enable them to be effective, even if less than central, members of the multidisciplinary team.

Many investigations are jointly undertaken by a child protection worker (usually a qualified social worker) and a police representative. The issue of male interviewers in child sexual abuse cases is controversial and has been reviewed by a number of researchers (Frosh, 1988; Narducci,1987; Raynes and Green, 1991). There are cultural aspects to be considered. Girls and women with certain ethnic and religious heritages would feel grossly violated if interviewed on their own by two men about intimate matters. Conversely, young males from some cultural backgrounds would not be comfortable being interviewed about sexual matters by a female worker. The consensus among practitioners appears to be that, ideally, the child should choose the sex of the interviewers, but as that is rarely feasible then in most cases at least one investigator should be female. Even that aspiration cannot always be met. This means that there may well be a role for a female health professional, such as a school nurse, in accompanying a girl whose mother is not available and who is to be interviewed by a male police officer and male social worker.

Another role that a health professional might take in an investigation is that of facilitator when a child has a disability that requires a skilled third party to promote good communication, such as someone proficient in sign language. Similarly there may be a role if the child's first, and possibly only, language is a minority one. A health professional who is familiar to the child and also fluent in that language is better than an unfamiliar interpreter.

A number of the principles discussed in the previous chapter on facilitating disclosures also apply to investigative interviews. These include provision of a comfortable setting where the child does not feel trapped, access to a functional vocabulary and avoidance of a display of emotion on the part of the interviewers.

Investigating professionals should not only obtain information but also give children appropriate messages. The key ones are those described in the previous chapter, from 'You are taken seriously' and 'You are not to blame', through to 'You were right to tell'. Children should be kept informed and have events and decisions explained to them in a way they can understand.

Nevertheless, there are significant differences between facilitating a child who is trying to disclose, and conducting an investigative interview. Investigators have to respond differently from the health professional who simply enables a child to 'tell'. Investigating professionals will be seeking, as far as possible, clear indicators that the child has been sexually abused and looking for evidence that will enable them to consider prosecuting the perpetrators.

They will be concerned to find out exactly what happened, when, where, to whom, by whom and how often. The questioning of the children will need to be more specific: rather than simply letting the victims unburden themselves, the investigators may have to be persistent in their questioning. This could cause some distress to a youngster who is being required to recall and recount events that have been painful, humiliating, frightening or embarrassing. Health professionals, present in a supportive role, should refrain from intervening even if the child shows signs of distress.

On the other hand, interviews should be brought to a close if the youngster shows prolonged, intense or recurrent upset or an obvious reluctance to continue. The investigators should never indulge in threats, shouting, swearing, sarcasm, bribes or derogatory remarks. All are totally unacceptable and the victim's supporter would have every right to intervene if this behaviour was displayed.

In 1992 the Home Office, in conjunction with the Department of Health, produced the *Memorandum of Good Practice*. Although it is intended to provide guidance in cases where video evidence is being obtained for criminal prosecutions, much of the information relating to the conduct of interviews is basic good practice and applicable to other interview settings. It advises that the child should be introduced to the people participating in the interview, for example. Although Scotland has its own self-contained legal system the following sections contain much that is relevant with regard to evidential interviews and video evidence.

In the initial stages of the investigation children may minimize what happened to them, thereby giving an inaccurate impression. They want to test the response of adults before they give full details. They may say something only happened once, in contradiction of what is known of the grooming process and perhaps another witness' account. Many victims believe that to 'admit' that the perpetrator was able to assault them repeatedly is tantamount to agreeing to the activity.

Children's accounts can also be incoherent because the grooming process has made it difficult for them to distinguish between abusive and 'normal' activities. They may have been assaulted so often that one experience merges into another. Victims abused at night-time, drugged or terrorized will have been confused by tiredness, narcotics or fear. Some will have repressed, denied and forgotten their worst experiences so that they only remember in a fragmented way. The interview itself and the fear of the consequences may also cause stress, so that the youngsters cannot think clearly.

Danya Glaser (1989) makes the point that by asking questions the interviewers are placing on children the burden of giving an answer. 'If details are requested, which from the child's point of view are peripheral to the event and therefore not recalled, the child may feel obliged to fabricate an answer'. This is because youngsters usually want to be helpful, not because they are lying to attract attention or cause trouble. The essence of what they are saying is likely to be the truth. Unfortunately, when investigating a crime the interviewers are likely to want exact details, such as times and places which the victims may not remember, so they may give a 'guestimate' to satisfy their interrogators. This may conflict with more accurate information given by another witness, lead to inconsistencies and throw their evidence into doubt.

Studies of children's memories demonstrate that they do not have poorer ones than adults, indeed in some circumstances they have better ones (Allport and Postman, 1947; Lindberg,1980). A study of 4-year-olds (Tobey and Goodman, 1992) demonstrated that although such young children were not very good at estimating ages and had difficulty answering time questions they were otherwise very accurate when answering questions suggesting abuse. They were not suggestible. Participation in events 'strengthens children's free recall concerning the action that occurred, heightens resistance to suggestion and reduces errors of commission to questions about abuse'. Despite this, there are many reasons why during an investigative interview children's statements may sound vague, confused and contradictory.

Nevertheless, investigators have to try to gain as coherent and comprehensive an account as possible. This means they have to seek clarification, which may require them to ask children to repeat their account several times. They will be particularly concerned to ensure that the correct people have been identified as the perpetrators. They will be equally keen to establish whether or not other children have been abused.

In seeking information the interview should be conducted in a way that is appropriate to the children's ages and abilities, as well as their culture. With young children, toys may be used to put them at their ease and to enable them to communicate. When interviewing black or Asian youngsters the pictures, dolls and play figures available should not represent only white people. Similarly, provision should be made for children with disabilities.

Using anatomical dolls

Trained and skilled interviewers may use anatomical dolls during an investigation. These are also called 'anatomically complete' or 'anatomically correct' neither term being an accurate description. Some workers refer to them as 'show and tell' or 'sexually explicit' dolls. The preferred phrase is anatomical dolls because it indicates the dolls have additional anatomical features that most other dolls do not have.

Assorted dolls with additional attributes have been used for many years by child therapists but it is thought that this particular type was first used specifically in child abuse cases in 1976 in Oregon, USA, by Marcia Morgan and Virginia Friedemann (Swann, 1985). They started being used in England by the Great Ormond Street team in 1982/3.

The dolls come in sets of at least four. They all have mouths that can open to pull out a tongue, fingers and toes, navels and nipples and an anal opening. In addition they have male or female genitalia as appropriate, plus pubic hair for the larger dolls. For an effective investigation they should also have assorted clothing available. One small boy, who lived alternately with his stepfather and natural father, would say nothing until he had burrowed into the clothes bag and found a vest. He explained it was the 'daddy' that always wore a vest who had abused him. Another girl was unable to give any details about what had happened until she had dressed the figures in track-suits.

The dolls are particularly useful for children who have limited verbal skills, those with severe speech impediments and those that may be inhibited or unable to give specific details. A 10-year-old said she was very angry about what her uncle had done to her. She said it was too rude to tell but was able to show anal penetration using the dolls. Ultimately she was able to describe events verbally and through drawings.

The dolls can be used in three main ways. The first is to help children name parts of the body. A word like 'bottom' may be used by girls to describe their buttocks, anus and vagina. 'He poked my bottom' can, if referring to the buttocks, be a careless gesture during horseplay, but if meaning the vagina is a strong indication of sexual abuse. The second function, particularly with very young children, is in free play to see if they act out scenes they could only have experienced or that mirror details given by another witness. The third role is to help children who have already given some details to show more precisely what has happened to them. This can act as a protection for the accused. In one case when anatomical dolls were not used a small girl described her father's penis as 'big' and the court assumed she meant that he had had an erection. Using dolls she could have shown that it remained hanging down and he had not attempted intercourse.

The dolls are effective but their very effectiveness has led to difficulties. In the courts defence lawyers have attempted to discredit them saying that because they are endowed with 'private parts' children will naturally play with them in a way that seems sexualized. This has, however, largely been disproved. Several studies, most notably those by Sivan *et al.* (1988) and Glaser and Collins (1989), have shown that non-abused children show no more interest in the anatomical dolls than in other toys. Out of 144 children aged from 3 to 8 years, none showed role-play of explicit behaviour in the Sivan *et al.* study, with only 1% showing any aggression. In the Glaser and Collins study of 91 children aged 3 to 6 years, only five showed sexualized play and in three of these the source of sexual knowledge later became apparent.

A second concern is that untrained, unskilled people have been using the dolls inappropriately. Some, for example, were naming the dolls for the children: 'This one is you and this one is daddy, now what did daddy do to you?' Children should be left to identify the dolls themselves. If an interviewer has a preconception that a child has been abused and uses dolls with a lot of pressure and hypothetical questions, there is likely to be apprehension about false indications or allegations (Vizard, 1991). Despite this, a study by Kendall-Tackett and Watson (1993) showed that professionals in the Boston, Massachusetts area were 'well trained and careful in their use of anatomical dolls' in contradiction to earlier studies.

An additional misgiving has been that children can be traumatized by the dolls. Some victims can certainly react very strongly to them, tearing off limbs and flinging them away violently. However, the studies by Sivan *et al.* (1988) and Glaser and Collins (1989) showed no evidence that children generally are traumatized. In some cases the dolls can have a therapeutic effect, even at the investigative stage, by giving a victim the chance to depersonalize and gain mastery over what has happened (Swann 1985). Nevertheless, to remove any possible risks the dolls should be carefully introduced, initially with clothes on, and no child should be pressurized into using them.

Anatomical dolls should not be used unless they are clearly required. The Cleveland Inquiry report (Butler-Sloss, 1988) was critical of their indiscriminate use at too early a stage. Sexualized role play with dolls by a child is an indicator of a possible problem but not by itself conclusive evidence of sexual abuse. Generally the dolls are a valuable tool for skilled investigators.

Video recording

Some children welcome the opportunity to discuss their experiences several times with a range of different people, but for many disclosure is painful and embarrassing, and repeated interviews will only cause them greater distress. Children under about 7 years old are likely to describe what has happened once, possibly twice, but can rarely be persuaded to do so again, at least not for a long time. In order to ensure that youngsters do not have to be questioned repeatedly, investigators are making increasing use of video recordings of interviews.

In the UK it has now been accepted that when children are likely to have to give evidence of certain sexual or violent offences in the criminal courts, a video recording of their 'evidence in chief' can be made. This refers to the basic account of events. There are a number of restrictions, including the type of offences and the maximum age in relation to the offence. The child must still be available for cross-examination, so it will not obviate the need for the youngster to appear in court. The *Memorandum of Good Practice* (Home Office, 1992) gives technical details about how best to set up the video equipment.

The investigators have to decide whether it is in the best interests of the child to make a recording. It is possible for them to decide to record in less than ideal technical circumstances, not for evidential purposes but instead to help colleagues who will be offering therapy to understand the victims' experiences without having to ask them repeatedly. However, the investigators have to be clear about why they are using the video. They must also be aware of the consequences if they choose not to make one, or make one that does not meet the evidential requirements outlined in the *Memorandum of Good Practice* (Home Office, 1992).

The Cleveland Inquiry report (Butler-Sloss, 1988) recommended that consent should be obtained from children before recording an interview. They should have an opportunity to see the camera. When a one-way mirror is used to enable others to view the proceedings, the children should again be consulted, as in most instances should parents.

There are considerable technical problems associated with using video cameras. Often they have to be fixed. If they are set to encompass the whole room they will fail to pick up detail. If they are set up to show only part of the room children will invariably wander 'off camera' at a critical moment. Colleagues controlling cameras through one-way screens can overcome this, but the presence of an additional person operating a camera in the interview room is not desirable. Sound quality has to be excellent with no intrusive noises like outside road traffic. Children tend to lower their voices or whisper when giving explicit descriptions. Good equipment and facilities cost a lot of money. Some areas now have purpose-built interviewing suites but even this can cause problems, meaning children are transported long distances or interviewed when they are not ready to talk.

A poor recording of a badly-managed interview can discredit what the child might have disclosed when not on tape. Courts have criticized inadequately-conducted and recorded video interviews but then given little weight to other non-recorded evidence. On the other hand, a clear disclosure captured on tape can leave abusers with no credible defence. In the USA perpetrators have sometimes pleaded guilty after seeing video tapes of children describing the abuse (Elias and MacFarlane, 1991).

Tapes must be kept safely. Again, the *Memorandum of Good Practice* (Home Office, 1992) gives details on how tapes of formal interviews should be kept. There are concerns that just as victims' written statements have found their way to paedophile rings, so video recordings in which youngsters describe their abuse could also become an off-shoot of the child pornography market.

Consent and presence of parents

Normally, parental consent is required for an assessment of a child. The Cleveland Inquiry report (Butler-Sloss, 1988) recommends that parents should be consulted and kept informed. But if a parent is likely to be an abuser, or if, despite strong indications of abuse, consent is not granted, then legal protective action may have to be taken. When parents are involved in the abuse, deferral to parental rights may be at the expense of the child, as witnesses are silenced and evidence destroyed.

Some youngsters are helped during interviews by the presence of at least one parent. But there are obvious problems with parental presence when the parent in question is the suspected perpetrator or the partner or close relative of the offender. It is like the victim of a mugging trying to give the police a statement while sitting in the same room as the alleged mugger.

Even when non-abusing parents are caring and supportive, children may be unwilling to talk in front of them because they are worried about upsetting them. Occasionally mothers or fathers inadvertently silence a victim because the child senses their distress. Sometimes it may be better, if non-abusing parents are worried about their child, to suggest that another person who is trusted by all parties acts as the child's supporter. Here, the choice could fall, for example, on a health professional known to the family.

Interview structure

While some professionals believe that investigative interviews should be rigidly structured, others favour an unstructured play technique to obtain a spontaneous response (Vizard, 1991). The *Memorandum of Good Practice* (Home Office, 1992) outlines the preferred progress of interviews. There should be four phases. The first is designed to establish a rapport between the child and the interviewers. It also enables them to gain insight into the youngster's developmental stage, understanding, emotional state and communication skills. The exchanges should focus on general discussion or play and should avoid reference to the alleged offences. On the other hand, this is only guidance and there are exceptions. One 8-year-old boy marched straight into the interview room and declared, 'Right, I'll talk now, play later' and immediately gave details of abuse by his father.

In the second phase the child is encouraged to speak freely and give an account, in his or her own words, of what has happened.

The third phase involves questioning in order to add to, and clarify, the information given in phase two. The fourth phase is the closing stage where there may be some final clarification, an invitation to the child to ask any questions of the interviewers and 'winding down' by reverting to neutral topics or some enjoyable free play. The youngster should be thanked and reassured that he or she has done the right thing by helping. Information should also be given about what will happen next.

Interviews should not be too long. It is tempting to keep a child in an interview until he or she discloses. This in itself is abusive; the child may not be ready to say anything or may have repressed and forgotten the abuse, or there may be nothing to disclose. It is sometimes better to have a few short interviews than one very long one, provided the child is protected in the interim (Gonzalez *et al.*, 1993).

Dealing with older children, the police may take formal written statements. These can take a considerable time to obtain. Four or five hours is not unknown. Here the comfort and welfare of the young people have to be balanced by the need to obtain evidence and protect other children by securing a conviction.

Retractions

Children usually disclose because they want the abuse to stop. They may want to avoid causing distress to anyone else. Those who have been abused within the family may well have 'accommodated' to the situation (Summit, 1983). This often means that they have taken on responsibility for protecting the family. In some cases non-family perpetrators can make victims feel they are responsible for sparing their family acute distress: 'Your parents will never live it down if the neighbours get to know'. During disclosure children temporarily abdicate this responsibility. Shortly afterwards they are made to feel guilty about their lapse. They see the family torn asunder or their parents pilloried by the neighbours. The only way to make amends is to pretend nothing really happened. So they retract, in the hope that their parents will be comforted or the family reunited. Having conducted research into children's patterns of disclosure, Gonzales *et al.* (1993) concluded: 'Judges, lawyers, parents and therapists must be helped to understand that recantation does not represent an end in itself and should not be equated with false allegation. Rather, recantation is more accurately viewed as a phase within the disclosure process for some children'.

Other interviews

The investigators will need to interview a number of other people. They may wish to see non-abusing parents to discover if they have any information that would corroborate the child's evidence. Other children associated with the victim are also likely to be interviewed, especially siblings in cases of intra-familial abuse.

Alleged perpetrators should be interviewed before they have time to destroy any evidence, intimidate witnesses or prepare a convincing story to contradict the victim. Hence the 'dawn raids' that attracted press attention in some instances.

Health professionals who may have relevant information may well be interviewed by investigating agencies. While mindful of the duty of confidentiality towards patients, they should be prepared to disclose any information that will protect the children in question. Subsequently, health professionals may be required to give evidence in court. This will be discussed later in this chapter.

MEDICAL EXAMINATIONS

Although evidence of sexual abuse in the form of physical damage is found in less than half the reported cases, a medical examination is frequently requested.

Benefits of a medical examination

The primary benefit of a medical examination is that evidence of sexual abuse may be detected. An asymptomatic child may still show signs such as reflex anal dilatation. Conclusive forensic evidence, such as semen or adult pubic hairs around a young girl's vagina, may come to light.

A medical examination could well reveal injuries or infections that require medical treatment. Similarly, pregnancies may be detected at an early stage and can then be managed more effectively than if discovered later.

A number of children who have been abused but not seriously damaged may benefit from the reassurance that the results of the medical examination can give.

Drawbacks of a medical examination

The most obvious drawback is that an intimate examination can recreate the sense of being abused, as the following accounts by victims all too clearly demonstrate.

I asked you for help
and you gave me a doctor
with cold metal gadgets and cold hands
who spread my legs and stared, just like my father.
(*MacFarlane, 1990*)

I climb onto Dr Miller's steel examining table, trying to keep my legs from shaking, seeing the doctor approach me matter-of-factly with a tongue depressor. It is then I notice, from the direction he is moving and the struggle my mother is having to disguise her familiar look of sexual distaste, that it is not my throat he is going to examine. As he spreads my legs, I disappear. My other self takes over, quivering in dread'.

(*Fraser, 1989*)

The problem is exacerbated by the lack of women doctors, especially female police surgeons, although children may still be upset even when the doctor is of a preferred sex.

Conduct of the examination

Children should be prepared for what is going to happen in a way they can appreciate and understand. They should not be led to think that the doctor is giving them a general examination, only to find he or she is suddenly 'interfering' with their private parts. They should be told step by step what is happening and why. Every attempt should be made to relax them because a tense, distressed patient cannot be examined properly. If victims have serious injuries requiring treatment, or complications requiring inspection by a number of doctors, a general anaesthetic may be required.

Examination should take place in a comfortable environment. Settings are sometimes far from ideal.

EXAMPLE: A 13-year-old girl, after disclosing abuse by her stepfather to a social worker and policewoman, was taken to the police station where she was questioned. She was then told to take all her clothes off and wait for the doctor. She started to tremble. The accompanying social worker asked if there was a robe or towel the girl could put on. The response was a polite and slightly surprised 'no'. The child was expected to stand naked in a cell-like examination room and await the arrival of the male police surgeon. When he did arrive it was hardly surprising that she refused the examination.

Children have the right to refuse a medical examination, and provision for this is made in the Children Act, 1989 (section 44). Parental assent should normally be sought. Emergency powers can be granted through the courts if this is refused and the child is clearly at risk.

The abuse makes the victims feel powerless and out of control of the situation. If the doctor lets them help, perhaps by allowing them to take their own vaginal swabs, they can gain a measure of control (Bamford and Roberts, 1989). Children aged from about 9 years are considered old enough to take their own swabs, although much will depend on the competency of each individual child. When the youngster is given this measure of control the doctor will provide careful supervision and will guide the youngster's hand to ensure that an appropriate swab is taken.

Children should also be able to choose a support person, who could be the trusted health professional to whom they disclosed. The rest of this section provides an outline of the main features of medical examinations for the benefit of health professionals acting as supporters.

The position the child is asked to adopt for the examination is thought to be important. Bamford and Roberts (1989) and Durfee, Heger and Woodling (1986) suggest that very young children sit on the knee of the mother or carer as she gently flexes and abducts the child's hips. This 'frog-leg' position is normally adopted for an examination of the vagina. For an inspection of the anus the knees-to-chest, face-down position is too reminiscent of an abusive position so children are now asked to lie on their sides and grasp the knees.

Examination starts with a general inspection for bruises or lesions to the body where the child may have been held, hit or tied. The mouth should be scrutinized for signs of oral abuse.

This is followed by a more detailed inspection of the genitals. Intrusive investigations are to be avoided if possible. However, Glaister's rods (small glass spheres on glass handles) may be used to examine the edge of the hymen vaginalis. Digital examinations of the pelvis through the vagina should not be performed on pre-pubertal girls. In the USA, in particular, a colposcope is used to clarify patterns of scarring to the hymen and vagina in cases of sexual abuse. It is a binocular optical instrument providing light and magnification and is non-invasive. It should not touch or penetrate the victim (Woodling and Heger, 1986; Durfee, Heger and Woodling, 1986).

The test for reflex anal dilatation is performed by separating the buttocks. A gloved finger may be inserted to assess the tone of the anal sphincter, however there are doubts about how necessary this is. If there is bleeding from the rectum and it is suspected that the lining is torn, a proctoscope or sigmoidoscope may be inserted under anaesthetic.

If the assault is likely to have been recent there could be forensic evidence present. Specimens from the oral pharynx, vagina and anus are collected. Swabs for testing for sexually transmitted diseases may well be taken. All materials for laboratory testing should be properly handled and labelled. Photographs might also be taken of positive findings. The necessity for these evidential processes make the examination all the more intrusive for the child but are sometimes necessary.

Medical examinations should be reduced to the absolute minimum. During the Cleveland controversy a few children were re-examined several times for the purpose of confirming or refuting a diagnosis of sexual abuse. In one family, three paediatricians and four police surgeons saw the children as second, third and further opinions were sought.

MULTIDISCIPLINARY WORKING

Although doctors may diagnose sexual abuse from physical signs, the conclusion that sexual abuse has occurred has to take account of all the other factors, such as the history given, the child's behaviour and family situation. Even when the investigating professionals are certain a child has been abused, it is often difficult to be equally sure about the identity of the perpetrator.

The information gathering and subsequent management of cases of sexual abuse usually have a multidisciplinary dimension. An incident like indecent exposure by a stranger may involve only the police, although in the case of a child the parents may seek support and understanding from family health professionals, such as the general practitioner or health visitor, and the school.

The closer the abuse is to the family the wider the range of workers involved. Each profession has different objectives and perspectives: the police have law enforcement as the main aim and operate within a legal framework; health professionals give priority to health promotion and operate within the medical model; child care social workers have child protection and child welfare as their main focus and work on principles drawn from the social sciences. These differences can be the strength of a child protection investigation because if, despite the varying perspectives, there is agreement about what has happened and should happen next, the decisions are likely to be the best possible in the situation. However, it can be a recipe for confusion and conflict as was seen in Cleveland (England) in 1986 (Butler-Sloss, 1988; Campbell, 1988).

Feelings are likely to be more charged the nearer the abuse is to the home. Families, even destructive ones, are very powerful. Different practitioners can find they are being courted by various members of the family. The perpetrator, in particular, is usually well-skilled at 'grooming' people outside the family as well as within. Social welfare agencies or child-oriented professionals such as paediatricians may well take up the cause of the victim, while the police or more adult oriented professions may appreciate the view of the parents. Here conflict may be the outcome (Furniss, 1987).

Case conferences

Case conferences first became popular in the early 1970s when it was realized that a range of individual workers from a wide variety of professions all had information about a particular child who was being physically mistreated. In some cases, such as that of Maria Colwell (DHSS, 1974), the failure of the professionals to communicate led to the death of the child.

Originally, conferences were held within a day or two of suspicious injuries so that decisions could be made about legal protection for the child. As the various professionals realized the significance of neglect, such as in the cases of Malcolm Page (Essex County Council, 1981) and Stephen Meurs (Norfolk County Council, 1975), families in which serious neglect was identified also became the subjects of case conferences. In the late 1970s sexual abuse was increasingly acknowledged and these cases started to be subjected to the same procedures.

What started as the most efficient and straightforward system for pooling all the information about a child has now become a somewhat unwieldy, quasi-judicial forum. Occasionally, some of the most important information is withheld, either because of the non-attendance of a key informant or because professionals are not prepared to share everything given the quasi-legal nature.

Case conferences tend to be held several days, possibly weeks, after the original complaint or concern was raised. All professionals involved in a case, including the police, will be invited, as foster-parents and volunteers may be, depending on local policy. Parents are asked to attend all or part of the conference. Children are rarely invited.

Parental attendance, despite initial misgivings, has appeared to work well in most areas. However, the exceptions are when a parent is also the perpetrator.

> EXAMPLE: At one case conference the father/perpetrator complained about the way his 12-year-old daughter had 'seduced' him, then 'made trouble' for him by disclosing. 'Has she apologized to you for her behaviour?' asked the senior police officer at the conference. His query went unchallenged by the rest of the members and by the end of the conference the daughter had been labelled a manipulative, promiscuous minx. The daughter, a very young-looking, withdrawn child did not attend, was only known to a few conference members and had no opportunity to correct the impression created.

In the UK the case conference is often chaired by a social work manager. This can create problems in relation to agency loyalty and colleague support if the case accountable social worker is also the chairman's subordinate. Moore (1985) recommends the appointment as chairman of an independent individual who has no agency responsibility or loyalties. Comments should be addressed to the chairman, although some conferences, despite being formal, allow for discussion between members.

Attending a case conference can be quite an intimidating experience the first few times, even for people who are normally confident in their professional abilities. Some agency representatives attend frequently and these regulars may know each other well. This can give the impression of an 'in-crowd', making the person who rarely attends feel isolated and even less self-assured. It is important to remember that every contribution is of value and good preparation will help increase confidence.

Health professionals should prepare themselves by ensuring they know what information they want to contribute. The chairman will be none too pleased if, after a two-hour conference and a decision to leave the children at home because the perpetrator has left, someone then announces that a new person, known to be a sex offender, has just moved in!

Health professionals should familiarize themselves with any reports or files that they take to the conference. Someone who spends several minutes scrabbling through endless notes and files simply wastes conference time. It is embarrassing to drop a file and find papers cascading everywhere. Punctuality is vital and workers with important information do well to arrive early so they can choose a prominent seat. Even at well-chaired case conferences people sitting on the periphery or in a very low seat are all too easily overlooked or over-ridden by a more powerful, better-placed contributor.

Case conferences tend to consist of three sections: the first is information gathering and sharing; the second is discussion and clarification; and decisions or recommendations are made in the third. It is usual to wait to be asked before contributing, although if another person makes an inaccurate or unacceptable remark it is possible, with the chairman's permission, to comment more or less immediately. If a member with information is not asked he or she should attract the chairman's attention before the information sharing section is drawn to a close.

The professional's contribution should be delivered clearly, confidently and audibly. There is a skill in being concise without excluding important detail. As far as possible, information given should be within the professional's direct experience, although it is possible to deliver reports on behalf of colleagues and to give information that is second or third hand. However, when this happens it should be made clear: 'My colleague, Mrs A, told me that the grandmother said the mother plays bingo every Thursday'. Value judgements and vague terms should be avoided: 'The house was dirty' needs qualification, such as 'There were urine-soaked mattresses on the beds and excreta on the carpets of every room'. Above all, it is essential not to drift off into talking about another case: 'It reminds me of a family I knew a few years ago . . .'. Finally, professional jargon should either be avoided or terms explained.

At the end, although members usually agree on the next course of action, it is possible to object to a particular recommendation by asking for dissent to be minuted. All conferences must include a minute-taker. Any professional attending the conference as a contributor should receive a copy of the minutes.

Individual agencies are not bound by conference decisions, which are in effect recommendations. It could be, for example, that conference members are unanimous in their agreement that a perpetrator should be prosecuted, but it is ultimately for the Crown Prosecution Service to decide if there is enough evidence and whether it is in the public interest to bring the offender before the courts. If one agency decides not to follow a particular recommendation then its representative should inform the conference chairman, who will in turn inform other participants. In some circumstances it may be necessary to reconvene the meeting.

Child protection registers

Child Protection Registers have variously been referred to as 'Child Abuse Registers' and 'At Risk Registers'. They are not to be confused with the 'At Risk' registers held by primary medical teams for vulnerable babies at risk of conditions that might cause problems, like cot-death or failure to thrive because of a variety of physical factors.

Case conferences held in the UK will recommend whether to place the child's name on the Child Protection Register. Registers arose in the days when non-accidental injury was the recognized problem. In the early 1970s it was realized that a number of professionals had evidence of mistreatment of children like Maria Colwell, the 7-year-old beaten to death by her steptfather in 1973, but they never shared their observations of bruises and distress. It was only when, after a death, the various agency records were collated that it became obvious that a tragedy had been inevitable.

Registers had been introduced in the USA in the 1960s. A DHSS circular acknowledged their value in the UK in 1970. By 1976 another DHSS circular confirmed earlier advice that central records should be kept in each Local Authority of children with signs of non-accidental injury or those at risk of abuse. Agencies still had their own records, but through the register professionals had access to significant supplementary information contributed by workers in other agencies.

In addition, registers served an important function in giving information not just about individual cases but about trends and incidence (Walton, 1989; Creighton, 1987). This had implications for resource planning and allocation. The various procedures for monitoring and up-dating register information meant that additional systems had to be developed to ensure that the different professionals worked together and shared new information. Neglect, sexual abuse and emotional abuse were categories added to registers during the 1980s.

The validity of registration in child sexual abuse is sometimes questioned. It can seem a purposeless exercise, particularly in cases where the victim is unlikely to be returned home. On the other hand, if children being removed from home are not registered then the statistics gleaned from the registers will exclude a significant number of the most serious cases and thereby present a misleading picture of the severity of the problem.

Registers are usually held by an independent agency, such as the NSPCC, or by a designated representative of the social services department. Health professionals should have access to the register although requests for information may have to be channelled through senior personnel. There should be systems in place to ensure confidentiality and to filter out illegitimate access to register records. Children and parents do not have access to registers, although in many circumstances they do have a right to see social service or medical files.

Parents and children should be informed that the child's name has been placed on the register. They should also know when and how it is removed. There is no right of appeal against this. However, the way in which information on a register should be used is limited. The fact that a child has been registered is not admissible as evidence of abuse, although the circumstances leading to the registration are. Parents who have had a child on the register should not automatically be prevented from working with children or from becoming child-minders or foster-parents. Registration may alert professionals to a problem, but the individual circumstances have to be examined. A child of very protective parents may be registered because of abuse by another family member. Children who are victims of abuse outside the family are not normally registered unless the parents are associated with the abuse.

LEGAL STEPS

There are a number of legal steps available in both the civil and criminal courts. The first consideration is usually the future protection of any children involved. In many cases protection can be assured on a voluntary basis. In abuse outside the family or when a relative is not in the household, the parents can provide protection. Where the alleged perpetrator leaves the home the children may subsequently be safe, although in some cases it is feared that, despite offenders saying they are not living at home, they are in fact doing so, or else they move back in after a week or two.

Voluntary arrangements

Sometimes parents may request that their children be removed from home. The youngsters may stay, on an informal basis, with relatives or friends, or they may be 'accommodated' with relatives, foster-parents or in residential units. In England and Wales 'accommodated' means being provided with accom-modation by the Local Authority. It is similar to being 'boarded out' or 'voluntary reception into care', the terms used before the Children Act, 1989.

Orders to protect children

The relevant orders relating to England and Wales are given in Appendix A. Suffice it to say here that in the USA, the UK, Australia and much of Europe there is provision for crisis intervention and some form of emergency protection. This is usually followed by legal means of securing a child's sub-sequent safety, although this may require removal from the home. The more desirable course of action – to legally remove the perpetrator from the scene – is less easily achieved.

Other civil proceedings

In many countries, despite the practical difficulties, there are ways in which an alleged abuser can be restrained from harming the child again. There are also ways in which the victims of crime can obtain compensation for their suffering. It is important that health professionals familiarize themselves with the broad outline of provisions so they can advise children or their families of the availability of civil action and suggest they discuss matters with legal advisors. They cannot, however, be expected to know the precise details as this is the role of solicitors. Details of additional civil proceedings are given in Appendix A.

Criminal prosecution

When a perpetrator is identified, he or she may be charged with a number of different offences (Appendix A). But only a small percentage of child sex abusers are ever prosecuted, and even fewer are found guilty. In the study by Abel *et al.* (1987) of sex offenders that were neither in prison nor on court order, the number of sexual acts against children was from 23.2 to 281.7 per offender. In a study of children on a county child protection register, of the 69 perpetrators, legal action was taken against 28%, with 21% being convicted (Doyle, 1987). This low figure is despite the fact that, in order to be registered, a group of experienced professionals including the police had to have before them enough evidence to convince them that the children had been the victims of sexual abuse.

A case in the criminal court has to be proved 'beyond reasonable doubt'. This is an essential safeguard for the innocent. It means proving that a particular person has molested a child. This can be very difficult because sexual abuse is usually a secret activity such that the only witnesses are the offender and the victim. The grooming of children means that they rarely want to give evidence or cause problems for the abuser. Even in the few cases where a child is prepared to speak out, it is the word of a child against that of an adult.

Perpetrators may well have collected 'respectable labels'. They are usually articulate and plausible, in contrast to children who usually have difficulty explaining their experiences. Courts are not designed for child witnesses and very few youngsters can cope with such a setting. This problem is discussed more fully below.

Even in cases where there is obvious physical damage the matter is not conclusive. The Cleveland controversy surrounding the validity of reflex anal dilatation amply demonstrated this. 'Although most experts agreed that anal dilatation may follow anal abuse, there was considerable disagreement as to the other circumstances in which it might occur' (Butler-Sloss, 1988).

In the proportionally few cases where the child has definite physical signs it may not be possible to say who has caused the injuries. Unless there is forensic evidence, such as blood on the child from a perpetrator with an unusual blood group, it can be impossible to state for certain that a particular person was the abuser.

A number of convictions are secured on the admission of the perpetrator, but there is little incentive for an offender to admit to the abuse. Some perpetrators have done so, only to find that their experience in prison is so horrific that they do everything in their power to conceal and deny any subsequent offences.

In cases where there are several victims and perhaps a number of abusers there is a greater number of potential witnesses, meaning that the perpetrators could be more vulnerable. This could explain why in cases with multiple victims – sex-rings, sibling groups, organized and ritual organized abuse – children are so often forced to commit offences against each other: the potential witness/victim is made into a perpetrator and is therefore less likely to disclose. The risks run by perpetrators in multiple abuse situations also explain the attraction of using supernatural terrors and bizarre ritual. Twenty children describing outlandish and grotesque experiences are less likely to be believed than one child disclosing events that sound more realistic.

Even if a conviction is secured, the sentence may be largely ineffective either in safeguarding children or helping the perpetrators. Furthermore, the attitude of courts and some judges may cause even more problems, endorsing the type of thinking that gives perpetrators 'permission' to abuse children. David Finklehor (1984) cites an example of a judge who, in 1982, described a 5-year-old as 'an unusually sexually promiscuous young lady'. The judge stated his belief that the father had not initiated the sexual contact (Nyhan, 1982). This was echoed by the English judge who, over 10 years later in June 1993, described an abused 8-year-old as 'not exactly an angel'.

COPING IN COURT

Health professionals who become involved in cases of child sexual abuse may find they have to give evidence in court. The most likely circumstances are where a court order is being sought to protect a child; however, they may be called to act as a witness in criminal proceedings.

Although most witnesses appear voluntarily, it is possible to be forced to give evidence – to be subpoenaed. A subpoena is a summons to appear in court 'under penalty'. Failure to appear despite the summons will be deemed a contempt of court, and the reluctant witness who continues to refuse to comply could end up serving a prison sentence.

Some people relish the chance to appear in court as a witness, but the majority of professionals find it a daunting experience. Those unable to convince the court that their evidence is reliable are not acting in the best interests of children.

Some health professionals find it difficult to understand lawyers who do everything in their power to discredit witnesses and thereby 'win' a case on behalf of their client, even when the client would seem to be quite clearly the perpetrator. It is hard to understand lawyers who know that, by their advocacy, offenders will be free to abuse again. There are, however, parallels with the medical profession. A doctor will attempt to save a person's life, even if that person is believed to be a sex offender. No doctor would be expected to think: 'If I save this man, he will only go and rape other children, so I will not operate and instead let him die'. By operating, a surgeon may, indeed, be enabling a child molester to reoffend. Both doctors and lawyers are expected to use their skills to the best of their abilities to achieve the best results for their clients or patients, without making moral judgements.

In continental Europe, the inquisitorial system of presenting evidence is used. Witnesses give evidence and it is the job of the court, rather than opposing lawyers, to test the evidence. In the adversorial system in use in the UK, each party to the case tries to persuade the court that its case is the 'correct' one. This tends to mean that discrediting the evidence of the opposite parties is an almost essential part of the process. It also means that witnesses are called by one or other of the parties, with whom they are then expected to take sides.

Another problem is that where there are several parties to the proceedings, a considerable number of lawyers have the right to cross-examine witnesses. In child care cases it is now usual to have at least four parties represented: the child, one parent, the other parent and the Local Authority.

Although appearing as a witness is a daunting experience, it is possible to cope effectively with all that it involves, including rigorous cross-examination. The following section provides guidance to assist in the presentation of evidence by health professionals.

Preparation

The acquisition of courtroom skills starts long before the actual appearance in the witness box. Health professionals need to ensure that whatever they do can be justified in court. Records of significant events should be kept and, when making them, it is worth ensuring that dates, places and details of individuals seen are correct.

Reports

Most courts require some form of pre-trial documentation, such as a report, affidavit or witness statement. Some employing agencies have a particular policy concerning court reports, and their employees should ensure that such policies are followed. Witnesses who want to take medical notes into court to aid their memories should be guided by the medical authority's policy on medical notes being available to the court. A witness has to ask the permission of the court to refer to notes.

They should be 'contemporaneous', that is, written as soon as possible after the event they record, preferably on the same day and certainly not more than 24 hours later. If permission is given to refer to notes the court may also wish to see them.

Written reports and statements should always be factually accurate including details such as the spelling of names and dates of birth. Inaccurate and badly written reports will lack credibility and so will their authors. At the end of the report there should be a conclusion and, in certain circumstances, a recommendation.

There are two types of witness, a 'witness as to fact' and an 'expert witness'. The former should confine both report and oral evidence to the facts of the case as the witness remembers them. Expert witnesses may give factual information but will also express an opinion. They can also rely on material given by other people, although they should distinguish between direct personal knowledge and second-hand information.

Health professionals may wish to incorporate diagrams or charts into their reports. There should be a clear explanation of what they are designed to illustrate. If percentile charts are included there should be an indication of the nature of the information they can provide. It is helpful if those taking the measurements sign the chart on each occasion so that their identity is known and they can be called to court to be asked directly about a particular measurement.

Familiarization

The report or statement should be reread before the court appearance and discussed with the lawyers who have called the professional in question. They should rehearse the points that are to be covered and try to anticipate the range of questions likely to be asked during cross-examination.

Witnesses should familiarize themselves with the issues surrounding any recent controversies or the recommendations from any relevant public inquiry. In relation to child sexual abuse it would be useful to read the *Report of the Inquiry into Child Abuse in Cleveland* (Butler-Sloss, 1988) and to become acquainted with its recommendations.

Professionals who are unfamiliar with the court may wish to visit it in advance in order to locate parking spaces and toilet and refreshment facilities. It makes it easier to remain calm and concentrate on the evidence to be given if witnesses know how to get to the court without getting lost, know where to park and arrive in plenty of time.

Special needs

Professionals may have special requirements which should be discussed beforehand with the lawyer. Wheelchair access, for example, may be a problem in some older, smaller courts. People with hearing or visual impairments may require special consideration.

Before giving evidence, witnesses will be required to swear an oath on an appropriate holy book for their faith, or to affirm if they have no religious affiliation. The New Testament, for Christians, and the Old Testament, for Jews, are readily available. The Koran is usually locked away for safekeeping. Other holy scriptures will have to be specially obtained. The relevant lawyer or court usher should be alerted if a holy book or scriptures other than the two Testaments is needed.

Witnesses who need to use audio-visual aids, such as slide projectors, tape recorders or even large diagrams, must discuss this well in advance with their lawyers.

Often there is a lot of waiting around outside the court and it is useful to have something to occupy the mind. The precise time at which witnesses will be called cannot be guaranteed, but some accommodation in relation to time for professionals with unavoidable commitments can be negotiated.

Appearance in court

Clothing is often a matter of concern to witnesses, especially since appearing in the witness box is rather like being centre stage. All the eyes in court are on the person standing alone in the box. In the interests of patients it is important for professional workers to dress in a manner that does not cause offence or derision. If unsure about what is acceptable, it is sensible to seek the advice of a friendly lawyer, probation officer, colleague familiar with court or maybe a magistrate.

While clothing should reflect a respect for the dignity of the court, it must also be comfortable. Members of minority ethnic groups will find that their traditional dress is usually accepted by courts. If in doubt, it is worth checking.

One of the keys to a satisfactory performance in the witness box is the ability to appear competent and confident. Competence will appear all the greater if the correct form of address is used. In England and Wales the following is a useful guide:

- 'Sir' or 'Madam' – chairmen of tribunals, individual magistrates;
- 'Your worships' – bench of magistrates;
- 'Your honour' – County Court Judges and Recorders, most Crown Court Judges;
- 'My Lord' (not M'lud!) or 'My Lady' – High Court Judges including those sitting in senior Crown Courts and Old Bailey Judges.

If in doubt, witnesses should check beforehand or listen carefully while in the box, as the lawyers may well address the bench.

Most witnesses wait outside the courtroom until called. Only those that are parties to the proceedings and some expert witnesses will sit through the whole case. When called it is important to walk confidently to the witness box. There will be an usher in a gown who calls the witnesses, shows them to the box and assists them in taking the oath or giving an affirmation.

Taking the oath/affirmation is an important opportunity to establish credibility. Taking it with clarity and confidence will immediately impress the court. Those taking the oath will hold the scriptures in the right hand. Witnesses choosing to affirm should let the usher know, when called, that an affirmation is to be taken. The words of the oath or affirmation are written on a card for witnesses to read from; witnesses who need spectacles for reading should make sure they take them into the witness box!

The lawyer calling the professional will open the questioning by asking the witness to state his or her full name, (work) address, occupation and probably qualifications and experience. Professionals should ensure their credibility is established by avoiding modesty and giving a brief but impressive account of their qualifications and experience.

The lawyer will then ask witnesses to give 'evidence in chief', which means their account of events. If this is already contained in a report available to the court, the lawyer will confine him or herself to asking for clarification or elaboration of certain points in the report. After this, lawyers for other parties will, in turn, question the witness.

At the end of the cross-examination the first lawyer may wish to re-examine the witness. This helps to remind the court of the main points of his or her evidence and may provide an opportunity to explain anything that seemed confused or contradictory during cross-examination. When all the lawyers have finished, the judge or magistrates may ask questions – usually for clarification.

Professionals do well to ensure that all replies are addressed to the magistrates or judge. Conventionally, witnesses turn to the lawyer when he or she is asking the questions, and then turn away to look at the bench when replying. Although this would seem to be mere convention it can be put to good use. By looking at the judges/magistrates it is possible to check whether they are hearing and understanding what is being said. They may well be writing and will appreciate replies that are delivered in a measured way, with pauses to enable them to catch up. It is also possible to control the pace of cross-examination by turning from the lawyer to the bench more quickly or more slowly before replying. Looking at the bench and away from the lawyer also makes it more difficult for the cross-examining lawyer to interrupt or intimidate by a hostile glance.

To assist in the turning process it is helpful to plant the feet, or if sitting to ensure the chair is turned, towards the bench. This means that if the witness turns to receive a question from the lawyer, he or she will almost automatically unwind back towards the bench. Fixing the eyes on the bench when replying also helps; too much eye movement can give a 'shifty' impression.

It is important not to be rushed into a hasty 'yes' or 'no'. If a question requires a fuller reply and the lawyer is seeming to demand a 'yes' or 'no', the witness needs to explain to the judge or magistrate that this is the case: 'Your Honour, I would be misleading the court if I were to give too simple a reply in relation to this complicated issue'.

If hectored and abused in the witness box, it is essential to stay calm and avoid becoming angry or unduly argumentative. Witnesses should recognize that personal insults can be a sign of 'victory' for them. It usually means that the cross-examining lawyer cannot discredit the evidence given and the only tactic left is to try to discredit the person. It is appropriate for witnesses to be assertive, but not aggressive, and to politely stand their ground.

On the other hand, witnesses can be thrown off guard by charm and flattery from cross-examining lawyers. Pleasant, gentle questioning with a tinge of praise and admiration is nearly always a warning sign that the lawyer is leading towards a thoroughly awkward question. Excellent guidance on how to cope with cross-examination tactics is given by David Carson (1990).

Once all the lawyers and the bench have finished their questioning, witnesses should not leave the box until being given permission to do so. Their lawyer will usually ask the bench if they may 'stand down'; if they are not being recalled they will be 'released', which means they may leave the court altogether.

Children as witnesses

There is considerable reluctance to use children as witnesses. Until recently there was doubt about their memories and their ability to understand the meaning of telling the truth. Many of the recent research findings on children's memories are discussed in Jones and McQuiston (1988). The idea that memory starts from minimal capability at birth and grows to adult capability is inaccurate. Different facets of memory and recall develop at different rates and, in later life, decline at different rates. In some memory tests children can be more accurate than adults. Children give the appearance of having memory deficiencies because they do not have the same experience and terms of reference as adults, and they usually have a vocabulary and language that is too limited to convey all they remember.

The problems for children trying to explain what has happened to them has been discussed in this and the previous chapter. In some cases children can give a clear account of what happened and should be credible witnesses, but often the courtroom experience disables children to the extent that they are often unable to continue to give evidence.

Finkelhor, Williams and Burns (1988) describe the experiences of a 4-year-old girl who was 'subpoenaed to answer questions about her previous "sexual history"'. The girl gave evidence until she could take no more: she 'had been yelled at by the defense attorney, called a liar, and told to look directly at him when she tried to look at someone else'. Maya Angelou (1984) describes her experiences in court. Raped at the age of 8 she was asked what the defendant had been wearing and did not know:

> "You mean to say this man raped you and you don't know what he was wearing?" He snickered as if I had raped Mr Freeman. "Do you know if you were raped?" ... "Was that the first time the accused touched you?" ... I didn't want to lie but the lawyer wouldn't let me think, so I used silence as a retreat.

Even before appearing in the witness box children can be distressed by the long wait to be called and by the possiblity of seeing the perpetrator, or perhaps relatives and friends of the perpetrators, in the waiting areas.

Children can be helped by being prepared for the court experience. In the UK there are a number of publications that can assist child witnesses such as that written by Madge Bray (1989). The Children's Legal Centre produces information sheets for them and the West Yorkshire Police have drawn up a cartoon pamphlet. An illustrated pamphlet can be obtained from the Crown Office in Edinburgh. In the USA there is a wide range of materials including video tapes (Flin and Boon, 1989).

Great care has to be taken when preparing a child witness. The Crown Prosecution Service or child's lawyer should be consulted. Defence lawyers have made considerable capital out of suggesting that children have been coached into saying certain things and their evidence is therefore unreliable.

A number of measures have been introduced to help children, although the use of these is totally at the discretion of the court and none is mandatory. The formality of the court can be reduced by the removal of gowns and wigs. The court may be cleared of all observers, although this sometimes has a deleterious effect because the child's (non-abusing) parents have also had to leave (Finkelhor, Williams and Burns, 1988). Even when the court is cleared, if there is a jury 20 or more strange adults will still remain.

A number of technical aids are available. Microphones mean the constant pressure for a child to speak up in order to be heard is relieved. Screens can be used to shield the victim from the alleged abuser. In both the USA and the UK video links have been introduced. A child sits in a room with a supporter. He or she is seen by the court through a video monitor, but the child will usually only see the person asking the questions on a monitor, although extra ones can convey additional images. The child can be cross-examined but will not be in the physical presence of the alleged perpetrator.

Even with these precautions children with limited vocabularies, comprehension and verbal skills are no match for the sophistication of the questioning techniques of cross-examining lawyers. 'Highly articulate lawyers who are steeped in the traditions and legal jargon of the courts may, understandably, experience difficulty in accommodating to the linguistic requirements of a child' (Flin and Boon, 1989).

Adult witnesses, whether victims, bystanders, professionals or experts, can all find an appearance in court a devastating experience. It is therefore hardly surprising that children can be severely affected by having to give evidence. Maya Angelou (1984) became mute for five years after believing that a lie she told in court had led to the death of the perpetrator. Other adult survivors have felt that the treatment they received in court was more abusive than the sexual assault. They have ended up feeling that they, not the perpetrators, were on trial. They have been ridiculed, verbally abused, harassed and hectored by lawyers. If, at the end of the day, the perpetrator is acquitted the victim's feelings of guilt, responsibility, anger and helplessness are all the greater. However, the fact that children have been subjected to such dire experiences is not a reason for preventing children from giving evidence, rather it is a reason for improving the treatment of child witnesses in court.

HELPING VICTIMS AFTER THE INVESTIGATION

All too often adults have believed that children can recover from distressing experiences by simply forgetting them – the 'least said soonest mended' philosophy. Unfortunately this has simply been the rationale for a solution that gives more comfort to the adults involved than the children. A more positive response is required if the victim is to be helped.

The amount of assistance each child needs depends on a wide variety of factors, the type of abuse, the circumstances in which it occurred, its duration, its frequency, the relationship with the perpetrator, the personality, sensitivity, sex and age of the victim, the consequences in terms of family cohesion and many more. The emotional distress caused is not necessarily related to what, in adults' eyes, appears to be the 'severity' of the abuse, meaning whether it was penetrative or violent. Professional workers have been heard to say with surprise 'but it wasn't that bad, he **only** fondled her'. However, the fear and breach of trust that persistent fondling by a trusted relative creates in a sensitive, insecure child, may be as damaging as a violent rape by a stranger on a youngster that has a basic sense of security and self-confidence.

Health professionals may come into contact with the victims of sexual abuse at the post-investigative stage in a variety of ways. Some might have been involved prior to the disclosure and have followed the case through its various stages. Others may have become involved at some time during the investigation. Yet others will only come into contact with the child some time after the investigation has been completed. Some health professionals will be involved specifically because they can give the child assistance with problems arising from the abuse.

Specialist staff, such as child psychiatrists or play therapists, will have specific training to help abused children; other health professionals may have a peripheral, but nevertheless significant, part to play in helping sexually abused children. Assistance is given directly and indirectly.

Coping with grief

Children who have been sexually abused are in a state of loss and mourning. They have lost their security, trust, sense of self-worth and dignity to name but a few of their losses. In cases of intrafamilial abuse they may have lost part of their family, and if moved into care will have lost their home, their friends, family pets and more.

Health professionals, perhaps above all other professionals, will be familiar with children suffering from losses such as family bereavement, amputation of a limb, loss of sight, hearing, or mobility and loss of material provision when the family bread-winner becomes ill and has to give up work. Some health professionals will have specific training in working with children suffering from losses. Others will have learnt through experience how to help such children. These skills, which so many health professionals have acquired, can be put to good use in helping sexually abused children.

Shock and anxiety

After the investigation some children will still be in a state of numbness or shock, and many will show signs of alarm. They can suffer severe separation anxiety, being unwilling to go out or to school. The physiological response to threat – increased flow of adrenalin, heart rate and muscular tension, and bowel and bladder relaxation – can result in insomnia, nightmares, enuresis, sudden aggression, weakness and exhaustion, and increasing susceptibility to illness (Jewett, 1984). Children in this state will need physical comfort and security. Strategies can include allowing a child a light or radio on at night and a comfortable place to retreat to, such as a floor cushion in their room to curl up in. The adults in their lives need to be thoroughly dependable and trustworthy. Health visitors, for example, can discuss this stage with parents or carers and help them devise ways of making the children more secure, comfortable and relaxed.

Denial

Children may remain in a state of denial and adults are all too ready to collude with this. Even if everyone has acknowledged the fact of the abuse they may deny the feelings that accompany it, which leads to difficulties in future relationships. Other children may become overactive; by keeping busy and boisterous they can avoid dwelling on what happened. In older youngsters loud music, telephone chat-lines, promiscuity with numerous partners, drink or drugs can all block out the pain. Some health professionals are in a position to talk to the victims spontaneously: 'You seem happier now but do you ever think about what happened?'. Other health professionals, who suspect a child may be in this state, could discuss their concerns with specialist colleagues or with the parents.

Regression

Children can experience a yearning and searching for that which they have lost. It is not unusual for them to regress to the age they were before the abuse occurred. A child abused from as far back as they remember may well become infantile, talking in a 'baby' voice and wanting a bottle or dummy, becoming enuretic and wanting to be carried; 10-year-old children can suddenly develop the egocentricity and tantrums of a 2-year-old, while cuddling teddy bears and demanding to drink out of their 'Peter Rabbit' beaker.

This regression can be very disconcerting and tiring for parents, teachers and health workers; one physiotherapist commented that she thought she was trying to help a teenager and felt instead that she was dealing with a toddler. It is a lot easier to be patient and allow the child to regress if the carer or helper understands that this is a natural phase in a healing process and the youngsters will eventually 'grow up' and return to nearer their physical age. Youngsters who have responded to the abuse in this way should not be told to 'grow up', 'stop acting like a spoilt brat' or 'act your age'. Instead they should be indulged for a while and then gently encouraged to move on: 'Do you still want your dummy? Why don't you just have it at night, not in the daytime?'. Children who seem to be stuck for a long time in a regressed state, particularly the infantile state, and children who already have some developmental issues to handle, such as those with severe learning difficulties, may need to be assessed for specialist help.

Anger and sadness

Abused children, like other people in a loss situation, become angry at some stage. An adult who has lost her purse will search for it and, sooner or later when it cannot be found, may be angry with someone she believes has stolen it or made her lose it: 'If he hadn't been rushing me to finish the shopping quickly I wouldn't have left the purse in the shop'. If no one else can be blamed, the anger is turned inwards against the self: 'I was stupid to leave my purse on the top of my shopping bag'. Similarly, the abused child will be angry once the extent of the loss has been felt. Children who have been helped to realize that they are not at fault will direct their anger towards the perpetrator or anyone else they can blame. Overtly angry behaviour may take the form of aggression, rudeness, being noisy and defiant or sulky with brooding silences.

Those who blame themselves carry a burden of guilt and shame. Turning their anger inwards, they despise themselves and become withdrawn and depressed (Koverola *et al.*, 1993). They can become careless of their own welfare, disregarding dangers. Some attempt suicide, some succeed. They may constantly inflict self-punishment by setting themselves up to fail, or invite retribution by behaviour that they know will get them into trouble.

Referring to bereaved children, Claudia Jewett (1984) comments: 'Even the supportive adult who tries to help a child in this stage of grief may face anger and hostility'. It is easier for parents and other concerned adults to cope with the anger or depression of victims if they understand that this is a natural and normal stage towards healing.

Youngsters can be helped to direct their anger against the perpetrator, with whom they have an absolute right to be angry. Children can be shown ways of expressing anger safely through play, punching cushions and vigorous physical activities. Unfortunately, when the abuser is an object of love or sympathy, victims have difficulty focusing their anger appropriately.

Children should be allowed to talk about their feelings while being given attention and understanding. Undue criticism should be avoided, but they can be gently checked for rudeness or aggression: 'I know that you have had a hard time and have a right to be pretty angry, but swearing at your teacher isn't being very fair to her'. This can lead to a discussion about what fairness is all about.

Exhaustion and disorientation

Their experiences can lead victims to a deep-seated physical and emotional exhaustion and disorientation. After disclosure and investigation, they are often easily distracted, find it hard to concentrate and fail at school. They may seem clumsy, forgetful, careless and lazy. A few go into a trance-like state which can irritate adults who think they are being defiant and rude: 'She just looks through me, takes absolutely no notice of me or of what I am saying'. Adults, particularly parents, need help to understand that this is a natural reaction to distressing experiences. Berating the victims, calling them lazy and stupid, or telling them to 'pull themselves together' are unhelpful responses. They require assistance to find interesting ways of coping with important tasks such as homework. They need plenty of pleasurable experiences that require little effort but generate enthusiasm.

Victims may continue to feel isolated and different from their peers. Referral to a therapeutic group for children who have been sexually abused, where they can share their feelings with peers in a similar situation can prove very beneficial (Hall, 1978; Paley and Cox, 1985; Furniss, Bingley-Miller and van Elburg, 1988; Nelki and Watters, 1989).

GENERAL COMMENTS

Anything that can be done to help raise a victim's self-esteem by way of genuine praise and positive comments will help. This means that a health professional, who may have no reason to talk directly to a victim or his or her carers about the abuse, can still be vigilant about avoiding criticism and seeking opportunities to give compliments.

Victims of abuse might need help and understanding well beyond the original abuse, disclosure and investigation. They could be reminded of their experiences some years later and find their feelings of distress and loss are re-awakened. Health professionals may have to respond to an older child or adult who is having difficulties coping with the aftermath of abuse that occurred, and was thought to have been dealt with, many years before. Guidance of how best to help in this situation is given in the final chapter.

Children who have been sexually abused can become more vulnerable to further abuse. Helping to protect children from re-abuse is an important piece of work that should be undertaken in the post-investigative phase. This is discussed in the next chapter.

Protection and prevention

Ultimately the only way that children will be protected and sexual abuse prevented is by ensuring that sex offenders no longer offend. As long as there are perpetrators seeking opportunities to molest children abuse will occur. The saying 'where there's a will there's a way' is all too true in this context. This is why the treatment of offenders has been placed in a chapter on prevention.

That is not to say that prevention programmes targeted at parents and children are not useful. They may help to protect some youngsters who would otherwise have been abused. The benefits and pitfalls of such programmes are included in this chapter.

SOCIETAL ATTITUDES

Sexual abuse only exists as long as perpetrators commit the assaults. Culpability for each instance of abuse is solely that of the offender, but some responsibility for the existence of child sexual abuse lies within society. Particularly accountable are those people in positions of power who hold values that nourish the fantasies of abusers and provide a rationale for their beliefs and excuses. The phrase 'pro-offender thinking' is used to describe attitudes that enable abusers to permit or excuse their behaviour.

Examples of distorted thinking were given in Chapter 3, as were societal arguments to explain why there appear to be more male than female abusers. Added to these are society's attitudes to children. Many Western cultures, and others influenced by British Imperial principles, view children as less worthy of dignity and respect than adults. When Valerie Yule (1985) observed adults with youngsters in the street, she noted that although they were generally polite to other adults, there was widespread rudeness towards children.

In the UK children are singled out as the only group in society that it is legal to assault physically. 'Army sergeants may not hit recruits in the interests of discipline and training for the defence of the realm. The police may not strike suspects except in self-defence, even those suspected of heinous crimes ... British law still positively asserts parents' rights to administer ''reasonable physical punishment'' to their children and nobody knows better than the child protection agencies how arbitrarily that line between ''reasonable'' and ''unreasonable'' is placed' (Leach, 1990).

What is more, many people argue that it is a positive disservice to children not to beat them. This argument is dangerously close to that of the sex offender who will argue that sexual activity with children is positively beneficial. 'Sex before 8 or else it's too late' is the paedophile's slogan. It is hardly surprising that much sexual abuse takes place within the context of physical punishment.

Babies and toddlers, in particular, require a lot of physically intimate care, as do some frail elderly people and adults with certain disabilities. In all these cases their bodies should be treated with care and dignity. Children, like adults, should be respected and their bodies should not be exploited or used to cause humiliation or pain.

Children are frequently objectified by adults. A child is often referred to as 'it': 'The baby was born a week ago, it has a heart defect', 'We have friends coming to stay. They're bringing their child. I don't know how we will cope with it'. Children are repeatedly stereotyped as 'little monsters'. In order to abuse, a perpetrator – whether a concentration camp commandant, a terrorist or a child sex abuser – has to objectify the victims or dismiss them as subhuman. Society therefore aids and abets child molesters in the way children are generally regarded.

In more recent years, the business and advertising worlds also have a case to answer. In pursuit of fashion, parents have been persuaded to buy sexy clothing for their pre-adolescent, even pre-school daughters. Perfumes and make-up have been specially manufactured for young children. Advertisements feature youngsters in provocative poses with slogans such as the one described in Chapter 3, 'Small ones are the juiciest', with its echoes of Jack who commented that the tight vaginas of young girls 'are the sweetest and most value' (Li, West and Woodhouse, 1990).

By making children sexually alluring and dressing them as rather cute, sexy little adults, manufacturers, marketing people and advertisers are feeding the paedophile's belief that children really want and need sex and are being deliberately seductive.

FOCUS ON PERPETRATORS

The problem of child sexual abuse only exists because some people want to have sex with children and are prepared to abuse any advantages, any power they have, in order to exploit youngsters in pursuit of their own needs. Protection and prevention has to start with the root cause, the perpetrators themselves.

Responding to adult offenders

The first obvious difficulty with trying to prevent child sexual abuse by starting with the perpetrators is that very few come forward to ask for help. Health professionals will be aware that people with relatively 'acceptable' addiction problems, such as smoking, alcoholism or gambling, find it difficult enough to seek assistance and maintain abstinence. Sex offenders have an added obstacle to seeking help because under many judicial systems, including that in the UK, they run the risk of imprisonment if they disclose their offences. Many are never detected, others simply deny what has happened and cannot be prosecuted because the courtroom setting militates against children giving evidence.

Some professionals have fondly believed that the shock of being caught will prevent a perpetrator from reoffending, even if the case does not end in a conviction. Health professionals are unlikely to be so ingenuous because they will be all too familiar with behaviour that has an addictive component. They know that a shock may cause a patient to abstain for a while, but eventually, as memories recede, the desire to resume the behaviour will return.

In Sacramento and some other parts of the USA, there is a policy known as pre-trial 'diversion'. This takes advantage of the motivation to change that is sometimes present in the immediate aftermath of disclosure. The evidence against a perpetrator is collected and kept but a prosecution is not proceeded with as long as the abuser engages in treatment and at no time reoffends. But if another offence is committed the perpetrator is prosecuted on both counts.

In the UK there is no parallel policy. Diversion before trial is possible, but for practical reasons the case would then have to be dropped entirely. Those opposed to the adoption in the UK of a similar pre-trial diversion argue that evidence could be hard to produce as witnesses' memories fade, and any confession would be deemed inadmissible because of the likelihood of its having been obtained in return for a promise of treatment. There would therefore be no realistic way of ensuring that the perpetrators kept to any commitment to engage in treatment.

In the UK offenders can, however, be diverted into treatment after conviction. It is possible to offer a probation order containing certain conditions in relation to psychiatric treatment and residence. But it is sometimes difficult to enforce. Moreover, if an offender pleads guilty and accepts responsibility there is no guarantee that the judge will agree to a probation order. No plea bargaining is allowed between lawyers and judge, although this does occur, to a modest degree, between prosecution and defence (Toth and Spencer, 1991).

A conviction may well result in imprisonment, and this is likely to exacerbate the problem as very few prisons have sufficient effective treatment facilities. Some perpetrators will choose to serve their sentence in the mainstream prison alongside a wide range of other offenders. If the nature of their offences becomes known they may be treated harshly by fellow inmates and prison officers. For some, this harrowing experience of the adult world makes them retreat into a world of fantasy activities with children; they resolve all the more firmly to avoid the company of adults when released.

On the other hand, perpetrators can choose to be grouped with other sex offenders in a prison segregation unit; this is commonly referred to as 'being on Rule 43'. The treatment on offer for these prisoners varies from prison to prison. In instances where treatment is limited there are dangers that, being grouped with other sex abusers, pro-offender thinking, attitudes and behaviours are likely to be reinforced. The prisoners share exploits and minimize the effects on victims. One cause for concern has been the circulation around prisons of victims' witness statements to police, serving to titillate and stimulate fantasies. Inmates will collude with the excuses their fellow offenders make and learn additional ways of evading detection in future. Protection for children is only guaranteed while the perpetrators are in prison. On release, far from having 'learnt their lesson', they will pose an even greater risk than before, having instead learnt some additional new grooming and concealment strategies.

An effective alternative to imprisonment without treatment is group therapy. This can be offered in prison, but it can also take place in non-custodial residential settings, such as the former Gracewell Institute in Birmingham, or in community programmes based in hospital out-patient clinics or probation service facilities.

This does not mean that custodial sentences and the imposition of strong penalties are of no value. As early as 1984 David Finkelhor had concluded that it was not true that effective treatment could only be undertaken when offenders were motivated to get help. 'Programs have been successful in treating offenders who were pressured into treatment through threats of prison or parole revocation'. Staff at the Gracewell Institute worked with offenders who denied they had done anything wrong. Some maintained that they only agreed to attend to 'prove their innocence'. A number of these appeared to make more progress and real positive change than those who seemed eager to admit they were in the wrong and needed to be 'cured'.

Group work has been shown to be effective in modifying denial in child sex abusers (O'Donohue and Letourneau, 1993). In addition, properly conducted group work requires offenders to examine the validity of their thoughts and attitudes. They will not be allowed to excuse or minimize their actions or the effects on the victims. Perpetrators have to accept responsibility for their actions. Initially it may be the professionals working with the group who question and confront, but gradually fellow offenders become aware of one another's strategies and will challenge what is being said. This sort of constructive confrontation is invariably more meaningful when delivered by peers who know the game than by professional workers who can be dismissed as not really understanding what life is like for a sex offender.

In group or individual work with perpetrators the aim is control not cure. They need to be helped to identify their own cycle of offending behaviour. Sex abusers have to become aware of the events, if any, that may act as a trigger, and appreciate subsequent behaviours and rationalizations. Only by understanding their thoughts and actions will they be able to exert control over themselves.

Psychodrama, such as that run by the Geest Theatre Company in the UK, has been used to apparently good effect with some sex offenders. This enables them to experience and understand events from the perspective of their victims by taking on board the role of a victimized child.

Work with perpetrators must only be undertaken by professionals who have had specialist training. Health professionals with general counselling skills are not equipped to deal with sex abusers and may do more harm than good. As Richard Purdie and Shirley Tordoff (1992) comment: 'We have had to unlearn some of our professional training with its emphasis on acceptance of the clients' material in order to maintain an attitude of vigilant scepticism'.

Working with sex offenders is emotionally draining and distressing. Those undertaking it have to be constantly alert to correct perpetrators' distorted thinking, minimizing and blaming of others. The attitudes and intransigence of some perpetrators can lead to anger and frustration. There is an added burden for those professionals whose colleagues question their motivation for wanting to work with offenders.

Much of the treatment work so far undertaken has been with male perpetrators. However, some intervention has been provided for female abusers, such as the group treatment in Styal prison, Manchester (Barnett, Corder and Jehu, 1989), the Gracewell Clinic, Birmingham (Eldridge, 1993) and work in the USA (Matthews, Matthews and Speltz, 1989; Matthews, 1993). Jane Kinder Matthews (1993), who has worked with both male and female sex offenders, has noted some differences between the sexes that have implications for treatment. Women are less able to forgive themselves, tend to stay longer in a state of shame and have a more deeply entrenched anger against themselves.

Treating adolescent offenders

In the field of juvenile justice it has been the policy to try to keep young people who commit 'commonplace' crimes out of court. There are indications that young men in particular are likely to 'grow out of' offending behaviour, especially crimes such as car thefts and burglary. Securing a conviction and emphasizing the deviant nature of their behaviour is likely to criminalize them and set them on the road to lifelong offending.

This strategy of minimizing the criminal aspects of certain offending appears to work well, and various juvenile justice schemes have produced good results. The same philosophy is, however, inappropriate when applied to juvenile sex offenders. Although some young people may simply be experimenting and will grow out of the behaviour, many more, as detailed in Chapter 3, will have already been caught up in a cycle of offending behaviour that is compulsive, and which they cannot control. It is likely to be reinforced and become more entrenched as they reach adulthood.

Like adult offenders, youngsters need help to control their behaviour. In the case of very young children this can be done largely on a behavioural basis. This does not mean that they should be severely or physically punished (Cantwell, 1988). Sexually acting out behaviour can be discouraged using firm words and actions with a simple explanation, or the youngsters' attention can be diverted and alternative behaviour rewarded.

Older children and adolescents may already have developed rationalizations to justify their behaviour, their attitudes and beliefs therefore have to be challenged. While this can be undertaken on an individual basis, great benefits accrue from group work. The views and opinions of their peers are, to most young people, of paramount importance, while those of an older generation may be rejected. In group settings youngsters who are denying, minimizing, excusing and blaming can be challenged by people of their own age.

Young offenders need to understand their sexual assault cycle. This concept, which is a modified form of the adult offender cycle, 'provides a framework on which offenders can attach their individual feelings, thoughts, and behaviours, seeing themselves as unique individuals while identifying what they have in common with each other' (Ryan *et al.*, 1987). As with adult offenders, the ultimate objective is to acquire a recognition of triggers and precipitating events and respond by employing more constructive ways of thinking and behaving so that the cycle is interrupted at the beginning.

Juvenile perpetrators are frequently victims themselves, and it is difficult not to become engrossed in helping them with their damaged and distressed emotions. However, the offending behaviour has to be addressed first, otherwise they may simply use their enhanced recognition of their own victimization to excuse present transgressions and seek sympathy for their abusive activities.

Young offenders may have additional problems which can damage their self-esteem and increase their sense of powerlessness and helplessness. It has been shown that many young people committing sex offences have serious impairments in other areas of their functioning (Saunders and Awad, 1988). For example, a significant number have specific learning difficulties and so will need specialist educational assistance.

The case for treating the young is strong (Knopp, 1985). Their attitudes and cognitive and behaviour patterns are less deeply entrenched than those of adult offenders. Moreover, they are still trying out a number of ways of gaining sexual satisfaction and can therefore be helped to discover less exploitive ways.

STRENGTHENING EXTERNAL INHIBITORS

Only in an ideal world could offending behaviour be totally eradicated. It is unlikely that the first two of Finkelhor's preconditions, namely the wish to abuse children and overcoming internal inhibitors (1984) will cease to exist. While there are men and women prepared to exploit children, prevention and protection has to rely on tackling, at least in part, the third and fourth pre-conditions, namely overcoming external inhibitors and overcoming the victim's resistance.

Law enforcement agencies

If children are to be protected, society must be unequivocal in showing that their exploitation for sexual gratification is totally unacceptable. As described earlier in this chapter, societal attitudes that endorse pro-offender thinking have to be challenged. In addition, society must give power to its agents to intervene when such exploitation is suspected. Potential perpetrators are less likely to offend if they believe they will be caught and called to account. Although not true in all cases, for many the fear of discovery is a powerful disincentive.

This means that laws protecting children have to be maintained or introduced. Legal prohibitions provide an unequivocal demonstration that the sexual exploitation of children – for whatever reason and whatever the circumstnaces – is unacceptable. Whenever the law is contravened the courts must ensure that, while protecting innocent adults, the scales of justice are tipped more fairly towards child victims and witnesses than they are at present. The judiciary, police and probation services must have training that enables them to understand the dynamics involved. In the UK judges have resisted health professionals' offers of training with regard to domestic violence and sexual abuse. However, in Canada the judiciary has welcomed such offers to good effect (Wade, 1993).

The role of helping professionals

Helping professionals, particularly those who come into contact with children in the course of their work, are in a position to help prevent sexual abuse. Those who have been trained to appreciate the issues at stake can share their knowledge with colleagues and educate those who harbour misconceptions about the subject or know very little about it.

Teachers, social workers and health professionals are frequently in a position to pick up the signs and symptoms of sexual abuse. They may be able to create an atmosphere in which children or non-abusing adults feel able to disclose their knowledge or fears of sexual abuse.

Health professionals command respect and are therefore ideally situated to influence other people. Those who are well-informed can enlighten others and press for improvements in the response to child sexual abuse cases.

The news and entertainment media

Professionals working for the media, such as journalists and TV programme-makers can have a beneficial influence by accurately reporting and portraying the problem of child sexual abuse.

The media can be a great force for good or ill. During the Cleveland crisis the news media was a mixed blessing. Members of the press who regularly attended the inquiry were thanked by Lord Justice Butler-Sloss for the responsible way in which they reported the daily evidence and protected the children concerned from undue publicity. However, this only served to highlight the less responsible news media representatives whose behaviour elicited criticism from the inquiry chairman (Butler-Sloss, 1988).

A similar mixed blessing was noted by Finkelhor, Williams and Burns (1988) in their research into abuse in day care settings. Some media coverage was biased – in favour of the accused perpetrators in four instances, and towards the victim in three. Identification of the victims by the press led to pressure and unwarranted attention from reporters, concerned friends and hostile allies of the accused. In the UK, under a voluntary code of conduct instituted in 1992, newspapers have agreed to try to avoid identification of victims in circumstances not already covered by legislation prohibiting the naming of child sex abuse victims. Nevertheless, there remains a danger that sensational, indeed any, media coverage can create fear and overprotection of children. On the other hand, reporters have alerted authorities to possible cases and have had a beneficial role in enhancing awareness of the problem and providing insight into the issues, as demonstrated by reporters David Williams (1987) and Julia Stuart (1993).

Non-abusing parents

Although professionals, law enforcers, neighbours and friends can all play a part in protecting children, the people in the best position to do so are usually non-abusing parents.

To say that being a parent is a difficult job may be a cliché, but it is never more true than in the area of protection. There has to be a balance between protecting children and yet not frightening or over-protecting them. Ways in which parents and other adults can help children to protect themselves are discussed in the last section of this chapter. Parents need to be aware of the strategies and programmes that can be used.

In the case of parents whose child has been abused and who wish to ensure protection from re-abuse, the situation is more difficult. The reactions of parents were discussed in chapter 4. Those who deny what has happened and express disbelief or those who vent their anger on the victim are exposing all the youngsters in the family to the risk of further exploitation. Abused children will have an increased sense of helplessness and worthlessness. Both victims and siblings, who witness the fate of their brother or sister, will feel unable to disclose future abuse for fear of the parents' negative reactions.

Health professionals may be approached by parents seeking advice because they are unsure of how to respond to their child. They want to stop something similar happening in the future but do not know how to do so. The following suggestions can be offered:

- The key to protection is good communication. This means that parents have to send helpful, positive messages to their children. It also means enabling youngsters to talk freely to both their mother and father. Anything that improves communications between parents and their offspring will enhance protection.
- Attempt to remain calm and avoid expressing strong feelings, especially negative ones in front of both the victim and any brothers and sisters. Children, who often lack a full understanding of all the issues, readily misinterpret a display of strong emotions in adults. They may believe anger against the perpetrator is an expression of anger against themselves. If parents show a lot of distress youngsters may not be willing to disclose in future for fear of upsetting their parents again. It is important to sound caring but matter-of-fact.

- What the children say should be taken seriously. They are unlikely to be lying. If later they are found to have made up a story they may well be trying to express fears and distress through what they are saying. Happy, contented children do not give detailed fictitious accounts of having been sexually abused.
- Children should be allowed to talk about the abuse. Listening and acknowledging their feelings is important. Parents can take the opportunity to look at what lessons can be learned for the future, but in such a way that blaming the victim is avoided. Parents must ensure that their children are not left with a burden of guilt. The youngsters must be told directly that only the perpetrator is responsible for what happened.
- Information about the abuse should be shared with other children. The nature and extent of this sharing must be appropriate to their age. It should be just sufficient to satisfy their curiosity. If they are not told the facts, sensing something is wrong they will imagine that something worse has happened. On the other hand, giving intimate details is usually best avoided because this could cause fear, or embarrass the victim. Youngsters need to know that their brother or sister was by no means the only child to have been molested. It is a risk to which every young person is exposed. The discussion should then progress to an exploration of how children can avoid dangers or seek help if they do get into difficulties.
- Abusers may have threatened their victims with dire consequences if they tell. Abused children should be encouraged to talk about their fears and about any threats made. The ways that perpetrators target and groom children can usefully be discussed with all the youngsters in the family.
- There is the temptation to withdraw from physical contact, particularly if the child seems reluctant to be held. Fathers sometimes fear that their actions will be misinterpreted as sexual. Abused children need to know that they are not rejected or untouchable and parents have to judge whether to cuddle or merely touch their child lightly on the hand or shoulder. Good, bad and inappropriate touching is another topic that may be discussed with both victims and siblings to the benefit of all.

- Parents can become over-protective and restrict the activities of all the children in the family. This may result in the victims blaming themselves or being reproached by siblings for disrupting the family and causing their loss of freedom. Parents need to be vigilant but not too restrictive.

Parents who are able to remain calm and avoid dumping their negative emotions on their children are more able to implement the guidance given above. Group and individual counselling for non-abusing care-givers contributes to the protection of children and prevention of further abuse. It helps parents to understand and cope with their feelings, thereby enabling them to support their children all the more effectively.

Some people will find that joining a support group for parents of sexually abused children is of considerable assistance (Hildebrand, 1988; Baghramian and Kershaw, 1989; Erooga and Masson, 1989; Wright and Portnoy, 1990). These are not available in all areas, however, and those that are running tend to cater for mothers only. Some groups restrict membership to mothers whose partners are the abusers. There is a general lack of support available for non-abusing fathers, and yet they usually have as many emotional needs as mothers.

Black or Asian parents and those from ethnic minorites may find appropriate support unforthcoming, particularly on a group basis, often finding themselves the only black, Asian or minority members in a group. In addition to other problems, they will have to deal with issues such as the racist attitudes of some white agencies and institutions, and these may not be properly understood and appreciated by other group members. On the other hand, involving other people from the same community is not always appropriate. White social workers were delighted when an Asian colleague agreed to be a co-worker for a mothers' group. They were taken aback when an Asian woman from the same background, whose child had been abused, refused to join. She felt that exposing her 'shame' to a group of strangers would be bad enough, but to expose it to a member of her own community was even more humiliating.

Health professionals may find themselves in a position to help parents by being prepared to listen and allow them to express their feelings. Alternatively, they may be able to refer them to an individual therapist or group. Those not involved in the abuse who have reasonably high self-esteem and the ability to trust are likely to benefit from relatively straight-forward, short-term help and may prove well able to protect their children in future.

When mothers and fathers are already struggling to cope with the demands of parenthood, their lack of ability can be a factor in their child's abuse. Sgroi and Dana (1982) describe some of the mothers in incest cases as 'psychologically absent', seeking to 'escape the frustration, unpleasantness and bore-dom of their roles by seeking companionship, distraction, or employment outside the home'. Others, whose children have been abused outside the home or by baby-sitters and lodgers, have shown a pattern of failing to provide adequate care and supervision. Such parents will need specialized longer-term help if they are to be relied upon ever to protect their children.

Parents who were themselves abused as children and who have not resolved the issues around their own mistreatment may prove effective protectors, but may equally need specialist help. The response to adult survivors is discussed in the final chapter.

PREVENTION PROGRAMMES WITH CHILDREN

The final pre-condition suggested by Finkelhor (1984) is that a perpetrator has to overcome a child's resistance. In some cases the grooming starts in infancy. Sylvia Fraser (1989) was eventually able to recall that her father must have started abusing her in her babyhood. In such cases prevention pro-grammes will only have a limited impact.

In other instances the exploitation occurs when children are old enough to be aware that something may be wrong. In these cases youngsters can be given guidance about what to do to protect themselves. For many years pupils in schools have been given 'danger–stranger' talks, often conducted by the police, and these have been useful in ensuring that they are on guard against certain types of targeting and grooming.

In recent years the revelation that abusers are usually known to their victims and not considered strangers has led to the development of more generalized prevention programmes to increase the resistance of children to approaches by all types of perpetrators.

There are some drawbacks if adults do not convey information to children in an appropriate way. In the past danger–stranger campaigns gave youngsters the impression that 'strangers' were ugly, frightening-looking men who did not know their name. This meant that potential victims were not on guard against pleasant, attractive people.

Children can be deceived by perpetrators who know their name into thinking they are friends of their parents'. It is all too easy to find out youngsters' names by spotting them on bags, badges or bracelets, or by hearing friends using them. Parents and schools should ensure that children do not have their names displayed conspicuously. School nurses, in particular, may be able to advise headteachers that insisting that pupils have name labels on the outside of uniform or bags is putting them in danger.

Prevention messages and programmes can deter children from disclosing abuse if too much emphasis is placed on the message that they should say 'no'. The grooming tactics of perpetrators are often so subtle that it is not until sexual activity has progressed some way that the victims recognize that something is wrong. Other children feel they have to comply because of the threats made: 'Do as you're told or you will be punished'. 'I'll kill your brother/kitten, if you resist'. Young people can find themselves in a 'catch-22' situation: refusal to comply means danger or condemnation for disobedience and impoliteness; compliance means that they are to blame for not having followed the instruction to say 'no'.

Prevention programmes can emphasize the risks so much that children feel unable to trust any adult and become generally fearful and anxious. On the other hand, if programmes are too superficial and minimize all the very real dangers, youngsters will not take them seriously and will not be sufficiently prepared for a significant incident. The programmes and materials used have to achieve a fine balance so as to provide sufficient detail to enable children to appreciate the risks without creating a pervading fear.

Some of the best programmes, such as Kidscape in the UK (Elliot, 1986), start from a point that young people can understand. Small children will not cope with a lengthy discussion about keeping safe, so the idea has to be introduced as and when appropriate. Stories such as Beatrix Potter's *The Tale of Peter Rabbit* can be used to introduce the idea of 'telling', even when they think they might have done something wrong. Feelings and touches can be discussed – good ones, bad ones and mixed-up ones.

Coping with bullies is an excellent starting point for school-age children; adults would do well to discuss this with youngsters as an important topic in its own right. It leads naturally to consideration of how to cope with a more powerful person and the importance of telling adults about what happens. The reason for this is that only people with more power can give protection against those who abuse their position of strength. How people exercise power is a useful topic to explore. Overt aggression is not the only means, it can be wielded by those eliciting sympathy or by using charm.

Children need to know that they have a number of rights. Some adults find this a threatening concept, fearing that if youngsters are given rights they will run amok and the world will be full of spoilt, uncontrolled, demanding brats. However, they should have the liberties that are fundamental to all human beings. In 1984 the United Nations formulated a charter of rights for children. Youngsters themselves can understand that they have the liberty to breathe, to drink, to eat and to go to the toilet. They also have the right to be safe, even if they are doing something wrong, like playing truant. This means they have the prerogative to say 'no' to an adult who is making them feel uncomfortable or uneasy. It needs to be emphasized that sometimes they may not feel uneasy until it is too late and they cannot say 'no'. Rights are usually something they can choose to exercise, but they will not be punished if they cannot or do not want to do so.

Older children may benefit from questionnaires about rights, appropriate responses and myths about sexual abuse. Books, games, videos and practice through role-play are all beneficial. Giving a 'one-off' session will only have limited value so it is preferable to have several or to reinforce a single session through reading, colouring books and other materials that can be taken home.

It is usual for schools and other agencies running prevention programmes to ask parents' permission for their children to attend. Many of the schemes involve the parents directly before undertaking work with the pupils. Although parental involvement is important, the rights of the child to be safe have to be considered. Parents are not usually asked for permission to allow their offspring to take part in a road or water safety talk or a class instructing them on how to handle chemicals safely in the chemistry lesson.

One of the best prevention strategies is basic sex education. Children need to be provided with a vocabulary for their private parts that is acceptable to both adults and young people. As they develop, information about how bodies work and how babies are made can be introduced. There are a number of excellent books on the market in Europe and the USA (Mayle, 1978a, 1978b; Blank, 1980; Rayner, 1989).

Youngsters who are able to understand what is happening to their bodies and know what should happen only between grown-up people, are less likely to be deceived by a perpetrator saying things such as: 'This is something that every daddy does'. Children will also be less haunted by mistaken beliefs. Young girls, for example, have lived in terror, fearing they have been made pregnant by a kiss or simulated intercourse. Having the words to describe their experiences not only makes it easier for youngsters to disclose and describe what is happening but also makes them more credible witnesses.

Health professionals are often in an excellent position to talk about bodies with children in a natural context. Youngsters may be brought with aches and pains in the area of the private parts. Some health professionals are called on to give formal sex education in schools. Others can give informal advice to parents on how they can educate their offspring.

VULNERABLE CHILDREN

Children who have been victims

Lightning can strike twice; professional workers frequently encounter children re-abused by a new perpetrator in a different context. This is illustrated by some of the biographies of survivors. Sylvia Fraser (1989), abused from infancy by her father, was molested by a lodger when she was 9 years old. Graham Gaskin (MacVeigh, 1982) was first exploited by a residential worker and then by Malcolm, a youth worker. Kathy Evert (Evert and Bijerk, 1987) was physically and sexually mistreated by her mother and raped by her mother's cousin, Ben.

This phenomenon is due to a number of factors. Sometimes a youngster is simply unlucky, in the wrong place at the wrong time on more than one occasion. Other children, like Graham Gaskin, are forced into a way of life that means they are likely to be exploited. Some youngsters are trapped in extended families in which sexual boundaries are poorly drawn and there is a pattern of indiscriminate multi-generational abuse.

Many victims are made more vulnerable by the effects of the abuse on their emotions, beliefs and behaviour. The protection advice and information given to non-abused children, although important and useful, is not sufficient for victims. They have additional difficulties which have to be addressed if they are to be protected in the future.

Self-esteem

One of the effects of victimization is a loss of self-esteem and a sense of worthlessness. This means that sexually abused children are likely to believe they are not worth rescuing or helping. They are all the more readily convinced that they are simply objects to be used by other people.

They sometimes feel they are 'soiled goods' and therefore fit for nothing else other than sexual exploitation. Conversely, they are all the more likely to be seduced by someone that seems to value them and treat them as special. One of the first aims of treatment is to enhance their self-esteem by showing them that they are worth helping, by drawing out positive characteristics and by putting negative ones in perspective. Lack of assertiveness is connected to low self-esteem. Youngsters can be taught assertiveness as part of a general programme aimed at tackling self-esteem issues. If youngsters are helped to value themselves and seem confident and self-assertive, they are much less likely to be future targets.

Some victims require specialist therapy, others can be helped in less formal ways. Health professionals can play a part by taking every opportunity to praise and value youngsters with whom they work, and can encourage parents and colleagues to do likewise. Disparaging comments should not be made to any child but must be assiduously avoided in the case of those that have been abused.

Isolation

Abused children feel they are different from their peers. They may also have such a sense of guilt that they draw away from other people. This can be alleviated if a victim is repeatedly assured that he or she is not to blame and not the only child to have had such experiences. A careful, age-appropriate explanation of perpetrator motivation and the cycle of offending behaviour can be very enlightening. Joining a therapeutic group for victims is often particularly helpful for isolated children (Hall, 1978; Hildebrand, 1988; Furniss, Bingley-Miller and van Elburg, 1988; Nelki and Watters, 1989).

Coping with emotions

The maelstrom of emotions, which often rapidly appear one after another, can make a victim's behaviour difficult to understand and tolerate. Anger and aggression can be quickly displaced by despair, suicide attempts, regression, then again sudden bouts of intense anger and a subsequent return to moroseness and melancholy. This may make people withdraw support and understanding. Maya Angelou (1984), who became mute after being raped, recalled:

> In the first weeks my family accepted my behaviour as a post-rape, post-hospital affliction ... the doctor said I was healed ... When I refused to be the child they knew and accepted me to be, I was called impudent and my muteness sullenness ... then came the thrashings, given by any relative who felt himself offended.

Sexualized behaviour

Kathy Evert (Evert and Bijkerk, 1987) asked herself: 'Does the early sexual experience block my ability to feel loved – loved just for me – and not sexually?'. Many victims, particularly those abused by parents and close relatives, may have the same doubts. They may appear to be seductive because they doubt that they will win affection and friendship in any other way. They may also have been taught to behave in a sexual manner at an early age, just as another child may be taught to swim or play the piano. These youngsters are particularly vulnerable.

Small children can be discouraged from behaving in a sexual manner by the various techniques used to redirect any undesirable behaviour, such as nose-picking or biting, combined with assurances of affection. Hitting and severe punishment will only make these youngsters more secretive or increase their sense of violation and decrease their self-worth. Older children also need assurances and redirection of behaviour, but in addition they may need counselling so that they can understand the context in which sexual behaviour is inappropriate.

Sexual knowledge

Many professionals assume that abused children have a good understanding of their bodies and sexual matters. This is rarely the case; they are often very confused about what was done to them. They need to be given an understanding of how their body works and what sexual activities involve. They will then be able to appreciate what is happening if approached for a second time and can resist more readily. They also need to be taught to respect their own bodies and insist that other people respect them too.

Black, Asian and minority ethnic children

Some prevention programmes ignore the special needs of black and Asian children and those of minority ethnic groups. They have to cope with the added burden of racism and with the sense of betrayal to their community that disclosure may engender.

These youngsters should be given the opportunity to discuss their concerns, needs and fears in relation to their colour, culture and community. Materials for prevention programmes should include images with which young people from a variety of backgrounds can identify.

Children with disabilities

Children with disabilities, including those with severe learning difficulties, frequently require additional help with intimate
personal care and may be cared for in institutions, both of
which may lead to an erosion of privacy. Their needs in
relation to this should be addressed and health professionals
working with people with disabilities should be prepared to
advocate on their behalf.

Sometimes the sexual requirements and need for information of children with severe physical restrictions are ignored.
They will only be able to protect themselves from exploitation
or draw attention to any abuse they suffer or witness if they
have the knowledge to understand what is happening and the
means to communicate their concerns readily and clearly.

Children with difficulties in verbal communication, including hearing impaired youngsters, need to be given a way of
describing intimate experiences.

> EXAMPLE: A severely physically handicapped boy with very
> limited speech had been taught through basic sex educa-
> tion how to spell words such as 'penis'. He was able to
> disclose by using a word-board. He managed to protect
> himself from further abuse and prevented the perpetrator,
> a member of the care staff, from molesting other residents
> of the home.

In some instances health professionals form the one group,
apart from parents, that can talk about the more intimate
aspects of life with the children who need their help. Physiotherapists, doctors and nurses working with those with
disabilities often have to talk about a patient's private parts,
and instead of using generalizations it is useful to ascertain
whether or not a child has a specific vocabulary for these areas:
'You have a pain here, do you? Doctors call it the vagina. What
would you call it?'

Prevention programmes must be flexible. Some available
materials address particular issues, by, for example, in-
corporating illustrations of children in wheelchairs. Other
programmes can be adapted by parents, health and other
professionals to ensure they meet the requirements of
children with disabilities. Sgroi, Bunk and Wabrek, (1988)

advocate using three-dimensional teaching aids for people with learning difficulties.

It may be unthinkable that people should sexually abuse children with disabilities. However, it is now apparent that these youngsters are particularly vulnerable and require both sex education and abuse prevention programmes tailored to their abilities and requirements.

Helping adult survivors

Whatever the age of their patients, health professionals are likely to encounter child sexual abuse in some form. Even those working solely with adults could still find themselves involved because of the increasing number of adult survivors who now feel able to talk about their experiences. Women about to give birth may talk to their midwives. Terminally ill people sometimes express a wish to unburden themselves of a weighty secret before they die. People who end up in hospital accident and emergency departments having taken an overdose want to explain why they have felt so despairing and worthless for so long. Stroke patients who find their occupational therapists or physiotherapists kind and helpful seek their advice on how to overcome the problem they have kept to themselves since childhood. The examples are endless. Health professionals, in all their varied occupations, are generally seen as supportive, caring, compassionate and trustworthy. It is hardly surprising that survivors seeking help and understanding should turn to health workers in whom they place so much trust.

This chapter will explain something of the experiences and feelings of adult survivors, many of which are shared by child victims too. It seeks to give guidance on effective responses, and lastly looks at the issues facing professional workers who are themselves survivors and have to work with cases of sexual abuse.

THE LONG-TERM EFFECTS OF SEXUAL ABUSE

Any exploration of the long-term effects of sexual abuse has to take into account the fact that it is difficult to disentangle the aftermath of the abuse from those of other childhood problems. Some survivors, like Kathy Evert (Evert and Bijkerk, 1987), have been physically, emotionally and sexually abused by a rejecting parent. Others were targeted because they were already suffering from other forms of abuse. One such was Ben (1991) who, having run away from physical mistreatment at home, fell prey to paedophiles for whose friendship he initially felt immense gratitude. Many survivors have had to cope in childhood with the trauma of bereavement, severe illness, racism, poverty or social deprivation.

Most of the research into long-term effects has looked at troubled populations. This can give the impression that all sexually abused children grow up into adults with severe emotional difficulties. Many youngsters are adversely affected at the time of the assaults and most former victims will have at least some residual burden of emotional pain or unpleasant memories. Yet there are probably countless survivors who live happy, contented lives. Sexual abuse as a child does not automatically condemn a person to a disturbed and disturbing adulthood.

People are born with different characteristics and have varying degrees of resilience. It is therefore difficult to determine whether a problem such as anxiety or aggression in a particular individual is all a result of the abuse or would still have been present in fairly large measure had the person not been mistreated.

Sexual abuse is not the only childhood experience to cause difficulty for people as they mature, and when the adverse long-term effects are listed they are often identical to the list of the consequences of other early developmental set-backs. The list can encompass almost any problems that adults experience, from homicidal impulses to sexual dysfunction, and from suicidal tendencies to nightmares.

Other forms of abuse, including over-protection, can have dire consequences. Furthermore, situations that nobody can be held responsible for can also cause emotional damage: the loss of a close relative, racist attacks, war, prolonged ill-health, disability and social deprivation can all leave their scars.

One of the differences, however, between all these traumas and child sexual abuse is that most of them can be talked about relatively freely without undue embarrassment. They are the very experiences that constitute the plots of many plays and books. Children who are war refugees, orphans or even physically and emotionally abused, such as Cinderella and David Copperfield, are likely to be shown sympathy and understanding. The person sexually abused in childhood is faced with the taboo of talking about sexual subjects, particularly when these involve children. They are left, perhaps for many years, burdened by a 'guilty' secret. They live in fear of exposure. Little courage is required for a man to mention that his father died when he was seven years old. It demands enormous bravery to disclose that his father sodomized him.

This has meant that ways of helping survivors have only been discovered comparatively recently. Moreover, most former victims have had to keep their experiences secret for many years. Consequently, their emotions are likely to run very deep. When they eventually surface, the effects can be devastating.

Low self-esteem

For many survivors the negative emotions generated by sexual abuse – shame, guilt, fear, betrayal and anger – corrode the sense of self-worth. The way that perpetrators objectify their victims leaves them with a vision of themselves as a 'thing' to be used, misused and then discarded. Unless they receive help at a very early stage, abused children are likely to carry this negative self-image into adulthood.

Some victims are fortunate, they have so many other positive experiences that they emerge into adulthood with a genuinely buoyant view of themselves. They are content with their lives and more or less reach their full potential.

Other survivors appear on the surface to have great self-confidence. They may be attractive, talented and successful in whatever they do. But they put themselves under a lot of pressure. Never content, they are always having to prove they are brilliant and loveable. Emotional pain is near the surface, unless they have made part of themselves numb. They either have periods when they have to withdraw to nurse the hurt and distress, or they live life so frenetically and superficially that the pain is never allowed to intrude.

Those in another, possibly large, group seem to be functioning well but they have pervading doubts about themselves and their abilities so that they constantly settle for second best. They hide their talents not wishing to attract the spotlight. They are passive and lack assertiveness skills. Although not actively or violently abused they are nevertheless used and imposed upon by those around them.

In some former victims their low self-esteem is immediately apparent. They take little pride in their appearance, they continue to allow themselves to be used and abused. They may behave in ways that reinforce their low opinion of themselves. They shuffle around like shadows, helpless, hopeless and unhappy.

Self-punishment

One of the aims of the grooming process is to ensure the victim takes the blame and feels guilty about what has happened. By this means the perpetrator ensures the victim's silence, because children rarely divulge secrets that will result in their being punished. Thus perpetrators can displace their own feelings of guilt. Occasionally, when children manage to disclose they are made to feel guilty for 'being rude', and the investigation process and its aftermath often make them feel that they are to blame.

Abused people will 'tend to continue a pattern of self-blame and self-punishment on a life-long basis' (Sgroi, 1988b). Self-punishing behaviours include self-abuse through drug and alcohol excess, eating disorders, self-mutilation including cutting and burning. Some suicidal behaviour is rooted in the belief 'I don't deserve to live'. A number of former victims invite punishment by law-breaking, placing themselves in dangerous situations or becoming involved with sadistic, punitive individuals. Another form of self-castigating behaviour is to reject opportunities for happiness. They will not use their talents to gain achievements or they constantly set themselves up for failure. They invariably place themselves in the victim role, and allow more powerful people to use and abuse them.

Health professionals working with people with learning difficulties need to be aware that developmental delay is no protection against the emotional aftermath of sexual molestation. A study by Cruz, Price-Williams and Andron (1988) of developmentally disabled women molested as children showed how some engaged in self-destructive, self-punishing behaviour and believed that they had 'deserved the abuse because they were retarded'.

Nightmares and flashbacks

Victims of abuse often have nightmares and these can continue well into adulthood. Some adults have nightmares with a recurrent pattern or theme throughout their lives.

> EXAMPLE: Leanora was sexually abused by an older brother. He would come into her bedroom at night and, as she approached adolescence, would subject her to anal and vaginal intercourse. She was in considerable pain but could not cry out in case she woke her parents.
>
> She had a recurrent nightmare of being chased, trapped and terrorized, and would scream out for help while knowing that no one could hear her. She would wake up at this point in a sweat of terror with a dry, sore throat.
>
> As she grew older she forgot about the abuse but the nightmares continued. In her 40s she suddenly recalled her childhood experiences. She felt able to confide in a friend, who was an occupational therapist and had had some recent training on child sexual abuse. The friend set time aside to let Leanora talk about what had happened to her. After two or three sessions of describing all that she could remember the nightmares, which used to occur several times a year, ceased.

Survivors, particularly those like Leanora who suddenly recall their abuse, can have flashbacks. Unlike nightmares, the person is fully conscious. They suddenly have a vivid memory of a particular incident or aspect of the abuse. It is not simply like watching the replay of a film because the flashbacks can involve any or all of the senses. When experiencing flashbacks Leanora could feel the sensation of being anally penetrated and could smell the sweat of her brother's armpits. The 'real' nature of flashbacks can cause intense physical and emotional pain. They are difficult to control since they occur suddenly, creeping up unawares and lasting for variable amounts of time.

Some survivors have found them so painful that they have contemplated suicide rather than face another one. Flashbacks usually lessen in frequency, duration and intensity over time, particularly if help is available.

Phobias and compulsions

Feelings of anxiety, even terror, can occur when a former victim is placed in a situation that has something in common with their abusive experiences. Sometimes the link is obvious, like the person who fears cellars because he was always abused in one. Sometimes the association is less clear. Fear can lead to compulsive behaviour: the dread of being thought dirty or defiled can result in an obsessive concern with bathing and cleanliness.

Anger, depression and despair

Abused children are in a state of loss. If not helped to come to terms with their losses they will carry this sense of loss into adulthood where it will be compounded by the sense of having forfeited a happy childhood.

Anger is a feature of all loss and mourning. Survivors will often project their anger on to other people or situations. They may become angry with any powerful authority figure, running foul of school, the police, the law, employers, religious authorities and politicians. Those who blame 'society' will embrace the politics of destruction or anarchy. Other former victims feel angry with those that represent their abusers, such as men in general. Some are easily angered by minor incidents, or target their anger against another person who had no responsibility for the abuse.

Disgust and anger can be turned against the self, causing not only self-punishing behaviour but also depression and despair as former victims feel themselves to be unworthy of happiness, help or self-regard. When this occurs suicide is again a very real possibility. Former victims, including those with learning difficulties (Cruz, Price-Williams and Andron, 1988), can have such a pervading sense of a ruined past, a miserable present and a hopeless future that they see no point in continuing to live.

Regression

Regression can occur in survivors who appear to have reached
a satisfactory level of maturity. Something, such as a television programme, the birth of their own child or a gynae-
cological examination, awakens memories of the abuse.
Flashbacks will ensue. The survivor then reverts to the
developmental stage, and age, they were at just before the
abuse started. It is as if the memories are so painful that
as a comfort they have to return to the emotions they experienced in the 'golden age' before their secure world was
destroyed. Adults in their 50s and 60s can find themselves
curling into a foetus-shaped ball and sucking their thumb just
like a toddler. A similar phenomenon was noted in Chapter
6 in the section examining the way children cope after
disclosure.

> EXAMPLE: Leanora, mentioned earlier, was first abused by
> her brother when she was 5. In her 40s after she had recalled
> and divulged for the first time the secret of her abuse, she
> began playing with dolls and eating jelly and blancmange,
> party treats when she was little. She cried easily and craved
> physical comfort.

Even where survivors cannot remember when the abuse
started, it is often possible to determine this by the stage to
which they return.

It can be difficult for friends and relatives of former victims
to understand their behaviour. Any adult who insists on going
to sleep with a dummy in the mouth is likely to be labelled
'mentally disturbed'. Survivors themselves can feel embarrassed and guilty about their desires and behaviours.

As the healing progresses the survivor may well pass
through all the other developmental stages; this can be difficult
for both the survivors and their relatives. Truculent, unreliable,
sulky behaviour may be acceptable in a teenager, but is less
than desirable in a 35-year-old with work and parental
responsibilities.

A variation on regression is a process by which survivors
get in touch with themselves as children. They can see their
child-self, perhaps frightened and crying in the corner of the
room. It is often a sign that the adult is more or less healed

when he or she can value and cherish the little child that they once were.

Sadly some adults never make positive contact with their child-self against whom they still feel anger and on whom they put all the blame. They displace their hatred of their child-self on to other children, often their own offspring, whom they may continually and unfairly punish and physically attack. Some assault children in order to comfort them, managing in this way to comfort their child-selves through a surrogate.

A few never function properly as adults. They have all the emotional features of a young child, with extreme dependency needs, a volatile nature and marked egocentricity. For them this is not a temporary regression but a more or less permanent state.

Impact on sexual functioning

A number of survivors have encountered problems with sexual functioning. In some cases sexual activity can be disrupted by flashbacks (Hall and Lloyd, 1989; Bass and Davis, 1990). Other problems relate to the arousal stage (McGuire and Wagner, 1978; Becker *et al.*, 1982). Some women experience difficulty with orgasm (Tsai, Feldman-Summers and Edgar, 1979). For some there will be pelvic pain on intercourse due to anxiety and tension, internal injury or chronic vaginal infection (Gross *et al.*, 1980).

In a study by Fromuth (1986) the sample did not demonstrate that there were significant differences between sexually abused and non-sexually abused female college students in relation to activities such as non-coital sexual behaviour, intercourse and experience of anorgasmia. But women with a history of abuse before the age of 13 were more likely to find themselves raped or otherwise coerced into non-consensual sexual relationships as young adults.

Men can encounter a variety of difficulties, with impotence being a common one. Some who have been subjected to male rape and molestation have problems with their sexual identity. Finkelhor (1984) found that 'boys victimized by older men were over **four times** more likely to be currently engaged in homosexual activity than were nonvictims'. Homosexuality is not generally considered a sexual dysfunction, but it can become a problem if, as in the case of Ben (1991) and Graham Gaskin (MacVeigh, 1982), early abuse by older males leads to confusion about sexual orientation and identity, or if a boy assumes he **must** be homosexual if other men have found him sexually desirable. Gilgun and Reiser (1990) describe the experiences of three men; one clearly felt that his sexual orientation had become confused because of abuse by a male teacher when he was aged 12.

Some victims, both male or female, turn to prostitution for a living. There is a variety of reasons for this. Bianca, raped throughout her childhood by her mother's boy-friend and her natural father, summarized the motivation of many former victims by her comment: 'I am numb from the waist downwards. When I was little, men took what I had for free, now they can pay for it'.

Both men and women can have problems with any form of physical touching. This creates a barrier to sexual activity and satisfaction. It also has implications for other forms of relationships, because the victims may be unable to tolerate social situations that necessitate accidental or purposeful touching, such as being in a crowd or being expected to shake hands when introduced.

Relationship problems

Partnerships

Sexual problems can damage relationships and potential partnerships. Moreover, the betrayal of trust, which is so often a feature of child sexual abuse, means that the developing person is unable to have basic trust in anyone and cannot form intimate relationships (Erikson, 1965). Sometimes they will only form affiliations with people they can control and dominate; they are able to trust their partners solely because they know that they have a complete hold over them. Conversely, submissive former victims make themselves indispensable to dominant partners who can only tolerate companions who are able to accept powerlessness. In this situation, counselling or therapy that improves the self-esteem and assertiveness of the submissive partner can lead to the end of the relationship. Very occasionally it results in a dangerous situation as the dominant partner attempts to reassert his or her power through violence and coercion and becomes increasingly angry and frustrated as the attempts fail.

Parenting problems

Adult survivors can run into difficulties as parents for a variety of reasons, including their need to be in control or, conversely, their inability to exert control (Cole *et al.*, 1992). They may either be over-protective or, on the other hand, be unwilling to recognize any dangers. A refusal to touch, obsessional behaviour, drug or alcohol addiction, suicide attempts or angry responses can all impair their ability to parent their own offspring. A few will sexually molest their own children, though it must be stressed that an abused child will not inevitably become an abusing adult and parent.

Isolation

Some former victims are evidently loners who remain aloof. Others continue to live with abusing parents or siblings well into adulthood, and make no attempt to form other relationships. But many survivors are in stable relationships and cope well as parents. They are surrounded by relatives and friends, but, despite this, some can feel very much alone and different from other people. They cling to friends and relationships to prove that they are likeable, yet have a pervading sense of insecurity. They harbour a guilty secret and are frightened of getting too close in case people find out, then reject or punish them. A shadow, a sense of distrust, pervades all their relationships. Survivors who have not been helped to cast off the spectre are forever haunted by their secret.

Personality disorder

Health professionals can find that they are working with patients who have relationship difficulties in all areas of their life and whose behaviour is so challenging that they tend to be diagnosed as personality disordered. Much of what they do appears to be 'madness' and yet they are not suffering from any clinically-recognized psychotic illness.

Dissociation

Many abused children use dissociation as a defence. They almost seem to move out of their body and either cease to exist during an assault or have a sense of watching themselves being abused in a detached manner. Either way, the physical and emotional pain is numbed. Adults in traumatizing situations sometimes report feeling no pain at the time and experience events as if they are watching a film. This is an aspect of denial. If it continues into adulthood and is transferred to other situations it can become a danger because at times there is a loss of a sense of reality. Moira Walker (1992) describes a young man who during periods of dissociation would injure himself badly.

Multiple personality

Denial, splitting off and dissociation can lead to what is now termed the multiple personality disorder. Sylvia Fraser (1989) developed three personalities by the time she was an adolescent, her 'shadow-twin' – her father's concubine, Sylvia – the good girl, and the fairy-tale princess, who later became a glamour girl called 'Appearances'. 'So now there were three of me, all vitally connected yet somehow separate. Like my other self, Appearances began as my servant and then I became hers.' Moira Walker (1992) describes Carol who at times has had some 20 or more personalities with their own names, preferences and experiences.

This development of personalities affords protection as a child, but as an adult can cause the individual confusion and distress. They will have difficulties relating to people and may appear to be untruthful and periodically detached from reality. They can end up with the label 'schizophrenic'. Although not suffering from a clinically-defined mental illness, they will nevertheless benefit from expert therapeutic help. Health professionals who do not have psychotherapeutic training can nevertheless assist by showing understanding and respect.

People that do well

By no means do all survivors have more problems than the average non-abused person. The study by Jennings and

Armsworth (1992) showed that a sample of women who had been sexually abused as children had healthier ego development than a similar sample of non-abused women. Fromuth's research (1986) showed that family background and lack of parental support have more effect on later psychological functioning than does the experience of abuse. In relation to sexual dysfunction, for example, Tsai, Feldman-Summers and Edgar (1979) found that many former victims had no more sexual problems than a control group of non-molested women. The study suggested that survivors who do well seemed to have support from sympathetic and understanding partners and from friends and relatives who assured them they were not to blame and were worthwhile.

Another factor is age. Tsai, Feldman-Summers and Edgar (1979) indicate that those last abused at 12 years or over are more adversely affected. This appears to be linked to older children's sense of responsibility and what is deemed inappropriate behaviour, and of the turmoil at that age in relation to sexual identity. Also badly affected were children who had a lot of negative emotions associated with the greater frequency and longer duration of the abuse.

This suggests that the earlier the intervention the better. If abuse can be stopped before a youngster reaches adolescence then healing is likely to be all the more satisfactory. It would seem that health professionals who encounter a case of sexual abuse should take action immediately to ensure that there is a speedy end to the activities.

HELPING SURVIVORS

It is clearly better to curtail any form of mistreatment and help the victim as soon as possible. However, in child sexual abuse some people cannot be helped in childhood because they do not disclose until well into adult life. Others may have sought help as children only to be dismissed as liars or to have been given too little assistance, too late. Moira Walker (1992) gives a catalogue of moving examples where this has occurred. A considerable amount of help can be given to adult survivors, particularly as many are already attempting to heal themselves.

Active listening

Health professionals who encounter a former victim who confides in them about their experiences need, as a first priority, to allow the person to talk. Survivors may have had memories and feelings haunting them for some time. Talking to an understanding listener can help to lay some of the ghosts of the past to rest. As when listening to children's experiences, the professional should not show shock, distress, anger or condemnation.

Positive messages

Once the victim has talked and explained as much as is necessary for the time being, the listener needs to take a more active role by conveying positive messages. As children, they had too little power and knowledge to resist and were not to blame. As adults, their childhood traumas do not diminish their personal worth.

Setting boundaries

It is perhaps a little flattering for professionals to feel that their patients or clients have chosen to seek help from them and them alone, and for compassionate people there is a great temptation to give as much help as possible. But it is important for health professionals to set appropriate boundaries and identify how far they are able to help given the constraints of their professional role.

There are great dangers in becoming too involved and turning a professional relationship into a friendship. Patients can become over-dependent and feel betrayed when their trusted helper changes jobs or has to prioritize other patients.

Moira Walker (1992) points to the benefits of establishing clear boundaries and levels of involvement. Firstly, it prevents the worker from becoming burnt-out and overwhelmed. Secondly, it provides a model for patients who may have had difficulty asserting themselves and saying 'no' without feeling guilty. A helper who does so appropriately 'demonstrates that limits can be enforced without harming the relationship and that the consequences need not be negative or destructive'.

As with children, the helper has to be very clear about limits in relation to physical touching. Again, it could be tempting to embrace a distressed patient, but the helper has to be clear of his or her motives for doing so, and must also ensure the adult does not feel that personal space and dignity are being violated. For their own sake health professionals must ensure their actions cannot be misinterpreted. Touch and physical comfort can, however, be a very healing experience for many adult survivors.

Sources of help

The next step is to decide with the survivors what sort of help they need now. There are several possibilities that are not mutually exclusive, different types of help may run consecutively or concurrently.

- It may be that another talk with the same health professional is requested.
- They may want to be referred to a specialist therapist or a sexual dysfunction counsellor.
- They may wish to join a group with other survivors (Tsai and Wagner, 1978; Bruckner and Johnson, 1987; Sgroi, 1988b).
- There are several books and tapes with which they can help themselves in their own time.
- The danger of suicide is very real for some, in which case they need to be encouraged to use a telephone help-line and possibly specialist psychiatric help. Antidepressants can be used to avert a tragedy with clinically depressed patients, although these are themselves not without risk.

Telling other people

Health professionals are ever-mindful of the issue of confidentiality. A survivor may well disclose to them because he or she knows that in this respect they are trustworthy. However, there may be a need to tell other people about the abuse.

The most obvious instance is when a referral for additional help is needed. The patient may be seeking this and so be more than happy for their details to be shared with another professional or helper. At other times they simply want to unburden themselves and do not want the information to go further. A health professional, however, may be able to see that they need more skilled help, so an element of persuasion may have to be employed, but not coercion.

Survivors sometimes do not know whether to tell their partners or friends. Their support and understanding can be very important, but some acquaintances can react unsympathetically or inappropriately to the news. Survivors should be enabled to feel they can share their experiences because they do not have to keep a guilty secret, but they also have to be made aware of the possibility of adverse reactions from some individuals. Some decide they will not deliberately tell their partners, but feel no need to hide their history if asked directly about it. In other instances it is sufficient for them to mention to their nearest relatives, without being specific, that they are trying to deal with some unpleasant experiences they had as a child or to explain that they are going through an emotional 'bad patch' and need a little space and understanding.

Another prospect is that of sharing the truth with other family members. Some survivors need to ask their non-abusing parents why they failed to protect them. They need to know if their brothers and sisters were also abused. They want answers which only other family members can give. This requires great courage, and sometimes the results are extremely hurtful if relatives respond with anger, rejection and denial. Survivors should not be discouraged from sharing with other adult family members, but they can be advised to wait until they feel emotionally strong and are able to cope with a negative outcome.

If the abuser is still alive the survivor may wish to confront him or her. Sometimes former victims can satisfy this desire indirectly: techniques involve using photographs, drawing pictures or making models of the abuser and then expressing all their feelings to this representation. Another option is to write letters, which are never sent, to the perpetrator. A role-play can be used to act out a confrontation scene. On occasion direct action has to be taken, in which case the survivor can be helped to think through and anticipate all the possible responses of the abuser and work out beforehand how he or she will react whatever the repercussions are.

If the abuser is still alive the adult survivor may have to be encouraged to consider reporting the matter to the police. As stated in Chapter 3, the perpetrator could still be abusing children. However, former victims should not be made to feel guilty and responsible for others if they feel unable to report the matter to law enforcement or child protection agencies. Those who manage to do so should be supported and their courage commended.

> EXAMPLE: Olivia was abused by a teacher at school when she was in her early teens. Ten years later, during treatment for a sports injury, she told her physiotherapist what had happened. The teacher was still at the school and Olivia had heard that a pupil had been expelled for making an allegation against him. She was encouraged to confide in her parents. They supported her in her wish to report the matter.
>
> The police had to reinvestigate the allegations of the expelled pupil. Olivia spoke about the matter to her former classmates only to find several had also been abused by the same teacher. Eventually some 20 girls, past and present pupils, came forward. The teacher was found guilty on numerous counts and sent to prison. It is unlikely that he will be able to obtain such a position of trust and authority on his release.

Finally, when survivors reveal details indicating that a specific child is being abused or is at risk, but refuse to report the matter themselves, the health worker has a professional and moral if not legal duty to protect the identified children. It may be possible to discuss the matter with senior colleagues and child protection workers without stating who the informant is. Where this is not possible it is very likely that the identity of the informant can at least be concealed from the perpetrator.

Coping with emotions

Many of the emotions felt by survivors can be dealt with by active listening and positive messages, but there are other strategies as well. Relaxation techniques, in particular, can help them cope with anxiety, and to some extent with anger.

Because of socialization processes, female victims usually have problems expressing anger and this can result in self-destructive passivity. Men, on the other hand, have difficulties acknowledging their feelings of fear and powerlessness; they may compensate by showing their anger as aggression or physical violence. They need to be helped to appreciate that it is the abuser who is weak and out of control, and that it takes courage and strength to survive abuse. Both men and women need to be helped to understand that anger can be a constructive emotion. Some of the greatest reformers have been motivated by anger.

Survivors have an absolute right to express anger against their abuser. They do not, however, have a right to project it on to other people, especially children. They might turn it against the health professionals trying to help them; this may be with good reason if the professional is insensitive or acting inappropriately, but more often it is a projection of hostiliy felt against the original abuser. In such cases, it is advisable not to react with aggression or take it personally, but to be patient and understanding.

There are a small number of instances when the projection of anger is so great that the professional worker is in physical danger. Medical staff, therapists and social workers have been attacked, and even killed, by angry patients. They need to be mindful of personal safety at all times and alert colleagues and managers to any potential dangers. Some organizations take a somewhat cavalier attitude to employees who express fear of attack, but to ignore the health and safety of their staff can result in managers and employers finding themselves subject to criminal prosecution.

Dealing with regression

Regression is one of the first steps on the road to healing. Survivors should be encouraged to indulge their 'child-self' without feeling guilty, as long as they do not hurt anyone else. If a man wants to buy a set of toy cars for himself, then why not? If he wants to go to sleep with his thumb in his mouth, he can be given, should he need it, permission to do so.

The most important aspect of healing is for survivors to cherish and forgive their child-self. Many do not condemn child victims and yet reproach themselves for their own victimization. They can be encouraged to form an image of themselves as a child. Early photographs can be of assistance here. They must then try to respond to the image in the way that they would if this was a child disclosing abuse to them. They need, metaphorically, to offer comfort and understanding to this child-self. They should tell the child that he or she is not to blame, not at fault and did not deserve to have been mistreated.

Eventually they will learn to love and forgive their child-self and then self-punishing behaviour will cease. Their self-esteem will be enhanced as they convince themselves that they were worth protecting and the perpetrator had no right to exploit them. This process is often helped by participation in a group for survivors where messages about being of value and being innocent are reinforced not only by professional helpers but also by their peers.

Looking forward to the future

For some, the past has damaged them so much that they have lost hope for the future. However, if the anger they feel with themselves and their past situation can be externalized, it can be used to good effect. One survivor, furious with the perpetrator, declared: 'He destroyed my childhood. He is not going to destroy my adult years'.

The experience of being abused is undoubtedly painful. It is one that no child should undergo. However, those unlucky enough to be victims have paradoxically been given a unique gift by their abuser. Only someone who has been sexually abused can completely understand what the experience entails. Survivors are in an excellent position to offer comfort, understanding and support to other victims. They are also in an excellent position to advocate on behalf of fellow sufferers. Anger, combined with empathy and understanding, has led some former victims to pioneer support schemes or press for resources and legislation to protect vulnerable children.

Some survivors choose to become helping professionals in order to assist other victims. Others enter these professions for other reasons, but find that when confronted with a case of child sexual abuse they have a unique gift, which they can use to good effect.

THE HEALTH PROFESSIONAL AS A SURVIVOR

Survivors come from all walks of life. It is hardly surprising that many choose to become health professionals. For some it is a family tradition and they have thought of little else in terms of career since their early years. They, and others who are caring and compassionate by nature, want to do a worthwhile job and if they have the ability to cope with the rigours of training are well suited to the work of a health professional. In a study by Dr Michael Wilson (1987) a substantial proportion of general practitioners was found to have experienced sexual abuse as children.

Victims who manage to become health professionals cannot have been unduly damaged by their experiences. They must have been able to retain sensitivity and compasssion, have a sense of being 'worthwhile' and have not been so distressed that they have forfeited their education. Nevertheless, they will share some of the emotional burdens carried by other victims. Furthermore, the fact that as an abused person they are working with abuse will add difficulties and stress.

The nature of stress

'Stress' is a widely used term, often having negative connotations. The Oxford English Dictionary defines it as 'hardship, straits, adversity, affliction'. Life itself, and particularly the work environment, makes demands on individuals. If these demands are perceived as positive they can be a source of satisfaction and a welcome challenge. This brings a feeling of contentment and well-being, which can generate enthusiasm. Demands that are felt to be negative become a source of

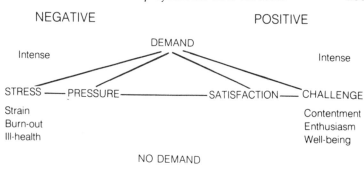

Figure 8.1 A model of stress and its antecedents.

pressure and stress and can lead to strain, ill-health and burn-out. Figure 8.1 provides a model of this definition of stress. Helping professionals are particularly susceptible to burn-out, usually caused when the emotional demands of the job exceed the emotional resources available (Cherniss, 1980; Maslach, 1982; Farber, 1983).

Health professionals who are survivors will inevitably find that working with child sexual abuse is demanding. Many, who have resolved their own difficulties and know they can use their own experience to help others, will perceive the demands as positive in nature and find the work challenging but satisfying. Others, who have not yet come to terms with their own history, will find the demands imposed by working with perpetrators, victims, survivors and their families produce a negative effect. They will experience strain and stress, which will lead to ill-health and burn-out (Doyle, 1986; 1991).

All survivors working as professionals have to face a number of problems in addition to those encountered by most former victims. These relate to the knowledge that they and their colleagues obtain about the subject, particularly when it is incomplete or one-sided.

Issues relating to the self

Former victims who now work in the health professions may

still have residual feelings of shame, guilt and lack of self-worth which are the legacy of sex abuse. On encountering a case of child sexual abuse in their work, negative feelings can be reawakened as they try to cope not only with the pain of the victims they meet but also with their own unresolved pain.

It is difficult for survivors to be sure that they remain objective when handling abuse cases. They might, on the one hand, over-identify with the victims, becoming uncontrollably angry with the perpetrators and non-protective parents. On the other hand, they may be unable to bear the victim's pain as well as their own, and so reject or ignore the needs of vulnerable patients.

Health professionals will inevitably become aware of all the research that indicates that a proportion of sexually abused children can reach adulthood with major emotional problems and dysfunctional personalities. This finding appears to be confirmed for these professionals because they are most likely to meet precisely the section of former victims who have problems and who are therefore seeking medical or psychiatric help. It can become difficult for health professional survivors to believe that anyone survives abuse unscathed since they encounter the relatively problem-free population of survivors far less frequently than those with problems. This could well lead them to speculate whether they are also damaged.

> EXAMPLE: Syreeta was sexually abused as a child. As a doctor she became exasperated by the lack of resources available for some of her patients. But she did not feel able to express her annoyance or make demands for extra resources. She was constrained by the knowledge she had about survivors' projection of anger and thought that her present wrath was a transference of the hostility she should be feeling towards her abuser. She had just cause for complaint, yet felt unable to express her views because she doubted her objectivity. This, in turn, compounded her feelings of powerlessness, injustice and guilt.

Some of the theories, fashionable in the late 1970s, about sexual abuse as a symptom of dysfunctional families and the role of the victim in their own abuse, are still floating around. Such ideas, coming to the attention of health professional survivors will only serve to make them worry about their loveableness and their own family relationships.

A further problem is the dilemma they may face if a patient should ask them if they were abused, or one who turns on them angrily with, 'You can't understand what it feels like to have someone do it to you'. Professionals can keep their own abuse a secret or deny it, but then they are being less than honest with the patients they are encouraging to talk, without guilt or shame, about their experiences. On the other hand, if they openly acknowledge that they were also victimized, their patients may view them as too vulnerable or 'flawed' to be effective helpers.

Issues in relation to colleagues

The colleagues of health professionals will also be aware of the various theories of long-term harm to victims and will be meeting, in the course of their work, an over-representative proportion of young people and adults that have been damaged. They may regard their survivor colleagues as blemished and less worthy of respect. Others may simply be embarrassed and avoid the survivor, in much the same way as some people do when they do not know how to respond to a recently-bereaved work associate.

Conversely, some health workers who have had an abuse-free childhood resent colleagues who have the 'advantage' of first-hand knowledge of the subject. They may attempt to invalidate the survivor's experience and use his or her victim status to undermine the insights gained: 'You won't be able to look at this case objectively', 'You will get over-involved', 'I think you might find this case too upsetting'.

Black or Asian professionals may already have to cope with discrimination and racism. They may be given a number of inaccurate labels and attributes based on stereotypical images of black people. If they are also female they will be subjected to double discrimination. Add to this the stigma still attached to having been sexually abused and some black professionals will be facing layer upon layer of prejudice and bigotry.

A final problem is the difficulty survivors encounter when they hear a work associate, perhaps quoting an 'expert' in the field, expressing confident opinions about child sexual abuse which they know from their own experience is inaccurate and insensitive. For male workers, especially, the blanket (and inaccurate) assertion that boys who are sexually abused themselves become abusers is particularly difficult to tolerate.

Issues relating to sources of help

Survivors who are also health professionals may find their sources of help are severely restricted. Their knowledge about the impact of disclosure on family and others close to the victims mean they will feel unable to risk seeking help from their family, friends or partners.

Furthermore, when seeking professional help, health workers are likely to find that the only sources of assistance are work associates. Accepting assistance from them could result in embarrassment, a sense of failure and role-confusion.

The third option is assistance from other survivors, especially in the form of self-help groups. Health professionals may again encounter embarrassment and an unacceptable role-reversal if the other members of the group are their own patients.

Issues relating to organizational climates

Not all health professionals work in organizations, but a sizeable proportion does. Helping professions and their organizations tend to divide the population into two groups, reminiscent of the Biblical 'sheep and goats'. The people they serve are seen as needy, vulnerable and weak. Their employees and representatives, conversely, have to be strong, robust and resilient. Helping organizations tend to be intolerant of professionals who appear to step over on to the vulnerable side of the divide. Many organizational climates are unsympathetic to employees with stress problems.

They are equally intolerant of people who openly acknowledge and seek help for their problems, despite the fact that to do so is a sign of professional responsibility and strength. Time and again employees who have referred themselves for stress counselling or psychiatric help have found they have been passed over for promotion or regarded with suspicion by their superiors.

SURVIVORS IN PERSPECTIVE

As indicated earlier in this chapter, everyone brings to adulthood some negative baggage from unfortunate experiences in childhood. Death, disease and natural disaster all cause distress. Children are so powerless that it is inevitable that somebody, somewhere and at some time, who is stronger or older will exploit their vulnerability. Therefore most people will have suffered some form of abuse, whether physical, emotional or sexual, whether it came from parents or non-relatives such as a school bully or a vindictive teacher. It is not realistic to divide the population into the abused and the non-abused. Everybody is a survivor in some way or another.

In Western society there is another way in which people are divided. We tend to label people 'copers' or 'non-copers'. People who have encountered a lot of emotional difficulties are generally seen as 'non-copers'. It would be more accurate to view all people as existing on a continuum, from a condition of weakness and vulnerability at one end to a state of strength and resilience at the other. Some people will spend a lifetime at the vulnerable end. But most of the population will move up and down the continuum, starting as vulnerable infants and returning to the same end if severely weakened by terminal illness or the fragility of extreme old age. Many survivors of sexual abuse will function towards the resilient end. However, there should be no shame or stigma attached to those who, recognizing their vulnerabilities, seek help in order to enhance their resilience.

In conclusion, health professionals spend their working lives helping people move up the continuum. They may be fighting alongside their patients to combat disease or to restore bodily functioning after injury. Because of this, they are ideally placed to understand and assist people whose emotional resources are being depleted by the aftermath of childhood sexual abuse.

Appendix A Legal steps in England and Wales

PROTECTION

The main source of legislation to protect children is the Children Act, 1989. This is a comprehensive piece of legislation dealing with a range of child welfare issues, not just those relating to abuse. It covers such matters as day care provision and the position of children in custody disputes. However, it also has a number of orders directly relating to child protection.

Emergency Protection Orders

In the past in England and Wales, Place of Safety Orders were used to remove a child to, or keep a child in, a safe place. The use of these caused controversy in the 1986 Cleveland crisis. The Children Act, 1989 replaced these with an Emergency Protection Order. Anyone, including health professionals, can apply for one when it is felt that a child is likely to suffer significant harm if he or she is not removed to, or kept in, safe accommodation. In practice these orders are usually sought by social workers. The court granting an order can, among other provisions, make stipulations in relation to a medical or psychiatric examination. The order lasts for eight days and is renewable for a further seven.

Children who are likely to suffer significant harm may be taken into police protection for a period of up to 72 hours.

Child Assessment Orders

Local authority or NSPCC representatives may apply for child assessment orders if they have reasonable cause to suspect that a child is suffering, or is likely to suffer, significant harm. This lasts seven days. It is not an emergency order but can enable a medical examination to be undertaken provided the child consents, assuming he or she is of sufficient understanding to make an informed decision.

Care and Supervision Orders

If concerns about children remain after the assessment and investigation, the matter can be placed before the court which may make a Care or Supervision Order. These are mutually exclusive. A child is either placed in the care of the local authority or is supervised by the local authority or a probation officer. Unlike an Emergency Protection Order, which can be sought by anyone, they can only be applied for by local authority or NSPCC representatives.

Additional Orders

Interim Supervision or Care Orders may be granted before a court is in a position to decide which order, if any, to make. There is also a range of provisions called Section 8 Orders, which are designed to comprise a flexible package of orders catering for any issue arising about the welfare of a child. They tend to be used more in custody cases, but may have a place in child protection.

Injunctions

These are not part of the Children Act, 1989, but can offer some protection to victims. A child or parent and child jointly may apply for an injunction to prevent an alleged abuser from assaulting, molesting or otherwise harming the child. This has its problems because a delay between an abusive incident and a request for an injunction may jeopardize the application. Children, particularly in cases where the perpetrator is close to the youngsters, may well not disclose immediately.

Other provisions under civil law can help to protect children and ensure that, if harmed, they are awarded some compensation.

The law of tort

In cases where a perpetrator has been convicted and he or she has assets, a victim may be successful in obtaining damages under the law of tort. Even when the perpetrator has not been convicted, damages may be obtained because in civil proceedings it is only necessary to prove that someone is responsible on a 'balance of probabilities', whereas in criminal proceedings proof has to be 'beyond reasonable doubt'.

Criminal Injuries Compensation Board

If the perpetrator has no assets, a child may still be able to gain compensation. For a case to be successful when placed before the Criminal Injuries Compensation Board, there must be evidence of a crime and proof that damage has ensued. Again, there is a problem in cases of child sexual abuse because there is at present a limit on the amount of time that elapses between the offence occurring and a claim being made.

CRIMINAL PROSECUTION

Prosecuting offenders is an indirect way of protecting children. The following shows the range of possible offences with which abusers can be charged.

- Incest is restricted to full intercourse within proscribed relationships.
- Rape requires full intercourse and is only an offence against girls or women.
- Indecency with children is an act of gross indecency against a child under 14 years or inciting such a child to commit a grossly indecent act.
- Unlawful sexual intercourse is an offence for men with girls under the age of 16 years. It is regarded as more serious if the girl is under 13 years.

- Buggery and anal intercourse is illegal whatever the age or sex of the child. When relating to human beings it is called 'sodomy' and when with animals it is termed 'bestiality'.
- Indecent assault is the commonest charge. It applies to any assault accompanied by circumstances of indecency (not covered by the other headings) against people of any age or sex.

Appendix B Female circumcision

Health professionals may encounter female circumcision in the course of their work. Comments on this have not been included in the main text because it is not sexual abuse in the sense that individuals with a sexual orientation towards children use and exploit them for their own sexual gratification. It is, nonetheless, claimed to be a form of sexual abuse in that it is the abuse of male power and is designed to restrict the sexual activity of women for the purposes of men. On the other hand, it is often older women who insist on girls undergoing the operation, and it is often women who perform it. They would argue that it is a cultural 'initiation ceremony'. It has been a tradition in parts of Africa for years and is part of the cultural heritage. A girl who has not had the operation will be a social outcast and is unlikely to be able to marry.

In the UK it is illegal but may well be occurring in private hospitals. Article 24(3) of the United Nations Convention on the Rights of the Child states that signatory countries 'shall take all effective and appropriate measures with a view to abolishing traditional practices prejudicial to the health of children'.

Female circumcision, also referred to as castration or genital mutilation, involves: clitoridectomy, the removal of the entire clitoris; excision, the removal of the clitoris and adjacent parts of the labia minora or all exterior genitalia except the labia majora; and infibulation, excision followed by the sewing together of the genitals to obliterate the entrance to the vagina except for a tiny opening, the size of a matchstick head, to allow for urination and menstruation.

Even under ideal conditions it is likely to result in painful intercourse and menstruation. It adds to complications at child birth because the perineum hardens and tears during delivery. It is often effected by means of broken bottles, knives or a razor blade. If not performed under anaesthetic it is extremely painful. Subsequently, it can lead to anguish due to the development of nervroma at the point where the clitoride nerve is cut. The girl experiences a severe flashing pain at the slightest touch similar to that encountered by some amputees. Other common results are haemorrhage, tetanus, urinary infection and septic anaemia. In some cases complications prove fatal.

It is usually performed on young girls between the ages of 6 and 13 years. It is found most commonly in parts of Africa including Nigeria, northern Sudan, Sierra Leone, Egypt, the two Yemeni republics, Somalia, Jibuti, Kenya, Togo, Iraq, Guinea and Ivory Coast. An analysis of infibulation as practised in the Islamic area of north-eastern Africa is given by Esther Hicks (1993). She demonstrates, from an anthropological perspective, that female circumcision cannot be eradicated in isolation from other social, political and religious factors within these societies.

There is a dilemma for white professionals because it is a custom practised predominantly by black people. There are many cultural aspects of child-rearing followed by white people that would be condemned by black parents; white parents do not have a monopoly on good childcare practices. It is important not to impose European values on people with African values and assume that white standards are superior to black. On the other hand, much of the opposition to female circumcision has come from black African feminists. As one black spokesperson said, 'Why are people refusing to condemn this practice? If this suffering had been inflicted on little white girls, would it have been allowed to continue for so long?'

A London-based organization called Forward is committed to eradicating the practice. Its members would argue that by failing to act to protect a girl from circumcision, a health professional was hiding behind fears of being seen as racist, but was in fact discriminating against young black girls.

An account of a young woman who chose female circumcision and facial scarification is given in *The Color Purple* (Walker, 1983). '"It is the way the Olinka can show they still have their own ways,", said Olivia, "even though the white man has taken everything else."' Somehow health professionals have to find a balance between children's rights, women's rights, parents' rights and the rights of black societies.

Appendix C Glossary

Although most of the words and phrases here have been described in the text, this list has been compiled so that a quick check can be made of words that tend to have a specific meaning within the context of child sexual abuse.

Many of the medical and anatomical terms that can be found in a good medical dictionary have not been included on the assumption that health professionals will be familiar with the majority of such words or will have ready access to a medical dictionary.

In many instances the meaning of a word or phrase in relation to child sexual abuse is given. In order to avoid confusion an indication is given of the other ways in which, particularly in the medical setting, the terms are applied.

Abuser   The person who sexually assaults or exploits a child victim; other terms include molester, offender and perpetrator.

Analingus   Sexual gratification through sucking, licking, or pushing the tongue as far as possible into the anus.

Androphile   Sexual preference for mature male partners, but this can also mean anthropophilic referring to parasites who prefer human to animal hosts.

Bestiality   Intercourse with an animal.

Black, Asian and ethnic minority   These terms have been used throughout because they are currently the most generally used and accepted terms for non-whites and those who do not have a white or Christian heritage. It is understood that in the USA some now prefer the term 'people of colour', that

Asian is a very loose term, and that ethnic minority can itself be a pejorative term, with many preferring minority ethnic, but for simplicity and to avoid confusion, we have chosen to use here the terms in widest current use in the UK.

Bondage   Sexual gratification through tying up a partner or being tied up.

Buggery   Anal intercourse with animals or other human beings, male or female. An offence under UK law.

Case conference   Any meeting of professionals to discuss a particular individual or 'case'. However, it often specifically means the gathering of investigating and helping professionals, sometimes with the family present, to collect information and plan for the future protection of a child who has been abused by other close family members.

Colposcope   A non-invasive instrument used primarily to study cervical pathology relating to early diagnosis of carcinoma; but may also be used to clarify the diagnosis of sexual abuse by assisting the examination of the vagina. It provides an excellent light source and can have a camera attached.

Coprolalia   Also known as cacolalia or scatologia, it means sexual gratification gained by using obscene words, especially nowadays via the telephone. It can refer to compulsive swearing, which can occur involuntarily as a symptom of Tourette syndrome.

Coprophilia   Sexual gratification gained through the use of faeces, excrement and dirt.

Co-victim   A person who is not directly assaulted but who is subjected to a similar process of targeting, grooming, exploitation and manipulation as the primary victim.

Cunnilingus   Act of sucking, licking, biting or kissing the vagina, or putting the tongue as far as possible into the vagina.

Disability   This has been used throughout because it is the generally adopted and accepted term. Nevertheless, it is accepted that it is a far from perfect word, focusing as it does on a person's lack of ability in certain areas rather than their abilities in others. Other terms have similar problems and so for simplicity the term disability has been used.

Disclosure A witness' first statement about what has happened. This usually refers to a child victim who tells someone about the abuse they have experienced.

Dual heritage This term has been used as it was considered to be more acceptable than the previous 'mixed race' or 'mixed parentage'.

Evidence-in-chief The main body of a witness' statements which can then be subjected to cross-examination.

Exhibitionism Sexual gratification obtained by a male through the exposure of the genitals. Often the perpetrator is a stranger exposing himself to women or children. The penis can be flaccid or erect. Exhibitionism may be accompanied by masturbation.

Expert witness A witness who is a recognized expert and specialist in a particular area. An expert witness can give opinions as well as factual evidence.

Extended family The whole family, not just parents and children but grandparents, uncles, aunts and cousins who may, or may not be resident in the household.

External inhibitors A range of factors external to sex abusers that can prevent them from committing an offence. This can be an abstract idea such as the threat of imprisonment or something more tangible such as a protective parent.

Familial Relating to the family, hence intrafamilial, something that involves or occurs within the family circle. Extrafamilial is something involving or occurring outside the family.

Fellatio Sexual gratification obtained by sucking, biting, licking or kissing the penis.

Flagellation Sexual gratification obtained through beating or whipping oneself or another person. In medical terms the word can also mean the formation or arrangement of the flagella, tentacles found in protozoa, amoebas, sporozoans and bacteria.

Flashbacks Sudden memories of earlier trauma. The memories are very vivid and can involve all the senses. The person is transported back and relives the experience. Flashbacks appear without warning and are difficult to control.

Frottage Sexual gratification by rubbing against a sexually desired person.

Grooming The process by which perpetrators make their victims submit to their will. This can range from subtle gentle bribery, through a type of seduction to a series of threats and intimidation.

Guardian *ad litem* An independent person, often a social worker, appointed by the court to represent the interests of the child.

Gynecomania Excessive desire in a male for sexual relations with females.

Gynophilia A sexual preference for mature female partners. But it is also sometimes equated to gynecomania, satyriasis, lagnosis or hypersexuality in males.

Hebephilia Sexual orientation towards young adolescent boys or girls rather than pre-pubescent children or fully mature adults.

Hypersexuality Above average or excessive sexual craving or preoccupation with sexual matters.

Homophobia An (irrational) fear, dislike or hatred of homosexuals and homosexuality.

Incest In legal terms, sexual intercourse between two people who are specified blood relatives. It is often more generally used to describe any form of sexual abuse within the family.

Internal inhibitors A potential perpetrator's conscience which holds him or her back from committing an offence.

Lagnosis From the Greek for lustful, extreme lust or sexual desire.

Masturbation Strictly speaking sexual activity on the self, especially rubbing one's own genitals. However, especially when referred to as mutual masturbation, the term is often used to denote the rubbing or fondling of the genitals of another person.

Molest   As a verb it means to sexually assault. In the USA it is often used as a noun. It can refer to any activity from non-contact voyeurism to sexual intercourse although it tends not to be synonymous with rape.

Molester Interchangeable with the words perpetrator, offender or abuser to denote someone who sexually assaults or exploits another person.

Necrophilia   Gratification through sexual activity with a dead body (corpse).

Nuclear family   A term applied to the most immediate family constellation, usually just parents and their offspring.

Offender   Anyone who breaks the law, but is used in this book interchangeably with abuser, molester and per-petrator to denote someone who sexually assaults or exploits a child.

Paederast   Having a sexual preference for young boys, but the term is sometimes used interchangeably with paedophile.

Paedohebephilia   The specific term for sexual preference for both pre-pubertal children and adolescents. Pedohebephilia is the American spelling.

Paedophile   Strictly speaking, an adult with an exclusive sexual preference for pre-pubertal children. However, the term is often used more generally to indicate anyone with a sexual orientation towards children and early adolescents. Pedophile is the American spelling.

Paraphilia   Sexual preferences often referred to as 'deviant'; certain conditions have to be met in order to gain sexual satisfaction.

Perpetrator   This can refer to anyone committing a crime, but is usually used to refer to the person sexually abus-ing a child. Interchangeable with abuser, offender and molester.

Registration Placing a child who is thought to have been abused on a child protection register. This usually only occurs after a case conference is satisfied that the child is likely to have been, or to be, abused. Parents and children should be informed of the decision. Professional workers from a variety of agencies can access information on the register.

Satyriasis Excessive sexual desire in a male.

Scatologia Coprolalia, sexual gratification gained by using obscene words, often associated with the misuse of the telephone. As a medical term it signifies the involuntary swearing that can occur as a symptom of Tourette syndrome.

Secondary victim A person close to the primary victim who has not been groomed, exploited or manipulated by the perpetrator but who nevertheless is adversely affected by the abuse of another, particularly a child.

Sibling A brother or sister.

Sodomy Attempted or forced anal penetration of females or males. This relates specifically to human beings; bestiality refers to anal penetration of animals. Under UK law sodomy is an offence.

Subpoena A writ commanding attendance in court as a witness under pain of a penalty for non-compliance. Documents and other pieces of evidence can also be required to be presented in court under subpoena.

Survivor People who have continued to live despite suffering a major deprivation or trauma. Specifically relates, in this book, to adolescents and adults who were sexually abused in childhood and have overcome many of the problems associated with sexual exploitation. This should be used as a positive term.

Target A particular child selected by a perpetrator to be the victim of sexual exploitation. Either sex and any type, personality, appearance or age of child can become a target, although perpetrators often have a personal target age or sex of child. They may also target vulnerable families, parents or institutions in order to obtain a position of power and trust, thereby gaining access to children.

Therapy   Systematic treatment. Often applied to psychological treatment similar to counselling.

Trauma   Medically this can be any injury to a person resulting from an outside force; however, it is used here specifically to refer to a psychological shock and the emotional disruption often caused by abuse.

Traumatic   Something that causes trauma (plural traumata); often associated with a shocking or emotionally disruptive experience.

Urophilia   Sexual stimulation obtained through the use of urine, especially drinking it or urinating on partners.

Victim   Although it can be anyone who is subjected to mistreatment or misfortune, it is applied in this book specifically to a girl or boy who is sexually abused by another person.

Voyeurism   Sexual arousal gained by watching other people, including children, undress or perform sexual and other intimate acts.

Witness as to fact   Witnesses in court who can give factual evidence of matters they experienced or observed. Unlike an expert witness, they are not expected to offer an opinion.

Zoophilia   Bestiality, sexual gratification through intercourse with animals. Zoophilic and zoophile can also refer to a parasite or blood sucking insect preferring animal to human hosts.

Appendix D Guide to additional reading

GENERAL WORKS ON CHILD ABUSE

There are a number of texts that give an overview of child abuse generally and provide good background reading. They help to put child sexual abuse in context for professionals for whom child protection is a new area.

A readable but comprehensive introduction to child abuse is provided by Jones *et al.* (1987). There are substantial contributions from two medical consultants, Peter Barbor and Margaret Oates, who have worked in the area of child protection since the late 1960s. A more recent authoritative book has been produced by Christopher Hobbs and Jane Wynne (1993). A series of articles from the *British Medical Journal* on a wide range of child protection issues are gathered together in Meadow's *ABC of Child Abuse* (1989). A lively presentation with a similar title, *The ABC of Child Abuse Work* is provided by Jean Moore (1985), while an interesting historical and political perspective is given by Parton (1985).

CHAPTERS 1 AND 2   DEFINITIONS, TERMS
AND SETTINGS

A useful, short but informative overview is given by Riley (1991). The collation of research findings by Finkelhor *et al.* (1986) up to the mid-1980s is still of value, as is the rather dated but authoritative text by Mrazek and Kempe (1981). Katherine Coulborne Faller (1990) covers many key areas including sexual abuse in day care settings, foster care and allegations in divorce proceedings. A collation of research, albeit based on small samples, covering a variety of topics such as adolescent offenders, victim resilience and female offenders is edited by Patton (1991). Dr Gill Wakley (1991), a principal in general practice, has written a guide specifically for doctors in primary care. For health professionals working in an educational setting, such as school nurses, there is Maher (1987).

Finkelhor, Williams and Burns' *Nursery Crimes: Sexual Abuse in Day Care* (1988) throws a clear and searching light on abuse in day care settings, and in the course of the research uncovers interesting findings on female perpetrators and organized ritual abuse.

A recent comment on ritual abuse is made by McFadyen, Hanks and James (1993) and a useful guide has been prepared by Hudson (1991). Ritual abuse was the focus of an enquiry into events in Orkney in 1991. Reflections on this are given by Anne Black (1993), an assessor to Lord Clyde's inquiry. The full report (HMSO, 1991) may also be of interest. There was also controversy about organized ritual abuse in Rochdale in 1990, and an interesting account and analysis of the subsequent wardship proceedings is given by Latham (1991).

The Kirkwood report (1993) makes very revealing reading for anyone interested in abuse in institutional settings.

CHAPTER 3 PERSPECTIVES ON PERPETRATORS

Finkelhor (1984), although apparently dated, nevertheless still contains large sections that have been validated rather than superseded by subsequent research. Clinicians and practitioners working with perpetrators will find the four preconditions he details in his book a particularly useful concept. Anna Salter (1988) has written a comprehensive guide to sex offenders, although one or two perceptions are now open to challenge. There are several useful chapters in Horton *et al.* (1990) and Hollin and Howells (1991).

A hard hitting and definitive text on child pornography has been written by Tim Tate (1990).

A varied and interesting set of perspectives on female offenders is provided by Michelle Elliot's 1993 book which followed the 1992 first British conference on women as sex abusers. A critique of the research on mother–son abuse is provided by Lawson (1993). The effect that the 'discovery' of female abusers may have on theories relating to the causes of child sex abuse is debated by Simon Hackett (1993).

The leading writers on juvenile sex offenders are Gail Ryan (1989; Ryan *et al.*, 1987), Otey and Ryan (1985) and Fay Honey Knopp (1985). For practitioners having to deal with abuse between siblings there are a number of articles including Fox (1962, dated but interesting for its intracultural perspectives), Finkelhor (1980), De Jong (1989), and Laviola (1992). A book on the subject that looks at issues of the abuse of power and control among siblings is by Wiehe (1990).

CHAPTER 4 VICTIM PERSPECTIVES

The entrapment of the victim and the Stockholm syndrome is explained more fully in Doyle (1990). Victim blaming and the perspective of the non-abusing parents is eloquently described by Anna Salter (1988). The classic article on the accommodation syndrome (Summit, 1983), which in its time revolutionized practitioners' understanding of the behaviour of sexual abuse victims, is still worth reading.

The book by Wendy Ovaris (1991) is one of the few works written specifically for and about non-offending mothers of sexually abused children. Two eminently readable books worth recommending to parents of molested children are by Corcoran (1987) and Hagans and Case (1990).

The plight of children with disabilities is discussed in a book by The Allan Roeher Institute (1988) and in a series of papers by Brown and Craft (1989). Volume 2 of Sgroi's book *Vulnerable Populations* (1988a) contains three chapters on adults with learning disabilities which are also relevant to children and young people with these disadvantages. Margaret Kennedy, a qualified nurse, has published a number of works (1989; 1990) on deaf children. She has also contributed to an edition of *Child Abuse Review* (1992, 1, 1) that is devoted to children with disabilities in relation to child protection. A further article on the issues for deaf children is provided by Ridgeway (1993).

Issues for black children are eloquently described by the works of Kadj Rouf (1990; 1991a; 1991b). Accounts of black American children who have been sexually abused are given by Maya Angelou (1984) and Alice Walker (1983). A discussion of the pitfalls of not taking cultural factors into account is given in an article by general practitioner Bashir Qureshi (1989).

CHAPTER 5 RECOGNIZING AND RESPONDING

There are several discussions of the distinction between play and abuse in relation to sexual activities between children. They include Waterman (1986), Sgroi, Bunk and Wabrek (1988) and an account of an absorbing research project by Lamb and Coakley (1993), although the authors restricted themselves to the play activities recalled by women.

A useful summary of medical findings is provided by Bays and Chadwick (1993). For school nurses, practical advice on how to be receptive to children who have been sexually abused can be found in a chapter by Michael Marland and Gill Malcolm (1990) in a book dealing with that topic.

CHAPTER 6 INVESTIGATION AND BEYOND

Guidelines to the investigative process are provided by Jones and McQuiston (1988), Glaser and Frosh (1993), Jones (1991) and the Home Office (1992). The Department of Health and Social Security (1988) has published guidance specifically for doctors on the diagnosis of child sexual abuse.

There are a number of helpful publications for professionals appearing in court as witnesses. A valuable handbook full of details on how to cope with the tactics of cross-examining lawyers is by David Carson (1990). Although written for expert witnesses, anyone who is appearing as a witness in a professional capacity will find it useful. There is a small but useful booklet written specifically for health visitors who have to go to court produced by the Health Visitors Association (1989). BASPCAN (British Association for the Study and Prevention of Child Abuse and Neglect) has also produced a handy booklet (Livesey, 1988) although some sections have been superseded by recent legislation. Myers (1991a) looks at hearsay evidence and subsequently (1991b; 1993) discusses the use of expert testimony in child abuse cases, although this is based largely on the American experience.

In recent years there has been a burgeoning of interest in the plight of children who are witnesses in child sexual abuse cases. There is a useful discussion of the stress on child witnesses in Flin (1991). Joyce Plotnikoff (Morgan and Plotnikoff, 1990) has undertaken extensive research in this area and was instrumental in producing the leaflets for adults and children from the Children's Legal Centre. Interesting discussions are provided by Flin and Boon (1989), Spencer (1990), Perry and Wrightsman (1991) and Graham Davies (1992).

Useful books giving an overview of intervention include Murray and Gough (1991), Blagg, Hughes and Wattam (1989) and Richardson and Bacon (1991).

Helena Kennedy's brilliant *Eve Was Framed* (1992) is essential reading for anyone coming into contact with the British judicial system. It examines the inequities of the system, especially in relation to women. The book embraces the fate of child sexual abuse within the system, the attitudes to female abusers and the additional problems encountered by black women. Kennedy explains: 'I have chosen in this book to look at the treatment of women in British justice as a paradigm of the faults and blindnesses of the legal system as a whole'. It is a truly memorable read.

CHAPTER 7 PROTECTION AND PREVENTION

The treatment of offenders is discussed thoroughly by Salter (1988). There is a short but very absorbing article on community-based group work with offenders written by Mezey *et al.* (1991) in the *Journal of Forensic Psychiatry* and this is preceded by a discussion of the treatment of offenders in prison (Seven, 1991). Three chapters of Sgroi (1988a) Volume 2 is devoted to this topic with four chapters relating to the treatment of victims.

There is often an assumption that the victims are female and many of the therapeutic groups are for girls. The perspectives of boys abused as children are discussed in Bruckner and

Johnson (1987), Krug (1989), Bolton, Morris and MacEachron (1989) and Pescosolido (1989).

The literature on helping victims is overwhelming; however, one book worth singling out is by Ann Cattanach (1992) and is devoted to play therapy with abused children. Ann Bannister is a talented child therapist and all works by her and her colleagues are well worth reading (Bannister, 1989; Bannister, Barrett and Shearer, 1990).

There are several discussions of the efficacy of prevention programmes by Berrick (1988), Budin and Johnson (1989) Conte, Wolf and Smith (1989) and Tutty (1993).

The role of the media is discussed by Keith Soothill (1991). Examples of responsible and informative journalism are provided by David Williams (1987) and Julia Stuart (1993). For health professionals who have to cope with the media there is a useful publication by Anne Fry (1987), which, although written with social services in mind, still has much that is relevant for other professionals.

CHAPTER 8 HELPING ADULT SURVIVORS

The publications devoted to helping adult survivors are plentiful and only a fraction can be mentioned here. Two thick but worthwhile tomes have been produced by Hall and Lloyd (1989) and Bass and Davis (1990). They are designed for survivors but the reader must be fairly erudite in order to understand them. Nonetheless, they are mines of information for more literate survivors, and are useful as a guide for helping professionals.

One modest book, which is directed towards adolescents but would also be valuable for older survivors, is by Bain and Sanders (1990). One of the most user-friendly books for adults who have suffered from any form of childhood abuse is by Elana Gil (1983). This is written in an accessible, congenial style and maintains a light touch with its cartoon drawings. The author has written a second book on treating adult survivors (Gil, 1988).

Comprehensive publications on how to counsel adults abused as children are by Christianne Sanderson (1990) and Clare Drauker (1992).

Finally, of relevance to both survivors and therapists, is a book on overcoming child sexual abuse by joint therapists Carol Jarvis-Kirkendall and Jeffrey Kirkendall (1989).

APPENDIX A LEGISLATION

For health professionals who wish to become more familiar with the Children Act, 1989, a clearly presented introduction has been produced by the Department of Health (1989).

Allen Roeher Institute (1988) *Vulnerable – Sexual Abuse of People with Intellectual Handicap,* The Allen Roeher Institute, Hexagon, Canada.

Angelou, M. (1984) *I Know Why the Caged Bird Sings,* Virago, London.

Bacon, H. (1991) Cleveland's children: seen but not heard, in *Child Sexual Abuse: Whose Problem? Reflections from Cleveland* (eds S. Richardson, H. Bacon, M. Dunn *et al.*) Ventura Press, Birmingham.

Bain, O. and Sanders, M. (1990) *Out in the Open: A Guide for Young People Who Have Been Sexually Abused,* Virago, London.

Bannister, A. (1989) Healing action – action methods with children who have been sexually abused, in *Child Sexual Abuse: Listening, hearing and validating the experiences of children* (eds H. Blagg, J.A. Hughes, and C. Wattam), Longman, Harlow, Essex, pp. 78–94.

Bannister, A., Barrett, K. and Shearer, E. (eds) (1990) *Listening to Children: The Professional Response to Hearing the Abused Child,* Longman, Harlow, Essex.

Bass, E. and Davis, L. (1990) *The Courage to Heal: A Guide for Women Survivors of Child Sexual Abuse,* Cedar, London.

Bays, J. and Chadwick, D. (1993) Medical diagnosis of sexually abused children. *Child Abuse and Neglect,* 17(1), 91–110.

Berrick, J.D. (1988) Parental involvement in child abuse prevention training: what do they learn? *Child Abuse and Neglect,* 12, 543–53.

Black, A. (1993) The Orkney Inquiry: a summary of some key comments and recommendations. *Child Abuse Review,* 2(1), 47–50.

Blagg, H., Hughes, J.A. and Wattam, C. (eds) (1989) *Child Sexual Abuse: Listening, hearing and validating the experiences of children*, Longman, Harlow, Essex.

Bolton, F.G. Jr., Morris, L.A. and MacEachron, A.E. (1989) *Males at Risk: The Other Side of Child Sexual Abuse*, Sage, Newbury Park.

Brown, H. and Craft, A. (eds) (1989) *Thinking the Unthinkable: Papers on Sexual Abuse and People with Learning Difficulties*, FPA Education Unit, London.

Bruckner, D.F. and Johnson, P.E. (1987) Treatment for adult male victims of childhood sexual abuse. *Social Casework: The Journal of Contemporary Social Work*, Feb., 81–7.

Budin, L.E. and Johnson, C.F. (1989) Sex abuse prevention programs: offenders' attitudes about their efficacy. *Child Abuse and Neglect*, **13**, 77–87.

Carson, D. (1990) *Professionals and the Courts: A Handbook for Expert Witnesses*, Venture, Birmingham.

Cattanach, A. (1992) *Play Therapy with Abused Children*, Jessica Kingsley, London.

Conte, J.R., Wolf, S., and Smith, T. (1989) What sexual offenders tell us about prevention strategies. *Child Abuse and Neglect*, **13**, 293–301.

Corcoran, C. (1987) *Take Care! Preventing Child Sexual Abuse*, Poolberg Press, Dublin.

Craft, A. and Hitching, M. (1989) Keeping safe: sex education and assertiveness skills, in *Thinking the Unthinkable: Papers on Sexual abuse and People with Learning Difficulties* (eds H. Brown and A. Craft), FPA Education Unit, London, pp. 29–38.

Davies, G. (1992) Protecting child witnesses in the courtroom. *Child Abuse Review*, **1**(1), 33–42.

De Jong, A.R. (1989) Sexual interactions among siblings and cousins: experimentation or exploitation? *Child Abuse and Neglect*, **13**, 271–9.

Department of Health (1989) *An Introduction to the Children Act 1989*, HMSO, London.

Department of Health and Social Security (1988) *Diagnosis of Child Sexual Abuse: Guidance for Doctors*, HMSO, London.

Doyle, C. (1990) *Working with Abused Children*, Macmillan, London.

Draucker, C.B. (1992) *Counselling Survivors of Childhood Sexual Abuse*, Sage, London.

Elliot, M. (ed.) (1993) *Female Sexual Abuse of Children: The Ultimate Taboo*, Longman, Harlow, Essex.

Faller, K.C. (1990) *Understanding Child Sexual Maltreatment*, Sage, Newbury Park.

Finkelhor, D. (1980) Sex among siblings: a survey on prevalence, variety and effects. *Archives of Sexual Behavior*, **9**(3), 171–94.

Finkelhor, D. (1984) *Child Sexual Abuse: New Theory and Research*, The Free Press, New York.

Finkelhor, D., Araji, S., Baron, L. *et al.* (1986) *A Sourcebook on Child Sexual Abuse*, Sage, Newbury Park.

Finkelhor, D., Williams, L.M. and Burns, N. (1988) *Nursery Crimes: Sexual Abuse in Day Care*, Sage, Newbury Park.

Flin, R. and Boon, J. (1989) The child witness in court, in *Child Sexual Abuse: Listening, hearing and validating the experiences of children* (eds H. Blagg, J.A. Hughes, and C. Wattam), Longman, Harlow, Essex, pp. 122–37.

Flin, R. (1991) Sources of stress for child witnesses in court, in *Intervening in Child Sexual Abuse* (eds K. Murray and D.A. Gough), Scottish Academic Press, Edinburgh, pp. 122–8.

Fox, J.R. (1962) Sibling incest. *British Journal of Sociology*, **13**, 128–50.

Fry, A. (1987) *Media Matters*, Reed Publishing, Wallington, Surrey.

Gil, E. (1983) *Outgrowing the Pain*, Launch Press, Walnut Creek.

Gil, E. (1988) *Treatment of Adult Survivors of Child Abuse*, Launch Press, Walnut Creek.

Glaser, D. and Frosh, S. (1993) *Child Sexual Abuse*, 2nd edn, Macmillan, London.

Hackett, S. (1993) Woman's place. *Community Care*, 26 Aug, 11.

Hagans, K.B. and Case, J. (1990) *When Your child Has Been Molested: A Parent's Guide to Healing and Recovery*, Lexington Books, Massachusetts.

Hall, L. and Lloyd, S. (1989) *Surviving Child Sexual Abuse: A Handbook for Helping Women Challenge their Past*, The Falmer Press, Basingstoke.

Health Visitors Association (1989) *Appearing in Court as a Witness*, Health Visitors Association, London.

Hobbs, C.J. and Wynne, J.M. (eds) (1993) *Child Abuse*, Bailliere Tindal, London.

Hollin, C.R. and Howells, K. (eds) (1991) *Clinical Approaches to Sex Offenders and Their Victims*, John Wiley and Sons, Chichester.

Home Office (1992) *Memorandum of Good Practice: on Video Recorded Interviews with Child Witnesses for Criminal Proceedings*, HMSO, London.

Horton, A.L., Johnson, B.L., Roundy, L.M., and Williams, D. (eds) (1990) *The Incest Perpetrator: the family member no one wants to treat*, Sage, Newbury Park.

Hudson, P. (1991) *Ritual Abuse: Discovery, Diagnosis and Treatment*, Safer Society Press, New York.

Jarvis-Kirkendall, C. and Kirkendall, J. (1989) *Without Consent: How to Overcome Childhood Sexual Abuse*, Swan Press, Scottsdale, AZ.

Jones, D.N., Pickett, J., Oates, M. and Barbor, P. (1987) *Understanding Child Abuse*, 2nd edn, Macmillan, London.

Jones, D.P.H. and McQuiston, M.G. (1988) *Interviewing the Sexually Abused Child*, Gaskell, London.

Jones, D.P.H. (1991) Interviewing children, in *Intervening in Child Sexual Abuse* (eds K. Murray, and D.A. Gough), Scottish Academic Press, Edinburgh, pp. 18–30.

Kennedy, H. (1992) *Eve Was Framed*, Chatto and Windus, London.

Kennedy, M. (1989) The abuse of deaf children. *Child Abuse Review*, **3**(1), 3–6.

Kennedy, M. (1990) The deaf child who is sexually abused – is there a need for a dual specialist? *Child Abuse Review*, **4**(2), 3–6.

Kirkwood, A. (1993) *The Leicestershire Inquiry 1992*, Leicestershire County Council, Leicestershire.

Knopp, F.H. (1985) *The Youthful Sex Offender: The Rationale and Goals of Early Intervention and Treatment*, Safer Society Press, Orwell, p. 10.

Krug, R.S. (1989) Adult male report of childhood sexual abuse by mothers: case descriptions, motivation and long-term consequences. *Child Abuse and Neglect*, **13**, 111–19.

Lamb, S. and Coakley, M. (1993) 'Normal' childhood sexual

play and games: differentiating play from abuse. *Child Abuse and Neglect*, **17**(4), 515–26.

Latham, C.T. (1991) Law report, family division: Rochdale Borough Council v. B.W. and others. *Local Government Review*, 26 Oct., 843–57.

Laviola, M. (1992) Effects of older brother–younger sister incest: a study of the dynamics of 17 cases. *Child Abuse and Neglect*, **16**(3), 409–22.

Lawson, C. (1993) Mother–son sexual abuse: rare or underreported? A Critique of the Research. *Child Abuse and Neglect*, **17**(2), 261–70.

Livesy, B. (1988) *Giving Evidence in Court*, BASPCAN, York.

Maher, P. (ed.) (1987) *Child Abuse: The Education Perspective*, Basil Blackwell, Oxford.

Marland, M. and Malcolm, G. (1990) Telling tales: in and out of school, in *Listening to Children: The Professional Response to Hearing the Abused Child* (eds A. Bannister, K. Barrett and E. Shearer), Longman, Harlow, Essex, pp. 40–50.

McFadyen, A., Hanks, H. and James, C. (1993) Ritual abuse: a definition. *Child Abuse Review*, **2**(1), 35–41.

Meadow, R. (ed.) (1989) *ABC of Child Abuse*, British Medical Journal, London.

Mezey, G., Vizard, E., Hawkes, C. and Austin, R. (1991) A community treatment programme for convicted child sex offenders: a preliminary report. *Journal of Forensic Psychiatry*, **2**(1), 11–26.

Moore, J. (1985) *The ABC of Child Abuse Work*, Gower, Aldershot.

Morgan, J. and Plotnikoff, J. (1990) Children as victims of crime, in *Children's Evidence in Legal Proceedings* (eds J. Spencer, G. Nicholson, R. Flin and R. Bull), Hawksmere, London.

Mrazek, P.B. and Kempe, C.H. (eds) (1981) *Sexually Abused Children and their Families*, Pergamon, Oxford.

Murray, K. and Gough, D.A. (eds) (1991) *Intervening in Child Sexual Abuse*, Scottish Academic Press, Edinburgh.

Myers, J.E.B. (1991a) Hearsay evidence, in *Intervening in Child Sexual Abuse* (eds K. Murray, and D.A. Gough), Scottish Academic Press, Edinburgh, pp. 137–9.

Myers, J.E.B. (1991b) Expert testimony in child sexual abuse litigation: the American experience, in *Intervening in Child Sexual Abuse* (eds K. Murray, and D.A. Gough), Scottish Academic Press, Edinburgh, pp. 105–21.

Myers, J.E.B. (1993) Expert testimony regarding child sexual abuse. *Child Abuse and Neglect*, **17**(1), 175–85.

Otey, E.M. and Ryan, G.D. (1985) *Adolescent Sex Offenders. Issues in Research and Treatment*, National Institute of Mental Health, Rockville, Maryland.

Ovaris, W. (1991) *After the Nightmare: The Treatment of Non-Offending Mothers of Sexually Abused Children*, Learning Publications, Holmes Beach.

Parton, N. (1985) *The Politics of Child Abuse*, Macmillan, London.

Patton, M.Q. (ed.) (1991) *Family Sexual Abuse: Frontline Research and Evaluation*, Sage, Newbury Park.

Perry, N.W. and Wrightsman, L.S. (1991) *The Child Witness: Legal Issues and Dilemmas*, Sage, London.

Pescosolido, F.J. (1989) Sexual abuse of boys by males: theoretical and treatment implications, in *Vulnerable Populations, Volume 2*, (ed. S.M. Sgroi) Lexington Books, New York, pp. 85–110.

Qureshi, B. (1989) Multicultural aspects of child abuse in Britain. *Journal of the Royal Society of Medicine*, **82**, 65–6.

Richardson, S. and Bacon, H. (eds) (1991) *Child Sexual Abuse: Whose Problem? – Reflections from Cleveland*, Venture Press, Birmingham.

Ridgeway, S.M. (1993) Abuse and deaf children: some factors to consider. *Child Abuse Review*, **2**(3), 166–73.

Riley, D. (ed.) (1991) *Sexual Abuse of Children: Understanding, Intervention and Prevention*, Radcliffe Medical Press, Oxford, p. 2.

Rouf, K. (1990) My self in echoes. My voice in song, in *Listening to Children: The Professional Response to Hearing the Abused Child* (eds A. Bannister, K. Barrett, and E. Shearer), Longman, Harlow, Essex, pp. 1–19.

Rouf, K. (1991a) *Black Girls Speak Out*, The Children's Society, London.

Rouf. K. (1991b) *Into Pandora's Box*, The Children's Society, London.

Ryan, G., Lane, S., Davis, J. and Connie, I. (1987) Juvenile sex offenders: development and correction. *Child Abuse and Neglect*, **11**, 385–95.

Ryan, G. (1989) Victim to victimizer: rethinking victim treatment. *Journal of Interpersonal Violence*, **4**(3), 325–41.

Salter, A. (1988) *Treating Child Sex Offenders and Victims: A Practical Guide*, Sage, Newbury Park, p. ll.

Sanderson, C. (1990) *Counselling Adult Survivors of Child Sexual Abuse*, London, Jessica Kingsley.

Seven, P. (1991) Treating sex offenders in prison. *Journal of Forensic Psychiatry*, **2**(1), 8–9.

Sgroi, S.M. (ed.) (1988a)*Vulnerable Populations, Volumes 1 and 2*, Lexington Books, New York.

Sgroi, S.M., Bunk, B.S. and Wabrek, C.J. (1988) Children's Sexual Behaviours and Their Relationship to Sexual Abuse, in *Vulnerable Populations, Volume 1* (ed. S.M. Sgroi), Lexington Books, New York, pp. 137–88.

Soothill, K. (1991) Child sexual abuse allegations: informing the public. *Journal of Forensic Psychiatry*, **2**(1), 1–4.

Spencer, J.R. (1990) Persuading the courts to listen to children, in *Listening to Children: The Professional Response to Hearing the Abused Child* (eds A. Bannister, K. Barrett and E. Shearer), Longman, Harlow, Essex, pp. ll0–23.

Stuart, J. (1993) When mum is to blame. *Northampton Chronicle and Echo*, 24 March, 10.

Summit, R.C. (1983) The child sexual abuse accommodation syndrome. *Child Abuse and Neglect*, **7**, 177–93.

Tate, T. (1990) *Child Pornography – An Investigation*, Methuen, London.

Tutty, L.M. (1992) The ability of elementary school children to learn child sexual abuse prevention concepts. *Child Abuse and Neglect*, **16**(3), 369–85.

Wakley, G. (1991) *Psychosexual Medicine Series 3: Sexual Abuse and the Primary Care Doctor*, Chapman & Hall, London.

Walker, A. (1983) *The Color Purple*, The Women's Press, London.

Waterman, J. (1986) Developmental considerations, in *Sexual Abuse of Young Children* (eds K. MacFarlane, J. Waterman,

S. Conerly *et al.*), Holt, Rinehart and Winston, London, pp. 15–29.

Wiehe, V.R. (1990) *Sibling Abuse: Hidden Physical, Emotional and Sexual Trauma*, Lexington Books, Lexington.

Williams, D. (1987) Suffer little children. *Daily Mail*, 12 June, 8.

References

Abel, G.G., Becker, J.V., Mittelman, M. *et al.* (1987) Self-reported sex crimes of nonincarcerated paraphiliacs. *Journal of Interpersonal Violence*, **2**(1), 3–25.

Ahmad, B. (1989) Protecting black children from abuse. *Social Work Today*, 8 June, 24.

Allers, C.T. and Benjack, K.J. (1991) Connections between childhood abuse and HIV infection. *Journal of Counselling and Development*, **70**, 309–13.

Allers, C.T., Benjack, K.J., White, J. and Rousey, J.T. (1993) HIV vulnerability and the adult survivor of childhood sexual abuse. *Child Abuse and Neglect*, **17**(2), 291–8.

Allport, G.W. and Postman, L. (1947) *The Psychology of Rumor*, Henry Holt, New York.

Angelou, M. (1984) *I know Why the Caged Bird Sings*, Virago, London.

Armstrong, L. (1978) *Kiss Daddy Goodnight*, Pocket Books, New York.

Bacon, H. (1991) Cleveland's children: seen but not heard, in *Child Sexual Abuse: Whose Problem? Reflections from Cleveland* (eds S. Richardson, H. Bacon, M. Dunn, G. Wyatt, M. Higgs, H. Cashman and A. Lamballe-Armonstrong), Venture Press, Birmingham, p. 81.

Baghramian, A. and Kershaw, S. (1989) We are all survivors like our children. *Social Work Today*, 10 Aug., 20–1.

Bain, O. and Sanders, M. (1990) *Out in the Open: A Guide for Young People Who Have Been Sexually Abused*, Virago, London.

Baker, A.W. and Duncan, S.P. (1985) Child sexual abuse: A study of prevalence in Great Britain. *Child Abuse and Neglect*, **9**(4), 457–68.

Baker, C.J. (1978) Sexually transmitted diseases and child abuse. *Sexually Transmitted Diseases*, **5**(4), 169–71.

Ballard, D.T., Blair, G.D., Devereaux, S. *et al.* (1990) A Comparative Profile of the Incest Perpetrator: Background Characteristics, Abuse History and use of Social Skills, in *The Incest Perpetrator: the family member no one wants to treat*, (eds A.L. Horton, B.L. Johnson, L.M. Roundy and D. Williams), Sage, Newbury Park, pp. 43–64.

Bamford, F. and Roberts, R. (1989) Child Sexual Abuse – II, in *ABC of Child Abuse* (ed. R. Meadow), British Medical Journal, London, pp. 31–6.

Barker, E. (1946) *The Politics of Aristotle*, Oxford University Press, Oxford, p. 325.

Barnett, S., Corder, F. and Jehu, D. (1989) Group treatment for women sex offenders against children. *Practice*, **3**(2), 148–59.

Bass, E. and Davis, L.(1990) *The Courage to Heal: A Guide for Women Survivors of Child Sexual Abuse*, Cedar, London

Bays, J. and Chadwick, D. (1993) Medical diagnosis of sexually abused children. *Child Abuse and Neglect*, **17**(1), 91–110.

Becker, J.V., Skinner, L.J., Abel, G.G. and Tracey, E.C. (1982) Incidence and types of sexual dysfunction in rape and incest victims. *Journal of Sex and Marital Therapy*, **8**, 65–74.

Becker, J. (1991) Working with perpetrators, in *Intervening in Child Sexual Abuse* (eds K. Murray and D.A. Gough), Scottish Academic Press, Edinburgh, pp. 157–65.

Ben (1991) *Things in My Head*, Blendale Publishing, Dublin.

Bennetts, C., Brown, M. and Sloan, J. (1992) *AIDS: The Hidden Agenda in Child Sexual Abuse*, Longman, Harlow, Essex.

Bentovim, A. and Boston, P. (1988) Sexual abuse – basic issues – characteristics of children and families, in *Child Sexual Abuse Within the Family: Assessment and Treatment* (eds A. Bentovim, A. Elton, J. Hildebrand *et al.*) , Wright, London, pp. 16–39.

Bentovim, A., Elton, A., Hildebrand, J. *et al.* (eds) (1988) *Child Sexual Abuse Within the Family: Assessment and Treatment*, Wright, London.

Berlin, F.S. (1985) Pedophilia. *Psychiatry*, **19**(8), 79–88.

Berry, G.W. (1975) Incest: some clinical variations on a classical theme. *Journal of the American Academy of Psychoanalysis*, **3**(2), 151–61.

Bettleheim, B. (1979) *Surviving and Other Essays*, Thames and Hudson, London.

Blank, J. (1980) *The Playbook for Kids About Sex*, Down There Press, Burlingame, CA.

Bolton, F.G. Jr., Morris, L.A. and MacEachron, A.E. (1989) *Males At Risk: The Other Side of Child Sexual Abuse*, Sage, Newbury Park.

Bray, M. (1989) *Susie and the Wise Hedgehog go to Court*, Hawksmere, London.

Brown, H. and Craft, A. (eds) (1989) *Thinking the Unthinkable: Papers on Sexual Abuse and People with Learning Difficulties*, FPA Education Unit, London.

Brown, M.E., Hull, L. A. and Panesis, S.K. (1984) *Women Who Rape*, Massachusetts Trial Court, Boston, MA.

Bruckner, D.F. and Johnson, P.E. (1987) Treatment for adult male victims of childhood sexual abuse. *Social Casework: The Journal of Contemporary Social Work*, Feb., 81–7.

Budin, L.E. and Johnson, C.F. (1989) Sex abuse prevention programs: offenders' attitudes about their efficacy. *Child Abuse and Neglect*, **13**, 77–87.

Burgess, A.W., Groth, A.N. and McCausland, M.P.(1981) Child sex initiation rings. *American Journal of Orthopsychiatry*, **51**(1), 110–19.

Butler-Sloss, E., Right Honourable Lord Justice (1988) *Report of the Inquiry into Child Abuse in Cleveland 1987*, HMSO, London.

Campbell, B. (1988) *Unofficial Secrets: Child Sexual Abuse – The Cleveland Case*, Virago, London.

Cantwell, H.B. (1988) Child sexual abuse: very young perpetrators. *Child Abuse and Neglect*, **12**, 579–82.

Carnie, J., Waterhouse, L. and Dobash, R. (1993) The abuser under the microscope. *Community Care*, 24 June, **(972)**, 24.

Carson, D. (1990) *Professionals and the Courts: A Handbook for Expert Witnesses*, Venture, Birmingham.

Cattanach, A. (1992) *Play Therapy with Abused Children*, Jessica Kingsley, London.

Celan, P.T. (1971) *Speech Grille and Selected Poems* (trans. Joachim Neugroschel), E.P. Dutton, New York.

Chasnoff, I.J., Burns, W.J., Schnoll, S.N. *et al.* (1986) Maternal Neonatal Incest. *American Journal of Orthopsychiatry*, **4**, 577–80.

Cherniss, C. (1980) *Staff Burnout: Job Stress in the Human Services*, Sage, Newbury Park.

Cole, P.M., Woolger, C., Power, T.G. and Smith, K.D. (1992) Parenting difficulties among adult survivors of father–daughter incest. *Child Abuse and Neglect*, **16**(2), 239–50.

Conte, J.R., Wolf, S., and Smith, T. (1989) What sexual offenders tell us about prevention strategies. *Child Abuse and Neglect*, **13**, 293–301.

Conte, J.R. (1990) The incest offender: an overview and introduction, in *The Incest Perpetrator: the family member no one wants to treat* (eds A.L. Horton, B.L. Johnson, L.M. Roundy and D. Williams), Sage, Newbury Park, pp. 19–28.

Cornford, F.M. (1941) *The Republic of Plato*, Clarendon Press, Oxford, p. 177.

Craft, A. and Hitching, M. (1989) Keeping safe: sex education and assertiveness skills, in *Thinking the Unthinkable: Papers on Sexual Abuse and People with Learning Difficulties* (eds H. Brown and A. Craft), FPA Education Unit, London, pp. 29–38.

Creighton, S.J. (1987) Quantitative assessment of child abuse, in *Child Abuse: The Education Perspective* (ed. P. Maher), Basil Blackwell, Oxford, pp. 23–34.

Cruz, V.K., Price-Williams, D. and Andron, L. (1988) Developmentally disabled women who were molested as children. *Social Casework: The Journal of Contemporary Social Work*, Sep., 411–19.

Dale, P., Davies, M., Morrison, T. and Waters, J. (1986) *Dangerous Families: Assessment and Treatment of Child Abuse*, Tavistock Publications, London.

Davies, G. and Westcott, H. (1991) Child abuse evidence abused? On Underwager and Wakefield's Training Manual. *Child Abuse Review*, 5(2), 7–8.

de Young, M. (1982) *The Sexual Victimization of Children*, McFarland & Co. Inc., Jefferson, NC, pp. 97–8 and 119.

Department of Health (1988) *Protecting Children: A Guide for Social Workers Undertaking a Comprehensive Assessment*, HMSO, London, p. 12.

Department of Health and Social Security (1974) *Report of the Committee of Inquiry into the Care and Supervision Provided in Relation to Maria Colwell*, HMSO, London.

Department of Health and Social Security (1979) *The Report of the Committee of Inquiry into the Actions of the Authorities and Agencies Relating to Darryn James Clarke*, Cmnd 7730, HMSO, London.

Dixon, K.N., Arnold, L.E. and Calestro, K. (1978) Father–Son Incest: Underreported Psychiatric Problem? *American Journal of Psychiatry*, 135(7), 835–8.

Dobson, C. and Payne, R. (1977) *The Carlos Complex: A Study in Terror*, Hodder & Stoughton, London

Doyle, C. (1985) *The Imprisoned Child, Aspects of Rescuing the Severely Abused Child*, Occasional Paper 3, NSPCC, London.

Doyle, C. (1986) Management sensitivity in CSA training. *Child Abuse Review*, 1(4), 8–9.

Doyle, C. (1987) Profile of Child Sexual Abuse Drawn from the Northamptonshire Child Protection Register, unpublished.

Doyle, C. (1990) *Working with Abused Children*, Macmillan, London.

Doyle, C. (1991) Caring for the workers. *Child Abuse Review*, 5(3), 25–7.

Durfee, M., Heger, A.H. and Woodling, B. (1986) Medical evaluation, in *Sexual Abuse of Young Children* (eds K. MacFarlane, J. Waterman, S. Conerly *et al.*), Holt, Rinehart and Winston, London, pp. 52–66.

Eldridge, H. (1993) Barbara's story – a mother who sexually abused, in *Female Sexual Abuse of Children: The Ultimate Taboo* (ed. M. Elliot), Longman, Harlow, Essex, pp. 79–94.

Elias, H. and MacFarlane, K. (1991) Legal and clinical issues in videotaping, in *Intervening in Child Sexual Abuse* (eds K. Murray and D.A. Gough), Scottish Academic Press, Edinburgh, pp. 129–36.

Elliott, M. (1986) *Keeping Safe: a practical guide to talking with children*, Bedford Square Press, London, p. 2.

Elliot, M. (ed.) (1993) *Female Sexual Abuse of Children: The Ultimate Taboo*, Longman, Harlow, Essex.

Ennew, J. (1986) *The Sexual Exploitation of Children*, Polity Press, Cambridge, pp. 122–3.

Enos, W.F., Conrath, T.B. and Byer, J.C. (1986) Forensic evaluation of the sexually abused child. *Pediatrics*, **78**(3), 385–98.

Erikson, E.H. (1965) *Childhood and Society*, 2nd edn, Penguin, Harmondsworth.

Erooga, M. and Masson, H. (1989) The silent volcano: groupwork with mothers of sexually abused children. *Practice*, **1**, 24–41.

Essex County Council and Essex Area Health Authority (1981) *Malcolm Page. Report of a Panel Appointed by the Essex Area Review Committee*, Essex County Council, Essex.

Evert, E. and Bijkerk, I. (1987) *When You're Ready: A woman's healing from childhood physical and sexual abuse by her mother*, Launch Press, Walnut Creek CA., p. 52.

Faller, K.C. (1990) *Understanding Child Sexual Maltreatment*, Sage, Newbury Park.

Farber, B.A. (ed.) (1983) *Stress and Burnout in the Human Service Professions*, Pergamon Press, New York.

Fillimore, A.V. (1981) *The Abused Child as a Survivor*. Unpublished paper presented to the Third International Congress on Child Abuse and Neglect, Amsterdam.

Finkelhor, D. (1979) *Sexually Victimized Children*, The Free Press, New York.

Finkelhor, D.(1984) *Child Sexual Abuse: New Theory and Research*, The Free Press, New York.

Finkelhor, D., Araji, S., Baron, L. *et al.* (1986) *A Sourcebook on Child Sexual Abuse*, Sage, Newbury Park.

Finkelhor, D., Williams, L.M. and Burns, N. (1988) *Nursery Crimes: Sexual Abuse in Day Care*, Sage, Newbury Park.

Flin, R. and Boon, J. (1989) The child witness in court, in *Child Sexual Abuse: Listening, hearing and validating the experiences of children* (eds H. Blagg, J.A. Hughes and C. Wattam), Longman, Harlow, Essex, pp. 122–37.

Fraser, S. (1989) *My Father's House*, Virago, London.

Freund, K. and Kuban, M. (1993) Toward a testable developmental model of pedophilia: the development of erotic age preference. *Child Abuse and Neglect*, **17**(2), 315–24.

Freud, S. (1979) *Case Histories II: The 'Rat' Man, Schreber, The 'Wolf' Man, A Case of Female Homosexuality*, Pelican Freud Library, Volume 9, Penguin Books, Harmondsworth.

Frewen, T.C. and Bannatyne, R.M. (1979) Gonococcal vulvovaginitis in prepubertal girls. *Clinical Pediatrics*, **18**(8) 491–3.

Friedrich, W.N. and Boriskin, J.A. (1976) The role of the child in abuse: a review of the literature. *American Journal of Orthopsychiatry*, **46**(4), 580–90.

Fromuth, M.E. (1986) The relationship of childhood sexual abuse with later psychological and sexual adjustment in a sample of college women. *Child Abuse and Neglect*, **10**, 5–15.

Frosh, S. (1988) No man's land? The role of men working with sexually abused children. *British Journal of Guidance and Counselling*, **16**(1), 1–10.

Furniss, T. (1987) Surviving child sexual abuse. *Child Abuse Review*, **1**(7), 3–4.

Furniss, T., Bingley-Miller, L. and van Elburg, A. (1988) Goal-orientated group treatment for sexually abused adolescent girls. *British Journal of Psychiatry*, **152**, 97–106.

Gaffney, G.R. and Berlin, F.S. (1984) Is there hypothalamic-pituitary-gonadal dysfunction in paedophilia? *British Journal of Psychiatry*, **145**, 657–60.

Gellert, E. (1990) Developing guidelines for HIV antibody testing among victims of paediatric sexual abuse. *Child Abuse and Neglect*, **14**, 9–17.

Gilgun, J.F. and Connor, T.M. (1990) Isolation and the adult male perpetrator of child sexual abuse: clinical concerns, in *The Incest Perpetrator: the family member no one wants to treat* (eds A.L. Horton, B.L. Johnson, L.M. Roundy and D. Williams) Sage, Newbury Park, pp. 74–87.

Gilgun, J.F. and Reiser, E. (1990) The development of sexual identity among men sexually abused as children. *Families in Society: The Journal of Contemporary Human Services*, Nov., 515–23.

Glaser, D. (1989) Evaluating the evidence of a child: the video-taped interview and beyond. *Family Law*, Dec., 487–9.

Glaser, D. and Collins, C. (1989) The response of young, non-sexually abused children to anatomically correct dolls. *Journal of Child Psychology and Psychiatry*, **30**(4), 547–60.

Glaser, D. and Frosh, S. (1993) *Child Sexual Abuse*, 2nd edn, Macmillan, London.

Goffman, E. (1968) *Asylums*, Pelican, Harmondsworth, p. 137.

Gonzalez, L.S., Waterman, J., Kelly, R.J. *et al.* (1993) Children's patterns of disclosures and recantations of sexual and ritualistic abuse allegations in psychotherapy. *Child Abuse and Neglect*, **17**(2), 281–90.

Gordon, L. (1986) Incest and resistance: patterns of father–daughter incest, 1880–1930. *Social Problems*, **33**(10), 253–67.

Gordon, L. and O'Keefe, P. (1984) Incest as a form of family violence: evidence from historical case records. *Journal of Marriage and the Family*, February, 27–34.

Gross, R.J., Doerr, H., Caldirola, D. *et al.* (1980) Borderline syndrome and incest in chronic pelvic pain patients. *International Journal of Psychiatry in Medicine*, **10**, 79–96.

Groth, N.A. (1978) Patterns of sexual assault against children and adolescents, in *Sexual Asssault of Children and Adolescents* (eds A.W. Burgess, A.N. Groth, L.L. Holstrom and S. Sgroi), Lexington Books, Toronto, pp. 3–24.

Groth, N.A. and Oliveri, F. (1989) Understanding sexual offense behavior and differentiating among sexual abusers: basic conceptual issues, in *Vulnerable Populations, Volume 2* (ed. S.M. Sgroi), Lexington Books, Massachusetts, pp. 309–28.

Hackett, S. (1993) Woman's place. *Community Care*, 26 Aug, 11.

Hagans, K.B. and Case, J. (1990) *When Your Child Has Been Molested: A Parent's Guide to Healing and Recovery*, Lexington Books, Massachusetts.

Hall, N.M. (1978) Group treatment for sexually abused children. *Nursing Clinics of North America*, **13**(4), 701–5.

Hall, L. and Lloyd, S. (1989) *Surviving Child Sexual Abuse: A Handbook for Helping Women Challenge their Past*, The Falmer Press, Basingstoke.

Halpern, J. (1987) Family therapy in father–son incest: a case study. *Social Casework: The Journal of Contemporary Social Work*, Feb., 88–93.

Hamilton, J.W. (1929) Multiple group rape: psychosocial considerations. *Journal of Nervous and Mental Disorder*, **167**(2), 128–30.

Harrison, H. (1993) Female abusers – what children and young people have told ChildLine, in *Female Sexual Abuse of Children: The Ultimate Taboo* (ed. M. Elliot), Longman, Harlow, Essex, pp. 95–8.

Heger, C. (1991) Physical examination, in *Intervening in Child Sexual Abuse*, (eds K. Murray and D.A. Gough), Scottish Academic Press, Edinburgh, pp. 40–63.

Herman-Giddens, M.E. and Frothingham, T.E. (1987) Prepubertal female genitalia: examination for evidence of sexual abuse. *Pediatrics*, **80**(2), 203–8.

Hicks, E.K. (1993) *Female Mutilation in Islamic Northeastern Africa*, Transaction Publishers, Plymouth.

Hildebrand, J. (1988) The use of groupwork in treating child sexual abuse, in *Child Sexual Abuse Within the Family: Assessment and Treatment* (eds A. Bentovim, A. Elton, J. Hildebrand *et al.*), Wright, London, pp. 205–37.

HMSO (1991) *The Report of the Inquiry into the Removal of Children from Orkney, February 1991*, HMSO, Edinburgh.

Hobbs, C.J. and Wynne, J.M. (1986) Buggery in childhood – a common syndrome of child abuse. *The Lancet*, 4 Oct, 792–6.

Hobbs, C.J. and Wynne, J.M. (1987) Child sexual abuse – an increasing rate of diagnosis. *The Lancet*, **11**, 837–41.

Home Office (1992) *Memorandum of Good Practice: on Video Recorded Interviews with Child Witnesses for Criminal Proceedings*, HMSO, London.

Howells, J.G. (1974) *Remember Maria*, Butterworth and Co., London.

Hughes, W.H., Patterson, W.J. and Whalley, H.J. (1986) *Report of the Committee of Enquiry into Children's Homes and Hostels*, HMSO, Belfast.

Hyman, S.L., Fisher, W., Mercugliano, J. and Cataldo, M.F. (1990) Children with self injurious behaviour. *Pediatrics*, **85**, 437–41.

Ingram, D.L., White, S.T., Lyna, P. *et al.* (1992a) Ureaplasma, urealyticum and large colony mycoplasma colonizations in female children and its relationship to sexual contact, age and race. *Child Abuse and Neglect*, **16**(2), 265–72.

Ingram, D.L., White, S.T., Lyna, P. *et al.* (1992b) Gardnerella vaginalis infection and sexual contact in female children. *Child Abuse and Neglect*, **16**(6), 847–54.

Jacobs, M. (1992) *Sigmund Freud*, Sage, London.

Jennings, A.G. and Armsworth, M.W. (1992) Ego development in women with histories of sexual abuse. *Child Abuse and Neglect*, **16**(4), 553–66.

Jewett, C.L. (1984) *Helping Children Cope with Separation and Loss*, Batsford, London.

Jones, D.N., Pickett, J., Oates, M. and Barbor, P. (1987) *Understanding Child Abuse*, 2nd edn, Macmillan, London.

Jones, D.P.H. and McQuiston, M.G. (1988) *Interviewing the Sexually Abused Child*, Gaskell, London.

Julian, V. and Mohr, C. (1979) Father–daughter incest: profile of the offender. *Victimology: An International Journal*, **4**(4), 348–60.

Kaliski, E.M., Rubinson, L., Lawrence, L. and Levy, S.R. (1990) AIDS, runaways, and self-efficacy. *Family and Community Health*, **13**, 65–72.

Kaufman, A., Vandermeer, J., Divasto, P. *et al.* (1976) Follow-up of rape victims in a family practice setting. *Southern Medical Journal*, **69**(12), 1569–71.

Kelly, S.J. (1988) Ritualistic abuse of children: dynamics and impact. *Cultic Studies Journal*, **5**(2), 228–36.

Kelly, S.J., Brant, R. and Waterman, J. (1993) Sexual abuse of children in day care centres. *Child Abuse and Neglect*, **17**(1), 71–90.

Kempe, H.C., Silverman, F.N., Droegemueller, W. and Silver, H.K. (1962) The battered-child syndrome. *Journal of the American Medical Association*, **181**(1), 17–24.

Kempe, H.C. (1978) Sexual abuse, another hidden pediatric problem: the 1977 C. Anderson Aldrich lecture. *Pediatrics*, **62**(3), 382–9.

Kendall-Tackett, K.A. and Watson, M.W. (1992) Use of anatomical dolls by Boston-area professionals. *Child Abuse and Neglect*, **16**(3), 423–8.

Kennedy, M. (1989) The abuse of deaf children. *Child Abuse Review*, **3**(1), 3–6.

Kennedy, M. (1990) The deaf child who is sexually abused – is there a need for a dual specialist? *Child Abuse Review*, **4**(2), 3–6.

Kirkwood, A. (1993) *The Leicestershire Inquiry 1992*, Leicestershire County Council, Leicestershire.

Knopp, F.H. (1985) *The Youthful Sex Offender: The Rationale and Goals of Early Intervention and Treatment*, Safer Society Press, Orwell, p. 10.

Knuston, J.N. (1980) The dynamics of the hostage taker: some major variants. *Annals of the New York Academy of Sciences*, **347**, 117–27.

Koverola, C., Pound, J., Heger, A. and Lytle, C. (1993) Relationship of child sexual abuse to depression. *Child Abuse and Neglect*, **17**(3), 393–400.

Krug, R.S. (1989) Adult male report of childhood sexual abuse by mothers: case descriptions, motivation and long-term consequences. *Child Abuse and Neglect*, **13**, 111–19.

Kubler-Ross, E. (1970) *On Death and Dying*, Tavistock, London.

La Fontaine, J. (1990) *Child Sexual Abuse*, Polity Press, Cambridge.

Landis, C., Landis, A.T., Bolles, M.M. *et al.* (1940) *Sex in Development*, Paul B. Hoebert, New York.

Lawson, E. (1985) *The Leeways Report*, London Borough of Lewisham, London.

Leach, P. (1990) The way forward, in *Listening to Children: The Professional Response to Hearing the Abused Child* (eds A. Bannister, K. Barrett, and E. Shearer), Longman, Harlow, Essex, pp. 172–84.

Li, C.K., West, D.J. and Woodhouse, T.P. (1990) *Children's Sexual Encounters with Adults*, Duckworth, London.

Lindberg, M. (1980) Is knowledge base development a necessary and sufficient condition for memory development? *Journal of Experimental Child Psychology*, **30**, 401–10.

MacFarlane, K., Waterman, J., Conerly, S. *et al.* (1986) *Sexual Abuse of Young Children*, Holt, Rinehart and Winston, London.

MacFarlane, K. (1990) Cindy's poem, in *The Incest Perpetrator: the family member no one wants to treat* (eds A.L. Horton, B.L. Johnson, L.M. Roundy and D. Williams), Sage, Newbury Park, pp. 147–9.

MacVeigh, J. (1982) *Gaskin*, Jonothan Cape, London.

Mannarino, A.P. and Cohen, J.A. (1986) A clinical-demographic study of sexually abused children. *Child Abuse and Neglect*, **10**, 17–23.

Marchant, R. (1991) Myths and facts about sexual abuse with disabilities. *Child Abuse Review*, **5**(2), 22–4.

Maslach, C. (1982) *Burnout – the Cost of Caring*, Prentice Hall, New York.

Mathis, J.L. (1972) *Clear Thinking About Sexual Deviation*, Nelson Hall, Chicago.

Matthews, J.K. (1993) Working with female sex abusers, in *Female Sexual Abuse of Children: The Ultimate Taboo* (ed. M. Elliot), Longman, Harlow, Essex.

Matthews, R., Matthews, J.K. and Speltz, K. (1989) *Female Sexual Offenders*, The Safer Society Press, Orwell.

Maxime, J.E. (1986) Some psychological models of black self-concept, in *Social Work with Black Children and their Families* (eds S. Ahmed, J. Cheetham and J. Small), Batsford, London, pp. 100–16.

Mayle, P. (1978a) *Where Did I Come From?* Macmillan, London.

Mayle, P. (1978b) *What's Happening to Me?* Macmillan, London.

McCann, J., Voris, J., Simon, M. and Wells, R. (1989) Perianal findings in prepubertal children selected for nonabuse: a descriptive study. *Child Abuse and Neglect*, **13**, 179–93.

McCarty, L. (1986) Mother–child incest: characteristics of the offender. *Child Welfare*, **LXV**(5), 447–57.

McElroy, L.P. (1992) Early indicators of pathological dissociation in sexually abused children. *Child Abuse and Neglect*, **16**(6), 833–46.

McFadyen, A. Hanks, H. and James, C. (1993) Ritual abuse: a definition. *Child Abuse Review*, **2**(1), 35–41.

McGuire, L.S. and Wagner, N.N. (1978) Sexual dysfunction in women who were molested as children: one response pattern and suggestions for treatment. *Journal of Sex and Marital Therapy*, **4**, 11–15.

Moore, J. (1985) *The ABC of Child Abuse Work*, Gower, Aldershot.

Mrazek, P.B., Lynch, M. and Bentovim, A. (1981) Recognition of child sexual abuse in the United Kingdom, in *Sexually Abused Children and their Families* (eds P.B. Mrazek and C.H. Kempe), Pergamon, Oxford, pp. 35–50.

Muller, D.A.F., McCluskey-Fawcett, K. and Irving, L.M. (1993) The relationship between childhood sexual abuse and subsequent onset of bulimia nervosa. *Child Abuse and Neglect*, **17**, 305–14.

Narducci, T. (1987) Breaking through the embarrassment barrier. *Community Care*, supplement, 25 June, iii–iv.

Nelki, J.S. and Watters, J. (1989) A group for sexually abused young children: unravelling the web. *Child Abuse and Neglect*, **13**, 369–77.

Norfolk County Council (1975) *Report of the Review Body Appointed to Enquire into the Case of Stephen Meurs*, Norfolk County Council, Norfolk.

Nyhan, D. (1982) For three girls justice takes a holiday. *Boston Globe*, 11 Feb.

Ochberg, F. (1978) The victim of terrorism: psychiatric considerations. *Terrorism*, **1**(2), 147–68.

O'Donohue, W. and Letourneau, E. (1993) A brief group treatment for the modification of denial in child sexual abusers: outcome and follow-up. *Child Abuse and Neglect*, **17**(2), 299–304.

Olafson, E., Corwin, D.L. and Summit, R.C. (1993) Modern history of child sexual abuse awareness: cycles of discovery and suppression. *Child Abuse and Neglect*, **17**(1), 7–24.

Oppenheimer, R. (1985) Implications for long term treatment. Conference seminar summarized by F. Groves in *Child Sexual Abuse – Report of the Inaugural Conference*, BASPCAN, Midlands Branch.

Oppenheimer, R., Howells, K., Palmer, R.L. and Chaloner, D.A. (1985) Adverse sexual experiences in childhood and clinical eating disorders: a preliminary description. *Journal of Psychiatric Research*, **9**, 357–61.

Paley, C. and Cox, K. (1985) Breaking the wall of silence. *Community Care*, 3 Oct., 16–17.

Palmer, R.L., Oppenheimer, R., Chaloner, D.A. and Howells, K. (1990) Childhood sexual experiences with adults reported by women with eating disorders: an extended series. *British Journal of Psychiatry*, **156**, 699–703.

Parker, T. (1970) *The Twisting Lane: Some Sex Offenders*, Panther, London.

Paul, D.M. (1977) The medical examination in sexual offenses against children. *Medicine, Science and the Law*, **17**(4), 251–8.

Pierce, L.H. (1987) Father–son incest: using the literature to guide practice. *Social Casework, The Journal of Contemporary Social Work*, Feb., 67–74.

Pierce, L.H. and Pierce, R.L. (1990) Adolescent/sibling incest perpertrators, in *The Incest Perpetrator: the family member no one wants to treat* (eds A.L. Horton, B.L. Johnson, L.M. Roundy and D. Williams), Sage, Newbury Park, pp. 99–107.

Pokorny, S.F. and Kozinetz, C.A. (1988) Configuration and other anatomic details of the prepubertal hymen. *Adolescent and Pediatric Gynecology*, **1**, 97–103.

Purdie, R. and Tordoff, S. (1992) Assault course. *Social Work Today*, **23**(43), 20.

Rayner, C. (1989) *The Body Book*, Piccolo, London.

Raynes, B. and Green, P. (1991) The role of men in child sexual abuse cases. *Journal of Training and Development*, **2**(2), 71–5.

Redding, D. (1989) Smashing a subculture. *Community Care*, 1 June, 14–15.

Rickford, F. (1993) Down memory lane. *Community Care*, 24 June **(972)**, 21.

Riley, D. (ed.) (1991) *Sexual Abuse of Children: Understanding,, Intervention and Prevention*, Radcliffe Medical Press, Oxford, p. 2.

Rouf, K. (1990) My self in echoes. My voice in song, in *Listening to Children: The Professional Response to Hearing the Abused Child*, (eds A. Bannister, K. Barrett and E. Shearer), Longman, Harlow, Essex, pp. 1–19.

Rouf, K. (1991a) *Black Girls Speak Out*, The Children's Society, London.

Rouf, K. (1991b) *Into Pandora's Box*, The Children's Society, London.

Ryan, G., Lane, S., Davis, J. and Connie, I. (1987) Juvenile sex offenders: development and correction. *Child Abuse and Neglect*, **11**, 385–95.

Ryan, G. (1989) Victim to victimizer: rethinking victim treatment. *Journal of Interpersonal Violence*, **4**(3), 325–41.

Salter, A. (1988) *Treating Child Sex Offenders and Victims: A Practical Guide*. Sage, Newbury Park, p. 11.

Saunders, E.B. and Awad, G.A. (1988) Assessment, management and treatment planning for male adolescent sexual offenders. *American Journal of Orthopsychiatry*, **58**(4), 571–9.

Schechter, M.D. and Roberge, L. (1976) Child sexual abuse, in *Child Abuse and Neglect: The Family and the Community* (eds R. Helfer and C.H. Kempe), Ballinger, Cambridge, MA, pp. 60 and 127–42.

SCOSAC (1984) Definition of child sexual abuse, in *Standing Committee on Sexually Abused Children*, SCOSAC, London.

Sebold, J. (1987) Indicators of child sexual abuse in males. *Social Casework: The Journal of Contemporary Social Work*, Feb., 75–80.

Seven P. (1991) Treating sex offenders in prison. *Journal of Forensic Psychiatry*, **2**(1), 8–9.

Sgroi, S.M. (ed.) (1982) *Handbook of Clinical Intervention in Child Sexual Abuse*, Lexington Books, New York.

Sgroi, S.M. (ed.) (1988a) *Vulnerable Populations, Volumes 1 and 2*, Lexington Books, New York.

Sgroi, S.M. (1988b) Healing together: peer group therapy for adult survivors of child sexual abuse, in *Vulnerable populations, Volume 1* (ed. S.M. Sgroi), Lexington Books, New York, pp. 123 and 131–66.

Sgroi, S.M., Bunk, B.S. and Wabrek, C.J. (1988) Children's Sexual Behaviours and Their Relationship to Sexual Abuse, in *Vulnerable Populations, Volume 1* (ed. S.M. Sgroi), Lexington Books, New York, pp. 137–88.

Sgroi, S.M. and Dana, N. (1982) Individual and group treatment of mothers of incest victims, in *Handbook of Clinical Intervention in Child Sexual Abuse* (ed. S.M. Sgroi), Lexington Books, New York, pp. 191–214.

Sivan, A.B., Schor, D.P., Koeppl, G.K. and Noble, L.D. (1988) Interaction of normal children with anatomical dolls. *Child Abuse and Neglect*, **12**, 295–304.

Snow, B. and Sorensen, T. (1990) Ritualistic child abuse in a neighbourhood setting. *Journal of Interpersonal Violence.* Dec., 474–87.

Solzhenitsyn, A. (1974) *The Gulag Archipelago, 1918–56*, Collins/Fontana, London.

Soothill, K. and Gibbens, T.C.N. (1978) Recidivism of sexual offenders: a re-appraisal. *British Journal of Criminology*, **18**(3), 267–76.

Spring, J. (1987) *Cry Hard and Swim: The story of an incest survivor*, Virago, London.

Stiffman, A.R. (1989) Physical and sexual abuse in runaway youths. *Child Abuse and Neglect*, **13**, 417–26.

Strenz, T. (1980) The Stockholm syndrome: law enforcement policy and the ego defenses of the hostage. *Annals of the New York Academy of Sciences*, **347**, 137–50.

Stuart, J. (1993) When mum is to blame. *Northampton Chronicle and Echo*, 24 March, 10.

Summit, R.C. (1983) The child sexual abuse accommodation syndrome. *Child Abuse and Neglect*, **7**, 177–93.

Swann, A. (1985) Therapeutic dolls. *Nursing Mirror*, **161**(17), 15–20.

Symonds, M. (1980) Victim responses to terror. *Annals of the New York Academy of Sciences*, **347**, 129–36.

Tate, T. (1990) *Child Pornography – An Investigation*, Methuen, London.

Terman, L.M. (1938) *Psychological Factors in Marital Happiness*, McGraw-Hill, New York.

The Research Team (1990) *Child Sexual Abuse in Northern Ireland: A Research Study of Incidence*, Greystone Books, Antrim.

Thompson, S.J. (1988) Child sexual abuse redefined: impact of modern culture on the sexual mores of the Yuit Eskimo, in

Vulnerable Populations, Volume 1 (ed. S.M. Sgroi), Lexington Books, New York, pp. 299–308.

Tipton, A.C. (1989) Child sexual abuse: physical examination techniques and interpretation of findings. *Adolescent and pediatric Gynecology*, **2**, 10–25.

Tobey, A.E. and Goodman, G.S. (1992) Children's eyewitness memory: effects of participation and forensic context. *Child Abuse and Neglect*, **16**(6), 779–96.

Toth, P.A. and Elias, H. (1991) Gathering legal evidence, in *Intervening in Child Sexual Abuse* (eds K. Murray and D.A. Gough), Scottish Academic Press, Edinburgh, pp. 65–75.

Toth, P.A. and Spencer, J.R. (1991) Diversion in America and England, in *Intervening in Child Sexual Abuse* (eds K. Murray, and D.A. Gough), Scottish Academic Press, Edinburgh, pp. 140–45.

Tsai, M., Feldman-Summers, S. and Edgar, M. (1979) Childhood molestation: variables related to differential impact on psychosexual functioning in adult women. *Journal of Abnormal Psychology*, **88**(4), 407–17.

Tsai, M. and Wagner, N.N. (1978) Therapy groups for women sexually molested as children. *Archives of Sexual Behaviour*, **7**(5), 417–27.

Unuigbe, J.A. and Giwa-Osagie, A.W. (1988) Pediatric and adolescent gynecological disorders in Benin City, Nigeria. *Adolescent and Pediatric Gynecology*, **1**, 257–61.

Vizard, E. (1991) Interviewing children suspected of being sexually abused: a review of theory and practice, in *Clinical Approaches to Sex Offenders and Their Victims* (eds C.R. Hollin, and K. Howells), John Wiley and Sons, Chichester, pp. 117–48.

Wade, A. (1993) The Canadian experience. *Community Care*, 4 Feb., 24–5.

Wald, E.R., Woodward, C.L., Marston, G. and Gilbert, L.M. (1980) Gonorrheal Disease among Children in a University Hospital. *Sexually Transmitted Diseases*, **7**(2), 41–3.

Walker, A. (1983) *The Color Purple*, The Women's Press, London.

Walker, M. (1992) *Surviving Secrets*, Open University Press, Buckingham.

Walmsley, S. (1989) The need for safeguards, in *Thinking the Unthinkable: Papers on Sexual Abuse and People with Learning Difficulties* (eds H. Brown and A. Craft), FPA Education Unit, London, pp. 5–17.

Walton, M. (1989) What use are statistics? - policy and practice in child abuse, in *Child Sexual Abuse: Listening, hearing and validating the experiences of children* (eds H. Blagg, J.A. Hughes, and C. Wattam), Longman, Harlow, Essex, pp. 152–62.

Waterman, J. (1986) Developmental considerations, in *Sexual Abuse of Young Children* (eds K. MacFarlane, J. Waterman, S. Conerly, *et al.*, Holt, Rinehart and Winston, London, pp. 15–29.

Weinberg, S.K. (1955) *Incest Behaviour*, Citadel Press, New York.

Wild, N.J. and Wynne, J.M. (1986) Child sex rings. *British Medical Journal*, **293**, 183–5.

Williams, D. (1987) Suffer little children. *Daily Mail*, 12 June, 8.

Wilson, M. (1987) Child sexual abuse histories among professionals. *Child Abuse Review*, **1**(7), 4–5.

Wolfe, F.A. (1985) *Twelve Female Sexual Offenders*. Presentation to Next Steps in Research on the Assessment and Treatment of Sexually Aggressive Persons (Paraphiliacs) Conference, St Louis, MO.

Woodling, B.A. and Heger, A. (1986) The use of the colposcope in the diagnosis of sexual abuse in the pediatric age group. *Child Abuse and Neglect*, **10**, 111–14.

Woodling, B.A. and Kossoris, P.D. (1981) Child sexual abuse: rape, molestation and incest. *Pediatric Clinics of North America*, **28**(2), 481–99.

Wright, E. and Portnoy, S. (1990) Helping mothers in crisis. *Community Care*, 25 Jan., 22–3.

Wyatt, G.E. (1985) The sexual abuse of Afro-American and white-American women in childhood. *Child Abuse and Neglect*, **4**, 507–20.

Wyatt, G. and Higgs, M. (1991) The Medical Diagnosis of Child Sexual Abuse: The Paediatrician's Dilemma, in *Child Sexual Abuse: Whose Problem? – Reflections from Cleveland* (eds S. Richardson, H. Bacon, M.Dunn, *et al.*), Venture Press, Birmingham, pp. 33–50.

Yates, A. (1982) Children eroticized by incest. *American Journal of Psychiatry*, **139**(4), 482–5.

Yule, V.C. (1985) Why are parents tough on children? *New Society*, 27 Sep., 444–6.

Zierler, S., Feingold, L., Laufer, D. *et al.* (1991) Adult survivors of childhood sexual abuse and subsequent risk of HIV infection. *American Journal of Public Health*, **81**, 572–5.

Index

Page numbers in **bold** refer to the Glossary of terms in Appendix C